MEDIEVAL YORK

MEDIEVAL YORK

GARETH DEAN

The
History
Press

First published 2008

Reprinted 2009

The History Press
The Mill, Brimscombe Port
Stroud, Gloucestershire, GL5 2QG
www.thehistorypress.co.uk

British Library Cataloguing in Publication Data.
A catalogue record for this book is available from the British Library.

ISBN 978 07524 41160

Typesetting and origination by
The History Press
Printed in Great Britain

CONTENTS

Preface and Acknowledgements   7

Introduction   9

1   The Lie of the Land   21

2   Portcullis and Palisade   47

3   For the Love of God   69

4   Merchant, Butcher and Candlestick-maker   105

5   Eating, Drinking and Shopping   135

6   A Matter of Life and Death   155

7   Life in Medieval York   177

    Select Bibliography   183

    Index   189

PREFACE AND ACKNOWLEDGEMENTS

'The addition of yet another, to the already considerable number of guides and histories of the City of York, would seem altogether unnecessary if there did not seem some very special reason for the undertaking', said George Auden in *A Handbook to York and District* in 1906. So what is the justification for another book? In this case it is about using archaeology as well as history to look at a period often seen largely through the eyes of the historian. Archaeology is more than capable of supporting, and even writing, episodes in the history of the medieval city.

The title, *Medieval York*, is in need of definition. Medieval conjures up different images to different people, from damsels in distress, knights on horseback, backward and oppressed people to the rounded jolly monk. Such characters may have existed in medieval York, but this is not what the book is about. The medieval period, or Middle Ages, in this book is taken as 1066–1550. The Norman Conquest in 1066 and the arrival of William the Conqueror in York in 1068 had a significant impact on the city's development. The closing date of 1550 covers the aftermath of the Dissolution of the Monasteries, when key institutions in medieval York ceased to exist and were replaced by new secular institutions that saw the city moving in new directions through the mid to late sixteenth century.

This book would not have been possible without the work of archaeologists in the city. The work of the pioneers of archaeology in York exposed the wealth of archaeological information that survives beneath the modern city. Most notably, York Archaeological Trust has been there since 1972, the beginning of the most recent threat to York's heritage. Since then others have worked within the city and their contribution to the recording of the city's past has been invaluable.

Special thanks to Patrick Ottaway who read early versions of the text and offered most astute insights. To Christine Kyriacou, who also read the text, Mike Andrews for sourcing the many photographs and Lesley Collett for producing the line drawings. Thanks also to other members of the Trust who have helped in the creation of this book, knowingly or unknowingly: John Walker, Ailsa Mainman, Jane McComish, Ian Milsted, Kurt Hunter-Mann and just about anyone who has listened to my thoughts, or prompted and inspired ideas. Thanks are also due to John Oxley and the publishers for their tolerance and patience. Last but by no means least to Frances Mee for her wonderful editing skills and patience and to Charlie, my wife, who supported me throughout the writing of this book.

Any reader inspired to look into the history and archaeology of medieval York should look in the select bibliography. This is divided according to chapter titles and will hopefully give a taster of the wide range of sources available for study. Ultimately, if this book makes one person say 'I never knew that' then it will have achieved its purpose. Any mistakes are, in the words of Chaucer 'that to the fault of my own ignorance and not to my intention which would gladly have been better said if I had the knowledge'.

INTRODUCTION

The modern city of York has developed for certain reasons. In 1068, on the eve of the arrival of William the Conqueror, the city was approaching the 1,000th anniversary of its foundation by the Romans. How had this city evolved and what was the legacy that William inherited? To answer these questions we must look back to York's origins. We will then look briefly at the post-medieval period to see how antiquarian interest and later research has shaped our understanding of one of England's most important towns, the ancient legacy of which still influences the city we know today.

IN THE BEGINNING: ROMAN YORK

In AD 71 the conquering Roman army crossed the Humber estuary. Passing through a well-ordered Iron Age landscape, the troops arrived at a slightly elevated area of ground at the confluence of a major tidal river and its tributary. This was a legacy of retreating glaciers and the land seems to have been unoccupied, but the Roman surveyors realised the potential of the site for a new fortress, Eburacum.

The fortress became a focus for an extensive network of roads and the Ouse provided a navigable route from the Humber estuary and the North Sea, a distance of some 40 miles, offering access to the rest of the Empire. The fort was also positioned on a natural east–west land route across the Vale of York that had been in use for some 2,000 years before the Romans and was to remain the principal crossing point of the Ouse until the eighteenth century.

The fortress, on the north-west side of the Ouse, was aligned north-west/south-east and enclosed an area of 50 acres (20ha). Within the fortress was a grid of streets, barracks and other buildings and at its heart where the medieval Minster now stands was the *principia*, or headquarters, which was partly excavated between 1966 and 1973.

Much of what we know of Eburacum is derived from excavations. The medieval walls now standing still follow the north-east and north-west sides of the fortress and the Multangular Tower incorporates much of a previous Roman tower; there is also a short stretch of the fortress wall in the Museum gardens.

Excavations show the buildings, public and private, were impressively built and many had fine mosaic floors. Inscriptions found near Nessgate were probably from temples dedicated to the emperors and the god Hercules. Civilian settlement developed on the land immediately outside the fortress towards the Ouse and the Foss, probably housing camp followers, soldiers' families and local people trading with the army. However the main civilian settlement developed on the south-west bank of the Ouse. It was linked to the fortress by a bridge that was to become a *colonia*.

Archaeology shows the importance of the rivers for bringing in raw materials such as building stone. Food, available from the hinterland of the Vale of York, was supplemented with produce such as olive oil and wine brought in by sea from the Mediterranean. Excavations in Coney Street identified two successive timber grain warehouses. Inscriptions from the burial grounds surrounding the city give a glimpse of the cosmopolitan nature of the residents of Roman York, drawn from across the Empire, including Marcus Aurelius Lunaris and his wife Julia Fortunata from Sardinia.

Occasionally the city played its part in major events; in AD 306 for example York was the site of the proclamation of a new emperor, Constantine the Great, the first emperor to allow Christianity to be practised, and in 314 York was made a bishopric, a home for the fledgling Christian Church.

Change is inevitable. During the fourth century the Roman Empire began to lose its hold on its northern and western provinces. The end of Roman Britain is traditionally dated to 410, but the shift to independence and the emergence of a new ruling elite would have been slow and gradual.

THE WILDERNESS YEARS: YORK IN THE FIFTH AND SIXTH CENTURIES

Few documents survive for this period so what was occurring in York in this period? The withdrawal of the influence and stimulus of Rome sees the disappearance of mass-produced pottery, glass and metalwork. Everyday items began to be made locally or even at home from materials such as wood and leather. These do not always survive well, which makes it difficult to date and interpret the archaeology of this period.

York gradually altered in appearance and some of these changes have been detected in the archaeology within the fortress and the civilian town. In the fortress different activities were carried out in the *principia* and barracks, and in the *colonia* timber buildings encroached on the main approach road to the bridge. The changes seen in the archaeology, their significance and dating are open to numerous interpretations, but it cannot be assumed that York was entirely deserted or without a role in the economy and society of the region.

Who lived in or around the city in this period? There is evidence for newcomers from the mid fifth and sixth centuries from cemeteries found in the area of the present Mount and Heworth, with urns decorated in styles distinctive of Denmark, Germany and the Low Countries. However it is unclear whether the cemeteries were used by inhabitants of the walled areas or the surrounding countryside.

THE CITY EVOLVES: YORK 600–866

Between 600 and 850 the four major Anglo-Saxon kingdoms, Wessex, East Anglia, Mercia and Northumbria were defined and Christianity was re-established. In York the

Anglian settlers were dominant and gave their name to this period in the story of the city. Increasing historical and archaeological information from this period makes York's role a little clearer.

In 627 Bishop Paulinus, one of the missionaries sent by Pope Gregory in 597, baptised Edwin, king of Northumbria, in a wooden church dedicated to St Peter. York may have been chosen because it was a regional centre or because Paulinus knew of the fourth-century Roman bishop's seat. In 1966–73 excavations below the Minster found no trace of Edwin's church. A high-status graveyard dating to the eighth and ninth centuries below the south transept may suggest the church was close by. A possible location for the Anglian Minster may be a semi-preserved square enclosure in Dean's Park. Alternatively the Minster may have been to the south of the present church in the area of St Michael le Belfry, in the courtyard of the Roman *principia*.

It is not clear how the defences of the fortress and *colonia* continued to be used or adapted. It is likely the gates remained in use and influenced the alignment of streets such as Petergate and Stonegate. Dating changes to the street pattern is difficult, but some streets such as Goodramgate that cut diagonally between the south gate and the blocked Roman north-east gate must have been introduced after Roman buildings had been removed.

Contemporary written accounts show the importance of the Church in York, especially after the city's elevation to archbishopric status in 735 and the founding of the internationally renowned York school and library mentioned by Alcuin. It is Alcuin who gives us a glimpse of the city in his poem *On the Bishops, Kings and Saints of the Church of York*, indicating it was a centre of commerce.

Early churches are indicated by the ninth-century carvings at St Mary Bishophill Junior and St Mary Bishophill Senior. St Gregory's, which stood near Barker Lane off Micklegate, was dedicated to the man who introduced Christianity to England, and was likely to have been founded in the centuries immediately after conversion. It is also likely that Holy Trinity Micklegate, pre-Conquest Christ Church, was immensely important.

Alcuin's trading settlement, reflected in York's eighth- and ninth-century names, *Eoforwic* and *Eoforwicceaste*, may have been part of a group of settlements with roles in manufacturing and trade called *wics*. Possible evidence for *Eoforwic* has been found in the areas beyond the Roman fortress on the south-east side of the River Ouse. The location outside the main Roman settlement is not unusual because many *wics* are close to Roman centres and not within them. London's Aldwych, the site of *Lundenwic*, is a mile from the Roman walled area which was used for high-status occupation by the Church and king. *Hamwic*, the precursor of Southampton, is outside a Roman settlement at Bitterne in Hampshire; Ipswich (*Gipeswich*) appears to be a new foundation along an old Roman road, though there is evidence of a villa close by.

Possible evidence for the *wic* comes from excavations at 46–54 Fishergate in 1986 and more recently at Blue Bridge Lane; Piccadilly and George Street also displayed a sequence of buildings, ditches and pits. These sites were used for manufacturing and craft activities such as bone and antler comb-making, metalworking, textile working and butchery. Animal bone suggests the residents were supplied with meat and other food, which implies control by a higher authority, something also observed at *Hamwic*. There is evidence for local and regional trade seen in the presence of pottery from East Anglia and Tating wares imported from the Rhineland.

But who controlled the *Eoforwic*? Was it the Northumbrian elite or the Church? If it was the Church *Eoforwic* could have acted as an important cultural and ecclesiastical centre and the ecclesiastical community may have encouraged trade in luxuries and other goods. Whoever controlled it, the *wic* established or enhanced the city's role as a centre of supply and redistribution which was to be a key part of York's future development.

INVADERS, SETTLERS AND DEVELOPERS: JORVIK 866–1068

On Friday 1 November 866 the Danish 'heathen great army' attacked and took the Anglian city of *Eoforwic*. It was to remain under Danish control, with only one brief interruption, until 954. Archaeology shows that the *wic* sites see a reduction in activity by the mid ninth century, with settlement focused around the Roman fortress again.

This is often referred to as the Anglo-Scandinavian period and was when York changed its name again to *Jorvik*. An unanswered question is: what did the Vikings inherit within the area of the Roman defences other than the ecclesiastical precincts and how did they, as pagans, react to the power of the Church in York?

Archaeology shows that by the tenth century a dense pattern of plots had developed at Coppergate and High Ousegate suggesting concentrated settlement, including property that has remained largely unchanged to the present day. Buildings on these plots combined living and workshop space, and the presence of crafts and industry is another important feature of Jorvik.

The principal streets of Jorvik focused on the crossing of the Ouse, but it is unclear when the crossing moved from its Roman position opposite the present Guildhall to the site of the modern Ouse Bridge. The most obvious legacy of the Viking replanning is the curving line of Micklegate, 'the great street'. Excavations at the intersection of Micklegate and Skeldergate showed structures of the tenth century fronted onto Micklegate on an alignment different from that of the Roman period.

A key question is when the defences were extended at the north-east and south-west corners to the banks of the Ouse and the Foss. The defences were probably a feature of the Anglo-Scandinavian city designed to protect the developing town and provide access to the rivers and vital trade routes. Included in these developments appears to be the raising of earth mounds over some of the Roman walls, perhaps topped with timber palisades. The defences on the Walmgate side of the Foss are not well understood, but the curving parish boundary of St Denys Church may represent the line of the defences forming a bridgehead with a crossing at the present Foss Bridge; such defended bridgeheads in towns are known to have existed in tenth-century England and Europe.

Walmgate possibly developed as a deliberate, planned suburb during the tenth century, built along the road following the ridge of higher ground and partially surrounded by a meander of the Foss. It is unclear what motivated the development of the Walmgate suburb that extended beyond the line of the later medieval defences, but the aim may have been to exploit trade passing along the principal road to the Humber estuary and the east coast.

George Street, ancient Fishergate, contrasts with the developed Walmgate frontage, although it was similarly busy, being the principal route south to Fulford, Ricall and Selby,

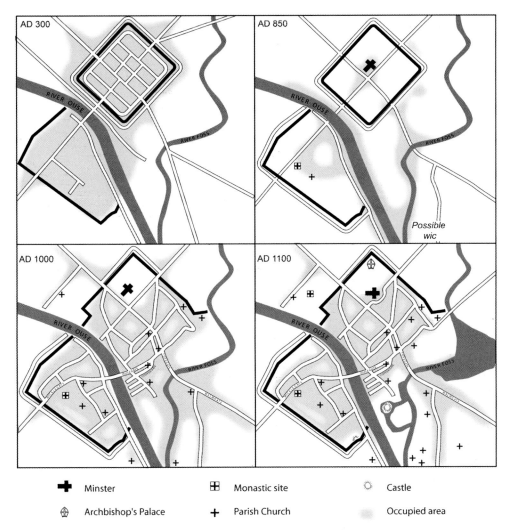

AD 300

AD 850

Possible
wic

AD 1000

AD 1100

✚ Minster	⊞ Monastic site	☼ Castle	
⬦ Archbishop's Palace	✚ Parish Church	▪ Occupied area	

1 The changing face of York from the Roman period to the Conquest

passing through the area of the Anglian *wic*. After the mid ninth century this route may have lost its significance as trade along the Ouse began to be focused further upstream. There is little evidence for occupation, although rubbish pits have been found underneath George Street.

The other approaches to the city such as Blossom Street, the main south-western route, and Bootham, the north-western, do not appear to have developed as extensive suburbs like Walmgate. Layerthorpe grew up on the eastern bank of the Foss as a small hamlet and Clementhorpe may also have its origins in the Anglo-Scandinavian period.

The rivers were key to Jorvik developing as an international port, and this is reflected in the range of imported Scandinavian goods such as silk, amber, schist and phylitte which have been unearthed in excavation. Regional trade enabled the import of jet from the North Yorkshire Moors and metal ores from across the British Isles. Little is known about Jorvik's waterfronts, but excavations along Skeldergate and North Street suggest that the Ouse was wider and shallower than it is today, perhaps allowing boats to be beached for unloading.

A wealth of artefacts has been found which can be associated with crafts practised in the town, providing evidence for textile making, metalworking in iron, copper alloy or gold and even glass-making. The uniform styles point to professional mass-production by specialist workers, perhaps a precursor of the guilds of later medieval artisans. Jorvik was the only town north of the Humber able to offer such a wide range of utilitarian and luxury products for sale.

The Anglo-Scandinavian Minster probably experienced continued use by the Anglian Church, with the high-status cemetery beneath the south transept continuing to be used through the tenth and eleventh centuries. The archbishop was powerful within the town and later documents, such as Domesday Book, refer to the archbishop's shire forming a large part of the pre-Conquest town.

Domesday Book mentions 13 churches: St Saviour's, All Saints Fishergate, All Saints Pavement, Holy Trinity, St Andrew Fishergate, St Crux, St Cuthbert, St Helen Fishergate, St Martin Micklegate, St Mary Bishophill Junior, St Mary Castlegate, St Michael Spurriergate and one belonging to Odo the crossbowman. Archaeology has shown many of the 40 churches of the later medieval city also had their origins in this period, examples being St Stephen's, George Street, St Helen-on-the-Walls and St Benet's Swinegate. These churches were founded by private individuals, as witnessed by the foundation inscription of Grim and Aese at St Mary Castlegate. Examples of private churches are found in other towns such as Winchester. The motive behind these foundations may have as much to do with money-making as an expression of faith.

But who was in charge of Jorvik? Was it truly the capital of the Northumbrian kingdom, whose traditional capital was Bamburgh, or an important trading settlement under the control of the archbishop or the king? The presence of a king would be expected to have an impact on the city, but it is only the Minster precinct that has left a lasting impression. If a royal residence existed within the city there is no definite evidence for it and it is perhaps significant that the later earls appear to have been based outside the walled area. If there was an established royal enclosure within the walls why was this not used?

The archbishop had extensive landholdings within the city and may have even been behind the development of the Walmgate area. Both Walmgate and Fishergate were listed as being owned by the archbishop in 1066 and it is interesting that two areas associated with the Anglian *wic* were in the possession of the Church. Whoever was ultimately in charge, however, does not change the fact that York developed into a leading town from the ninth century.

Danish rule ended with the death of Eric Bloodaxe in 954. York came under the influence of the kings of Wessex who established earls in the city to rule for them. The eleventh-century documentary references show the earls had a base in York; however, this period is still poorly understood. The penultimate earl, Siward (1033–55), left his mark by founding St Olave's Church in Marygate, which was to form the basis of St Mary's Abbey. The last earl, Tostig, was the brother of the king, Harold Godwinson. Tostig proved unpopular and was replaced by Morcar, brother of Edwin, Earl of Mercia. However, Tostig was not so easily dealt with and sided with the Viking king Harald Hardrada who invaded via the Humber, sailing along the Ouse to Ricall in September 1066. Morcar and his brother Edwin raised an army and met Hardrada and Tostig at the village of Fulford, outside the city. They were defeated and York was captured. Tostig and Hardrada moved to Stamford Bridge where Harold Godwinson surprised and defeated them.

However Harold Godwinson's victory was to be his last. In response to the threat of William of Normandy, Harold travelled south. William landed at Pevensy on 28 September and on 13 October Harold was defeated, decisively ending an era for Anglo-Scandinavian York and the rest of the country.

ALL CHANGE: 1068–1550

York's first dealings with the Conqueror came at Christmas 1066. Stigand, Archbishop of Canterbury, fled the country, leaving Ealdred, Archbishop of York, the dubious honour of crowning William at Westminster. After the coronation William focused on gaining control of southern England and York became a frontier town on the limits of the Normans' northern control.

William had to focus on the north of his new kingdom when rebellion broke out in 1068 and 1069. Each time he marched north to suppress the rebels and ordered the construction of two castles on opposite banks of the Ouse. These two testaments to the Norman assertion of power still stand at Baile Hill and York Castle (Clifford's Tower), making York the only city outside London to have two castles built by the Conqueror.

William's final assertion of control was the 'Harrying of the North'. We cannot take on face value the accounts of chroniclers such as Orderic Vitalis or Simeon of Durham, who describe the ground as remaining uncultivated for many decades for a distance of over 60 miles. However it is likely that the social, economic and psychological impact of the Conqueror's brutal assertion of power was significant. By the end of 1070 the Conqueror had firmly stamped his identity on York, with the new, raw earth mounds of the castles as a potent statement of the new power.

Following the Conquest, York continued as the focus for an extensive hinterland. Domesday identifies 84 carucates of land associated with the city that formed the later Ainsty, an area of farm land controlled by the city on the western side of York. The surrounding countryside was held by many different people, from the Church to powerful local families. This led to a complex pattern of pasturage with rights of access to areas of common land or strays being fiercely guarded. Much of the land belonged to the Church, with an extensive area on the south-west bank of the Ouse known as the Bishopfields. Another area of fields recorded around Walmgate, 'Bean Hills', was first mentioned in 1368.

The nearest royal forest to the city was called the Forest of Galtres. In 1316 it comprised 60 townships and 100,000 acres (40,000ha), and it was administered from a head office in Davygate. The extensive woodland formed a royal hunting reserve, but was also a source of raw materials for the city. The forests were at their largest extent under Henry II (1154–89), but were declining by the fifteenth century when concerns were voiced over the amount of deforestation.

Despite the early rebellions York continued to be a political and administrative centre. Domesday Book tells us the city was divided into seven shires with hereditary law men. Such internal divisions are only recorded in three other towns: Cambridge, Stamford and Huntingdon. Descriptions of York by contemporaries are far from flattering. In the 1120s William of Malmesbury described York as having high walls and churches but stated that 'All the language of the Northumbrians, and especially York, is so sharp, slitting and frothing and unscape [crude], that we southern men can scarcely understand it'.

York was barely troubled by national events following the Conquest, but the city briefly featured on the national stage when Archbishop Thurstan rallied the citizens and nobles against the Scots and was victorious at the Battle of the Standard in 1138. In the 1170s, during the reign of Henry II, the city involved itself in arms smuggling which resulted in a heavy fine from the king. The wars with the Scots during the reigns of Edward I to Edward III brought York back into the limelight. The seat of government moved from London to York on several occasions from 1298 to 1335.

Perhaps one of the most trying of events of the period was the Black Death from 1348. However, the impact of the disease on the development of the city, though poorly understood, does not seem to have been long-term and the fourteenth and early fifteenth centuries may have seen the city at its most affluent. The fifteenth century opened with the deposition of Richard II by Henry IV in 1399. The city became involved in the rebellions against the new king and Archbishop Richard Scrope went through the streets preaching against Henry. He was executed at Clementhorpe on 8 June 1405. York played a minimal role in the Wars of the Roses although the Duke of York made a bid for the crown and was killed at Wakefield in 1460, after which the heads of the leading Yorkists were set up over the city gates. The city found royal favour under Richard III who was killed at the Battle of Bosworth in August 1485. This event was recorded with an entry in the city annals stating Richard was 'pitiously slane and murdered, to the grete hevynesse of this Citie'.

The new king, Henry VII, visited the city in 1486 and again in 1487 with the intention of making the citizens submissive subjects. In July 1503 the city hosted a royal reception for Princess Margaret as she travelled north to join her husband the King of Scotland. The Reformation in the 1530s, during the reign of Henry VIII, saw the break with the established church. By 1550 the city had changed beyond recognition from the time of William the Conqueror and the closure of the religious houses and some parish churches and the fundamental changes in religious practice effectively ended the medieval period of the city as it had to find a new direction.

A NEW WORLD

Following the succession of Elizabeth I in November 1558, the second half of the sixteenth century was to pass in relative calm that allowed the economy to recover. The city found a new role as a political and administrative centre in 1561 with the establishment of the Council of the North at the King's Manor and a new Ecclesiastical Commission. York was to continue as a centre of administration and commerce throughout the late sixteenth and early seventeenth century.

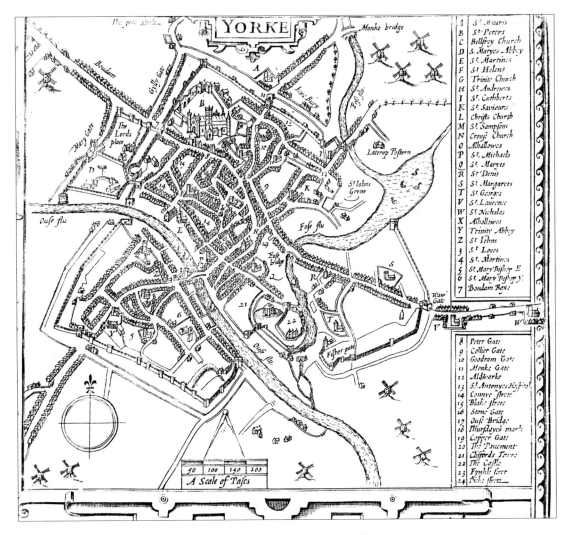

2 John Speed's map of York *c.*1610: a glimpse of the end of medieval York

The English Civil War had a profound impact on the city despite minimal damage to its historic monuments following the siege of 1645. The Council of the North was closed down, despite the pleas from the city for its reinstatement after the Restoration in the 1660s. York remained important as a legal and administrative centre and county town, however it no longer acted as a major trading centre and had to find a new strength.

The writer and journalist Daniel Defoe noted in the 1720s that wines from France and Portugal came along the river, and as such, were the only form of trade being driven by the needs of the gentry rather than the economy of the town as a whole. The Annual Assizes became a key feature of the social calendar with races and other events organised by the city. Perhaps the clearest statement of this new role for York were the Assembly Rooms in Blake Street which were opened in 1732.

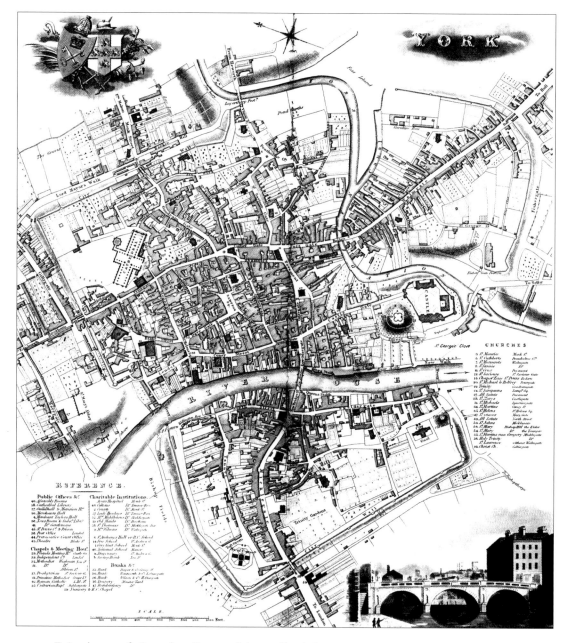

3 Baines's map of 1822: a last glimpse of the medieval city

Study of the medieval past was largely overlooked during the late sixteenth and seventeenth centuries although antiquaries such as Roger Dodsworth began recording ancient monuments. The main legacy from this period are maps, of which the earliest surviving example is one of York dating from *c.*1547; the most significant is John Speed's which was published in 1610. From the seventeenth century maps were increasingly accurate and show the city remained remarkably consistent in size until the early nineteenth century. Baines's map of 1822 gives one of the last glimpses of the medieval city before the campaigns of street-building and infilling with housing, processes which took place to provide for the rapidly growing population. The buildings produced as a result are shown on the First Edition Ordnance Survey map in 1851.

Study of the Middle Ages was avoided because the period was seen as barbaric and restrictive, an attitude which still prevails today. Interest in the medieval period developed towards the end of the eighteenth century due to its romantic rather than its historic appeal. However, Thomas Gent, a printer, was responsible for one of the first purpose-written guide books to a medieval monument, York Minster. Perhaps the most significant of these early guides was Francis Drake's *Eboracum: Or the History and Antiquities of the City of York* published in 1736.

While the country as a whole underwent the Industrial Revolution, these developments were taken up slowly by York. However, by the nineteenth century the arrival of the railways put the city in a position to advance. Changes to the city included the rebuilding of Ouse Bridge, once described as the 'fairest arch in all England', in 1820. In 1860 and 1878 two new bridges were built across the Ouse: Lendal Bridge and Skeldergate Bridge. Road widening was carried out from 1806 and new streets created, such as Parliament Street in 1836.

A growing interest in the past led to the foundation in 1822 of the Yorkshire Philosophical Society. Nevertheless the rapid growth of the city threatened its historic fabric. Changes made included the removal of three of the barbicans on the gates and several of the smaller posterns between 1807 and 1840. A section of the walls was removed in 1831–35 for the creation of St Leonard's Place. The artist William Etty wrote in 1839 'beware how you destroy your antiquities, guard them with religious care. They are what give you a decided character and superiority over other provincial cities. You lost much – take care of what remains'. Much of what has been lost was recorded by artists such as Cave, Halfpenny and Etty and supplemented from the 1850s by photographs.

The contribution of archaeology at this time remained slight and until the twentieth century urban excavation was almost unheard of. One of the earliest excavations of a sort was of St Mary's Abbey when Charles Wellbeloved cleared the ruins and published his findings. After the fire of the Minster in 1829 which was followed by restoration, the choir was excavated by John Browne. Works appeared such as Robert Skaife's plan of *Roman, Medieval and Modern York* in 1864. In the late nineteenth and early twentieth centuries the architect George Benson often visited building sites and recorded workmen's discoveries, writing books on the history of the city.

The excavations which took place during the 1920s and 1930s focused on the Roman period. Fortunately York survived the Second World War with only one serious bombing raid that destroyed its medieval Guildhall on Coney Street. The site for the new telephone exchange in Hungate in 1948 was the scene for York's first true urban excavation directed by Kathleen Richardson.

Post-war redevelopment encompassed some of the last sweeping changes which have been made to the appearance of the city, including the creation of the Stonebow and the clearing of the medieval Little Shambles to provide space for the building of Newgate Market. Interest in the medieval period continued and Angelo Raine published *Medieval York* in 1955. This work was based on research using the city archives and bore references to archaeology; it was one of the first to look solely at the medieval period.

To counter the post-war redevelopment threat, a short-lived York Excavation Committee was formed. It was funded by the Ministry of Works and again the emphasis was on the Roman period. The largest excavation at this time was that of Derek Phillips at the Minster which took place between 1966 and 1973. The year before it ended the Yorkshire Philosophical Society and the Council for British Archaeology oversaw the creation of York Archaeological Trust for Excavation and Research that finally made medieval archaeology an important area of study.

Through the Government funding of excavations during the 1970s and 1980s many sites from Roman times through to the present were explored. In the late 1980s the government reduced and finally withdrew funding and since 1992, funding of archaeological work has been the responsibility of the developer. York City Council appointed an archaeologist to its planning division who determines the level of archaeological work required. The biggest consequence of this has been a change in the nature of excavations, with the emphasis on limiting below-ground disturbance. The time is now right to review what has been learnt about the medieval city.

1

THE LIE OF THE LAND

If William I had stood at the top of York Castle in 1069 and looked over his newly acquired city, he would have seen the broad ribbons of the Ouse and Foss, the web of streets lined with low timber buildings with thatched roofs, punctuated by the towers of the parish churches and, competing with each other for dominance of the skyline, the castle and the Minster. The view in 1500 would have been familiar in some respects, but changed beyond recognition in others. Dominance of the skyline was contested between the castle, the Minster, St Mary's Abbey and the religious houses, with streets lined with a variety of timber-framed buildings. Fifty years later the city would look different again, with many of churches and religious houses closed and the sites cleared or full of buildings falling into disrepair. It is these changes that archaeology and historical documents allow us to trace to build up a picture of the medieval city.

TOPOGRAPHY OF A CITY

The medieval city of York consolidated the area of its Anglo-Scandinavian predecessor. The main expansion was the incorporation of part of the Walmgate area within the defensive circuit in the thirteenth century. Once complete, the defences enclosed *c.*263 acres (106 ha), less than half the area of London or Norwich.

Within the walls was the framework of streets and lanes, lined with the shops, homes, workshops and the larger institutions, both ecclesiastical and secular. Influences on the organisation of space were the gates, quays, bridges and areas of specialist craft activities. Less obvious, but equally influential, were wards, liberties and parishes associated with the many churches. The wards were administrative areas into which the city was divided and were probably derived from the shires into which the city was divided as recorded in Domesday. The liberties developed in assocation with larger institutions such as the Minster and St Leonard's Hospital, within which they exercised influence politically, juris-dictionally and economically and were seen as a major threat to the developing civic authority that had no authority there. The compact nature of York was financially benefi-cial in facilitating close regulation of tolls levied on goods bought and sold in the city.

However, it was the natural geography that was the main determining factor in the development of the city. The dominant natural features are the Rivers Ouse and Foss, dividing the city into three zones: the central area within the extended defences of the Roman fortress; the area centred on Micklegate; and the area east of the Foss centred on Walmgate. Bridges

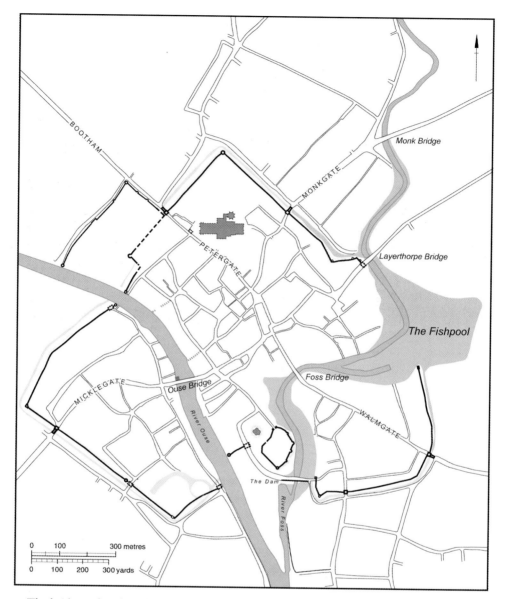

4 The bridges of York and the possible maximum extent of the King's Fishpool

were a vital part of York's infrastructure linking the zones together, the only other option being the ferries that crossed the Ouse where the Lendal and Skeldergate bridges now stand.

THE OUSE

The Ouse was the lifeblood of the medieval city, connecting York to the sea and inland waterways, enabling merchants to bring in goods and materials that were used by the city to develop its capacity as an important port. Indications of the importance of the river

5 An unusual, circular trench for the construction of new pumping station at North Street that exposed wattle and timber river-front revetments. © *York Archaeological Trust*

are seen in the efforts the Corporation made to keep it free from financial and physical obstructions; the area around it, especially near Ouse bridge, formed the commercial heart of the city with some of its wealthiest parishes.

The river ran within a steep-sided channel, much of which is now almost invisible due to later development, but can still be seen in the steep slope from Bishophill to Skeldergate and the noticeable slope at the rear of Coney Street. At the time of the Conquest the Ouse was much wider and excavations have shown that in the early twelfth century the bank was within 3m of the streets of Skeldergate and North Street.

Changes to the river banks were caused by reclamation, although when this commenced is unclear. In 1288 it was considered an ancient custom for those with property backing onto the river along Coney Street to enlarge their holdings by encroaching onto the banks. River fronts did not develop in one campaign, but plot by plot, giving the river front its uneven appearance.

Along North Street and Skeldergate excavations have shown land reclamation commenced in the ninth century, but more concerted efforts began in the eleventh and twelfth centuries. In Skeldergate wattle fences were set at right angles to the river, possibly acting as breakwaters to encourage silt to build up. A possible quay was identified in North Street with timbers defining a rectangular space backfilled with rubbish. Elsewhere the banks were covered with dumps of material stabilised by timbers driven into the river banks.

The process of reclamation intensified in the late twelfth and thirteenth centuries and along Skeldergate timber planks, posts and hurdle work was found 5m from the present street front. The area behind this was backfilled with vast quantities of material containing leather, brushwood and domestic rubbish. Similar revetments have been found in London at Billingsgate and Queenhithe. This period also saw limestone used for river walls instead of timber in places along Skeldergate. At the rear of Coney Street, a substantial stone wall of late twelfth- or early thirteenth-century date may indicate a previous river wall 25m closer to the street than the present river front.

The process of reclamation and rebuilding is clearly demonstrated in North Street where successive limestone river walls have been found with buildings constructed on the newly reclaimed land. Reclamation in some plots was a long process. At Albion Wharf in Skeldergate, sequences of reclamation associated with a limestone river wall parallel to the Ouse were overlain by dumps of clays and silts spanning the fourteenth to sixteenth centuries, probably associated with walls pushed further out into the river.

Through the late thirteenth and the fourteenth centuries reclamation continued, perhaps driven by the development of ships capable of carrying larger cargoes. A documented campaign of reclamation involved the Franciscan Friary on the north-east bank of the river that had built a river wall in 1288. This apparently caused problems for the residents in Skeldergate who petitioned the king for permission to build a river wall of their own. This was granted in 1305 and was paid for from the *murage* (building tax) of the city. Part of this river wall was excavated close to Skeldergate Bridge at City Mills where a substantial limestone wall with a foundation of timber piles was found 8m behind the present river wall. Access through the limestone river walls was through gates, known as water gates, and it is possible that the warehouses built on the river fronts had cranes allowing ships to be unloaded directly into them.

The river wall excavated at the City Mills bore evidence of a warehouse and steps to a water gate with a vaulted passage. Another water gate was excavated at the rear of Coney Street and probably dated to 1575. These limestone river walls represent the ultimate development of the river front and are still visible, most notably between Ouse bridge and Lendal bridge on the north-west side of the river, with their many blocked and altered water gates.

King's Staith was the most important, as it was the only public quay in the city and is located on the north-east side of the river adjacent to Ouse Bridge. Little is known about the development of King's Staith and no excavations have been carried out there. It was constructed shortly before 1366, when a charter states that it was 'newly constructed between Use Bridge and the inn of the Friars Minor' and repairs were carried out in 1453 by the city mason, Robert Couper. It was extended after the Dissolution and rebuilt in 1774 and 1820.

Cranes were an important feature of the river front and common cranes are recorded in York and Hull. York's Common Crane was on Skeldergate, adjacent to the modern Skeldergate Bridge in an area known as the Crane Garth. It is first recorded in 1417 as a newly rebuilt timber structure on a stone footing which implies that it was originally considerably older. Here goods imported by 'foreign' traders (non-freemen) were unloaded and tolls levied.

Wharves also belonged to the ecclesiastical establishments along the north-east bank of the Ouse. The abbot of St Mary's Abbey had a wharf at the bottom of Marygate and the Augustinian and Franciscan Friaries had landings. There is also evidence for a water gate in the surviving precinct wall of the Franciscan Friary. The Ouse therefore changed dramatically from the late eleventh century through the piecemeal reclamation of the river front with the limestone river walls of the fourteenth and fifteenth century, forcing the river into a narrower course.

6 River-front archaeology on the Ouse. © *York Archaeological Trust*

7 The excavation and recording of a water gate in Skeldergate. © *York Archaeological Trust*

OUSE BRIDGE

Ouse Bridge was the most important in the city, on one of the principal streets to the market, and surrounded by wharves and warehouses. It is not known for how long the Anglo-Scandinavian bridge survived after the Conquest, but a timber bridge collapsed on the return of Archbishop William in 1154, under the weight of the crowd that had come to greet him. Its replacement was stone and antiquarian drawings of the civic buildings on the bridge suggest it was constructed *c.*1170–80.

The construction of a new bridge was a lengthy and costly business and little is known of how it was funded. London Bridge was rebuilt between 1176 and 1209, through gifts and endowments administered through the Church until control was passed to the bridge wardens. A similar situation could have existed in York. In 1307 Archbishop Greenfield supported raising charitable contributions for the maintenance of the bridge.

It was also a common act of piety to leave money for the repair of bridges and bequests were made in wills of York's wealthier citizens. Funding for the bridge was formalised when Richard II granted the city the right to acquire land and tenements to the value of £100 to pay for the upkeep of both Ouse and Foss Bridge, and the chapel on Ouse Bridge. This was managed by the bridgemasters and their accounts for Ouse bridge survive from 1400 and for Foss bridge from 1406.

The grand views along York's river fronts that we have today from Ouse Bridge would have been unfamiliar to the medieval residents. The bridge was a continuation of the street and was lined with buildings that hung over the edges of the bridge so as not to obstruct the carriageway. From the fourteenth century it had 23 buildings on the north side and 18 buildings and a cross on the south side. This increased through the later fifteenth and early sixteenth centuries, when there were between 20 and 30 houses on the south side.

Most of what we know of Ouse bridge comes from documentary sources, antiquarian drawings and paintings that depict it as it was after the centre of the medieval bridge collapsed in 1565 and before its total replacement in 1820. The medieval bridge had six piers, the outermost on dry land with only the central arches used for navigation; these were flanked by arches called the King's and Queen's Bow. The arch at the eastern end was called the Salthole and steps known as the 'salthole *grese*' led from the bridge to the river.

The bridge also housed some of the principal civic buildings of the city. On the north side of the west end was the chapel, the Council Chamber, the Exchequer and the civic prisons. The chapel originated as the King's Free Chapel, but it was rededicated to St William of York in 1228. The tower of the chapel had a clock and bell that set the time for the enforcement of market regulations and from 1246 there was a toll booth on the south side, where payments were taken for the transfer of goods from one side of the river to the other.

Other civic buildings included the city *maison dieu* (hospital), a charitable foundation of uncertain date, but re-founded in 1302, which stood opposite the chapel. The bridge had public toilets below the *maison dieu*, mentioned in 1367. In 1544 there was a female attendant who was paid two shillings for '*kepyng cleyn the pyssing holles*'. These toilets were removed in 1579/80 when all toilets that discharged into the Ouse were removed.

THE FOSS AND THE KING'S FISHPOOL

The Foss, like the Ouse, ran in a steep-sided channel. An area of high ground running along its northern side was followed by St Saviourgate and Coppergate where excavations have shown the river bank was 6m lower than the street level. In the Peasholme Green area ridges aligned roughly north–south ran towards the river and may have encouraged areas of marshy ground to form, dictating areas of occupation. Walmgate and George Street (medieval Noutgail) follow the higher ground along the spur of land surrounded by a loop of the river. Centuries of infilling, landscaping and modification have hidden much of the old river channel, but it is still detectable in the steep slope from St Saviourgate to Peasholme Green and from the present Lead Mill Lane to Piccadilly and Navigation Road.

Domesday Book and the *Rights and Laws* suggest the Foss had an important commercial role in the Anglo-Scandinavian period. This changed when a dam was built as part of the construction of the castle in 1069, creating a vast artificial lake known as the King's Fishpool (the *Stagnum Regis*). The dam was washed away in 1315 and needed constant repair during the fourteenth and fifteenth centuries. Excavations suggest it raised the water level in excess of 2m, although this steadily dropped through the twelfth century. Domesday Book lists the destruction this caused and excavations in Piccadilly showed that Roman, Anglian and Anglo-Scandinavian features were sealed by layers of river silt.

The extent of the Fishpool during the medieval period is unclear and the earliest map shows it after a period of reclamation. Clues can be found in medieval place names: the Marsh (*le Mersc*) around Hungate is recorded in the late twelfth century and St Saviour's Church is described as being on its edge. Other place names included Marsh Street and Pond Lane that led to Pond Garth indicating the area was far from dry. Peasholme Green (the islet or low-lying area where peas grow) is recorded by *c*.1270 and gives another clue as to the nature of the area. This information and evidence from excavations show the Fishpool covered a vast area around modern Coppergate, Walmgate, Peasholme Green and the land now called Foss Islands.

Water level in the Fishpool fluctuated due partly to reclamation, but also because the climate became wetter in the later fourteenth century. Another factor to affect water level would have been the small tributaries or becks that fed into the Foss on the eastern side of the city. The Fishpool acted as a royal fishery and fish sales are recorded from 1221 to 1399 after which it declined as a fishery, and the Foss and the Fishpool became the responsibility of the Corporation in 1537.

Several landings are recorded on the edges of the Fishpool at Layerthorpe Bridge, the Carmelite Friary and St Margaret's Landing near the Red Tower. By 1504 a quay existed at the Merchant Adventurers' Hall and the first landing at Coppergate is mentioned in 1546 as owned and let by the Corporation.

Changes to the management of the Fishpool are reflected in the archaeology, with the absence of silting from the eleventh to thirteenth centuries implying careful maintenance which may reflect its use as a fishery. During the fourteenth century this changed, perhaps motivated by a need to dispose of the city's rubbish as much as by a desire to gain more land. The Marsh was one of the principal locations for the dumping of rubbish, despite complaints made by the residents.

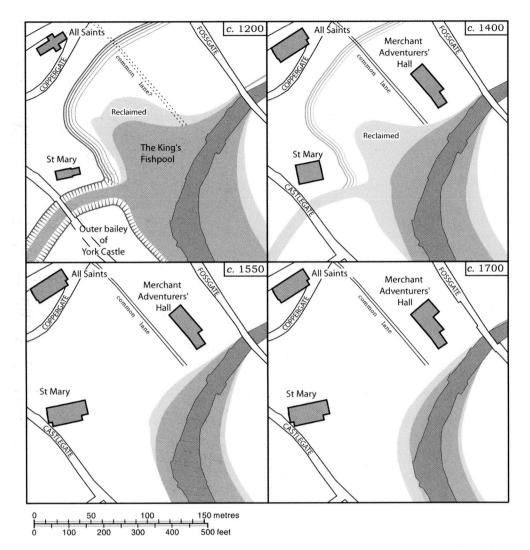

8 The process of reclaiming land as identified in the Coppergate area

Reclamation was carried out by individuals or groups of properties and increased the risk of flooding elsewhere, creating a self-perpetuating cycle of flood and reclamation. This often led to disputes with the keeper of the Fishpool. In the thirteenth century the keeper himself was accused of seizing flooded meadows and the jury decided he could cut on the banks, so long as his men used a little scythe and kept one foot in the boat. William Bowes in 1420 was accused of allowing filth, sedge and grass to accumulate in the pond to the rear of his properties in Peasholme Green and many fish had died. He was ordered to enclose his land and remove waste from the water.

Some of the best evidence for reclamation has come from Coppergate where a concerted attempt was made to raise the ground level, infilling the steep natural slope to the Foss from the late eleventh to twelfth century. Further campaigns of reclamation from the thirteenth century saw one area totally reclaimed, coinciding with alterations to the castle defences associated with the arrival of the Franciscan Friars established in the outer bailey of the castle.

The fourteenth to sixteenth centuries saw further reclamation. One of the largest encroachments was by the Carmelites in the early fourteenth century, who built a quay on the banks of the Fishpool. Evidence for this may have been found in excavations in Carmelite Street where a quay was found consisting of dumped material revetted with horizontal, edge-laid planks held in place with substantial posts. Excavations at Coppergate identified three further phases of reclamation: the later fourteenth, later fifteenth and early sixteenth centuries.

Reclaimed land was stabilised in Piccadilly by a substantial revetment consisting of rows of vertical posts, horizontal timbers and wattle work. At Coppergate the river front was consolidated with clay reinforced with piles and one revetment had substantial timbers, some of which had come from a boat. The reclaimed land does not appear to have been intensively used, perhaps because of the risk of flooding. A few buildings have been identified in Coppergate and on the Walmgate side of the Fishpool; the evidence suggests it was open ground used for wells and rubbish pits. This corresponds with a description from 1584 stating that land bordering the Foss was used for orchards and gardens.

FOSS BRIDGE

Foss Bridge is not as well understood as Ouse Bridge and, despite the medieval bridge surviving until 1811, it did not receive a great deal of attention from antiquaries or artists. Nevertheless it was no less important, being the only route to the important suburb of Walmgate and the road to the coast. In contrast to Ouse Bridge, a statement of civic pride, Foss Bridge was to become a statement of religious belief.

The origins of Foss Bridge may have been as a fortified gateway to the Anglo-Scandinavian city. The earliest references to the bridge date from 1145–48 and it was sometimes referred to as the 'bridge over the Fishpond'. Presumably the bridge started out as timber and was subsequently replaced in stone. Leland described the stone bridge as having three arches.

The bridge was positioned at the narrowest point of the Foss and the wider Fishpool was either side of it. The water within the Fishpool was not fast moving, and mud and silt constricting the river at the bridge was a serious problem – there were frequent complaints about the arches silting up. Measures to limit this included forbidding the occupiers of the houses on the bridge from throwing anything into the river, and grates were secured at the ends of the bridge to prevent rubbish from the street ending up in the river.

Like Ouse Bridge it was a continuation of the street and was lined with houses and shops. In 1376 there were 26 properties; by the mid fifteenth century there were 23 buildings on one side and 19 on the other. This number was maintained into the sixteenth century, but by the next century the number of buildings had been reduced.

Some evidence for the rebuilding of the bridge occurs in the charter issued by Richard II in 1393 that set up the bridge fund. The mayor and citizens were granted permission to build foundations for a chapel on Foss Bridge which appears to have been consecrated by 1424. It may be at this point that the bridge was also rebuilt in stone. The new chapel, dedicated to St Anne, was located at the north-east end on the northern side of the bridge. It was intended to house altars for masses for the souls of the royal family, the mayor and the citizens, and was managed by the Corporation.

THE STREETS AND LANES

The street names of York reflect its history and can be used to identify characteristics of its topography. The later medieval city was heavily influenced by the Anglo-Scandinavian layout and three principal routes can be defined, influenced by the orientation of the Roman fortress and the location of the crossings over the Ouse and Foss.

One route, roughly east–west, runs from Micklegate Bar, along Micklegate, over Ouse Bridge and to the oldest market of Pavement. The second passes across the south-east side of the fortress represented by Lendal, Coney Street, Nessgate and Castlegate. Radiating off these streets were numerous narrow streets, lanes and alleys, many of which still survive in one form or another. The third major route connected the two Roman gates at Bootham Bar and King's Square along High and Low Petergate then via Fossgate into Walmgate.

Important areas such as the markets and the river front were accessed by lanes running off the main thoroughfares and some can be traced back from the eleventh and twelfth centuries. King's Staith was served by lanes that ran down from Castlegate although these are now truncated by Clifford Street: First Water Lane or Cargate, now King's Street; Middle Water Lane or Thursgail, now Cumberland Street; Far Water Lane or Hertegate, now Friargate. Water lanes also existed off Skeldergate and North Street. Some lanes indicated their function such as Fish Landing Lane that runs down the side of St Michael Spurriergate, and in 1375 there was a reference to Lime Landing off North Street.

The medieval thoroughfares have suffered from street widening with only the famous Shambles and a few adjacent streets left to give a feel of the medieval city. This process of road-widening can be traced through maps and archaeology. Excavations at Coppergate showed the street frontage was up to 5m in front of the present street line. Maps from 1852 suggest the south-western end of the street was barely 2m wide. Even All Saints Pavement was altered to aid the widening of Coppergate and Pavement. Churchyards were popular targets for the road improvers and St Helen's Square was formed from the churchyard of St Helen's in 1733. All of the central churches have had their graveyards reduced for road-widening.

The Norman Conquest had a major impact on the established street pattern through the creation of the castles and the alterations to the Minster. York Castle (Clifford's Tower) and the creation of the Fishpool split one of the commercial districts, cutting off the route along Castlegate and resulting in a new route which skirted the defences, crossing the Foss over the dam. This replanning is perhaps reflected in early church redundancies such as St Stephen's, and the merger of St Mary's and St Margaret's by c.1308, combined with the initial abandonment of some plots during the twelfth century in Fishergate.

The network of streets was vital for the functioning of the city, but the Corporation was not directly responsible for their upkeep. Maintenance was down to the residents in each street who were responsible for the area adjacent to their building. Religious houses and lay landowners were often negligent in repairing roads and devised schemes to persuade the public to contribute to funding their repair.

Some people viewed road maintenance as a pious act. For example Robert de Howm, mayor in 1368, left money for the repair of Gillygate, Monkgate and the pavement beyond Monk Bridge in his will of 1396. An alternative was a toll called *pavage*, raised with the consent of the king, in 1308, 1319 and 1329 on merchandise brought into the city. Finally there were private agreements, such as that made by the abbot of St Mary, responsible for repairs to Gillygate, Bootham and Monkgate, who gave part of the tolls from fairs and the gift of two areas of stray to the mayor, on the condition that the latter maintained the streets.

Maintenance of roads was carried out by the pavers, who appear in the Freemen's Register in 1387. It appears they had a regular supply of work and one paver, John Bryg, worked for the city paving Hosiergate (Pavement near St Crux), Nessgate, the market and Ouse Bridge in 1440. He was again employed by Ouse Bridge in 1442 and 1454 and worked for the Minster mending pavements in 1447 and 1456.

That these streets were made of hard-wearing surfaces is reflected in the increasing use of horseshoes from the eleventh century, but occasionally archaeology gives us a glimpse of the handiwork of the medieval pavers. Excavation has shown that Goodramgate was surfaced with cobbles in the eleventh century, and then overlain with successive layers of gravel. In High Petergate cobbled surfaces 1m below the present street are thought to represent medieval street levels.

Excavation suggests cobbles were the favoured surface across the city. A lane that ran down the side of the Merchant Adventurers' Hall to the Foss was surfaced with cobbles. Away from the city centre excavations across the line of Hungate identified sequences of road surfaces dating to the mid fourteenth century consisting of closely packed cobbles. On the south-west side of the river excavations have identified cobble surfaces associated with Fetter Lane.

Lanes, alleyways and yards were more prone to being built over or altered as properties developed. Alleys divided plots and were provided for in title deeds as they gave access to the areas at the rear of properties. Excavations show they could be surfaced with a variety of materials. In Walmgate properties had cobbled alleyways and cobbled yards whereas in Coppergate, where alleyways were significant features from c.1300, they were surfaced with cobbles or limestone rubble. At the Bedern foundry off Goodramgate an alleyway was surfaced at different times with mortar and limestone, clay, rubble, mould fragments from the foundry, sand or cobbles.

What the documentary and archaeological evidence suggests, therefore, is that the streets, while not up to modern standards, were at least surfaced, predominantly with cobbles.

URBAN REAL ESTATE

While streets provided the skeleton of York, property, whether open land or buildings, secular, institutional or religious, gave the city its form. It has been argued that by the end of 1069 York was in need of rebuilding and again following the alleged fire of 1137, the record of which has been reinterpreted from reading *combustia* for fire to *consecreta*, meaning religious event.

The secular medieval buildings in York date from the fourteenth century and later, and many were surveyed by the Royal Commission on Historic Monuments of England. Since then further buildings have been identified during renovation and alterations. For example at 48 Stonegate the roof of a timber-framed building of c.1400 was exposed. At 36 Coney Street part of the timber frame of a building was found hidden behind seventeenth-century alterations.

Urban property, as it is today, was valuable and frequently changed hands. Value depended on size, location, occupation and usage. Town property also included open land available for rent, used as gardens, orchards or yards, and there are numerous references to these in the Bridgemasters' and Vicars Choral accounts. Medieval property markets were vigorous and became increasingly complex from the thirteenth century, a phenomenon which coincided with an increase in documentary sources. One clear feature of the average medieval neighbourhood is that the houses of the rich and the poor, as well as open spaces, could all be found along the same street.

Rebuilding was often the result of the changing needs of landlords and tenants combined with improving methods of construction. Owning and renting properties for cash income was to become an important source of wealth for some of York's citizens. The built environment reflected social values and institutional or personal initiatives, and was not simply a reflection of economic wealth and prosperity. New buildings were erected in times of financial and political insecurity, perhaps in a symbolic act to boost self-image and prestige.

Periods with an apparent lack of building activity may not signify economic decline. People may simply have invested in other expressions of wealth, such as internal fittings and fixtures. As such the vast majority of building activity was not new builds, but alterations and repairs which provided employment for carpenters, tilers and plasterers. The chance survival of archaeological sequences means large areas of medieval plot development are rare, but with documents and the surviving buildings, something of the character of the medieval townscape can be recreated.

Medieval building in York and other towns followed a basic yet highly adaptable pattern. However the extent to which designs and styles of buildings in town and country borrowed or copied from one another through the Middle Ages is a matter of debate. Documentary sources such as building contracts, rent accounts and title deeds give a glimpse of the character of the medieval streets. In the Petergate area, for example, shops had living accommodation above and alleys giving access to yards or property that stood at the rear.

Before the thirteenth century documentary and architectural evidence is rare and buildings are mainly known through their foundations. This is a problem since foundations can be open to several interpretations and we know nothing of the appearance of the buildings above ground which can be vital to the understanding of how they were used.

Documents suggest building regulations were introduced to York in the thirteenth century, and were perhaps similar to the London Assize of Buildings in 1200 that regulated everything from wall construction to roofing material. In York building contracts such as one in 1335 stating 'foundations to be made from firm piles and stones and above-ground level to be one foot broad under the sill beam' and the recurrence of similar construction methods across the city suggest that there was an element of control in construction.

9 A York building style: timber piles and cobbles. © *York Archaeological Trust*

Property was referred to as *messuage*, *tenement* or *burgage*, each term potentially reflecting some difference in the property or the tenants. Buildings on these plots might be described as house, hall or cottage. Documents refer to *dingis* in York from the late eleventh century to the fourteenth, which are thought to be cellars. Excavations have identified two thirteenth-century cellars. One was in Feasegate and re-used the Roman fortress wall accessed by a flight of stone steps; the other was at Coppergate and was timber-lined.

Plots were sometimes amalgamated to form larger units or subdivided to increase the number of properties. Excavation shows that plots were defined by ditches, fences, hedges or brushwood. Rubbish pits also clustered along property boundaries. These plots could be very long-lived and many, with only minor variation, survive into the present day.

Excavated sites in York, Southampton, London, Northampton, Lincoln and Durham show buildings were laid out either gable-end to the street or parallel to it. The most elaborate buildings were arranged around a courtyard with the main house at the rear of the plot and rows of shops at the front, such as Barley Hall in Stonegate. These belonged to wealthy families or institutions and were the town houses of lay or ecclesiastical lords who resided out of town. They were a residence for the lord when in town on business, but also provided accommodation for the lord's representatives engaged in everyday affairs such as selling produce, collecting rents or buying goods especially luxuries. Large buildings may also have functioned as taverns, alehouses, inns and almshouses.

More common were smaller properties with two rooms on two or more floors along the main streets. The majority of these properties were gable-end to the street, allowing the maximum amount of the street frontage to be used for retail units with alleys accessing the yards at the rear. These buildings were used as shops, warehouses, workshops and homes. Living accommodation was often on the first floor, with kitchens in a detached building at the rear, although in London examples are known with the kitchen above ground within the main building.

Stone began to be used for private buildings in the twelfth and thirteenth centuries with a shop or warehousing on the ground floor and a residence above. These buildings in York, Norwich, London, Winchester, Lincoln, Salisbury and Southampton were concentrated near the cathedral or commercial areas. Stone houses are recorded in York in the twelfth and thirteenth centuries in Coney Street where one was given to the prior of Durham. John Selby had a stone house in Micklegate and Kirkham Abbey owned stone houses in Walmgate. The bridgemasters' accounts mention stone houses close to Fishergate Bar into the fifteenth century.

Standing remains exist in Gray's Court and there are parts of a fourteenth- or fifteenth-century stone house in Precentor's Court incorporated into later buildings. The 'Norman House' in Stonegate is the most complete example and was exposed and partly excavated in 1939. A stone building was found below the Merchant Adventurers' Hall, re-used as foundations for part of the fourteenth-century guildhall.

Excavations have identified stone buildings in Skeldergate and Aldwark dated to the late eleventh century. They had foundations consisting of broad trenches into the base of which were driven piles, overlain by clay and cobbles, and were demolished in the late twelfth or thirteenth century. The demolition of stone buildings to make way for rows of timber cottages let out by their owners during the thirteenth and fourteenth centuries matches a trend seen across the country.

Timber was the primary building material for the cottages of the urban poor and the impressive medieval buildings that still line the streets of York were timber-framed. Some timber-framed buildings had a stone ground floor and are shown in paintings of the late eighteenth and nineteenth centuries. A much-altered survivor stands at the corner Newgate and Patrick Pool, with its upper floor replaced in brick.

How timber was used in buildings in urban and rural settings saw considerable change through the medieval period. In York buildings continued the pre-Conquest tradition of timbers driven directly into the ground or laid within shallow trenches until the thirteenth century. One change at Coppergate saw the wood-lined cellars characteristic of the Viking buildings disappear in the Anglo-Norman period. Other changes in construction at Coppergate saw buildings with posts in pits dug into trenches along both side walls. Posts could be set on limestone blocks with carefully constructed foundations consisting of a pit into which timber piles were driven. The pit was then filled with rubble. This was a common form of construction from the mid twelfth century, and was seen in excavations in Petergate, Skeldergate and Aldwark.

From the late twelfth century a continuous sill wall made of cobble or limestone began to be used. This indicates the use of fully timber-framed buildings and documents record the presence of two-storey buildings from the thirteenth century, and by the fourteenth century of buildings with two or three storeys. Padstones and dwarf walls were used to raise timbers off the ground, reducing the risk of rotting, and the above-ground framing was covered with plaster – both features of the buildings along Petergate and Stonegate. Documents and archaeology show the increased use of tile from the twelfth century for roofing and wall infill and by the fifteenth century tilers were constantly employed. These changes increased the durability of buildings and reduced the risk of fire.

10 What lies beneath: the archaeologist's contribution to understanding buildings at Back Swinegate. © *York Archaeological Trust*

An extensive area of medieval streetscape was excavated along Swinegate (medieval Patrick Pool), Little Stonegate and Grape Lane. Tenements were of uniform size and some were associated with the development of the demolished church of St Benedict. The excavations showed the graveyard was sealed by a levelling deposit in the late twelfth century before the construction of buildings that became known as Benets Rents. In Grape Lane properties were defined by alleyways leading to backyards or gardens. These alleys survived for varying lengths of time and some may have connected to Petergate, as the surviving Mad Alice Lane does today.

The complex nature of plot development was seen in excavations on the corner of Denys Lane and Walmgate. After the Norman Conquest the site fell into disuse until the thirteenth century when new property boundaries were laid out. In the fourteenth century timber-framed buildings were constructed; two gable-end to the street and one parallel to it. The early fifteenth century saw the site cleared and new buildings erected. The excavation of this area highlighted the problems which arise from the use of construction style to date buildings which are still standing. The survey of one of the buildings prior to demolition dated it to the early fourteenth century, but excavation showed it was 100 years older, suggesting it had re-used timber from one of the earlier buildings. This is a practice that can find parallels in the bridgemasters' accounts for the demolition and re-use of building materials.

Timber-framing introduced an element of pre-fabrication and flexibility, allowing additions and alterations to be made. Two-storey rows were adapted to form three-storey structures in Stonegate. For example, a row built *c.*1325 had garrets added in the late fifteenth

11 The surviving timber-framed buildings can also tell us much. © *York Archaeological Trust*

or sixteenth century and Mulberry Hall, built as a two-storey range in the mid fifteenth century, was heightened and given additional rooms in the sixteenth century.

The change from thatch to tile for roofing and better construction probably made buildings drier and saw a reduction in the amount of organic rubbish from roofing and floor coverings. This would also have seen a general improvement in living and working conditions. The bridgemasters' accounts record that three cartloads of earth were used for floors in the house of Richard Polyngton in 1472 and excavations show that clay or mortar was also used. The durability of buildings meant that even though floors were re-laid, the raising of ground level within buildings occurred at a slower rate than in previous centuries. As a result centuries of occupation can be compressed into a few centimetres that are often erased by later developments.

Buildings materials such as limestone had to be imported if a convenient source for recycling stone couldn't be found. Tile and brick supply was partly controlled by the religious institutions such as the Carmelite Friary and the Vicars Choral that had their own tile and brick works. Merchants also controlled the supply of material as in 1449 the Corpus Christi Guild obtained wood from John Marshall, merchant, and Marion Kent, a merchant's widow. Some merchants dealt in a variety of building material such as Thomas Gishop who supplied wood and tiles for a building project.

Modernisation of houses occurred in the late fourteenth and fifteenth centuries, and was recorded in the bridgemasters' accounts and the records of the Vicars Choral. Buildings were having chimneys inserted and internal subdivisions. Chimneys were often made not of brick, but of timber and plaster, which raises issues for their identification in the archaeological record. Nevertheless excavations have identified modifications to buildings in this period.

In Aldwark buildings that may have formed part of a row built in the mid fourteenth century underwent a programme of structural alterations which was followed by rebuilding in the late fifteenth to sixteenth centuries when the building was subdivided with service rooms, screens passage and hall. The buildings at the corner of Denys Lane and Walmgate went through a programme of renovation in the late fifteenth or early sixteenth century. The presence of fireplaces with plaster flues may have been identified at Newgate where fireplaces in the fifteenth-century tenements were built near the walls. The presence of post-holes around them may indicate the position of supports for plaster or timber cowl flues.

Rows are one of the most distinctive forms of York's buildings. These consisted of a uniformly sized sequence of houses-cum-shops under a single roof built from the fourteenth century. Rows probably developed when landlords decided to standardise the buildings along street frontages to maximise rents. Many rows were built by ecclesiastical institutions, coinciding with the development of the belief in purgatory and the founding of chantries, with the rents from the rows providing the funds for a chantry priest. The Church may also have been motivated by the restrictions on gifts of land except under royal licence in 1291, with rows serving as a way of maximising the income from static urban estates.

Our Lady Row, Goodramgate, is the most famous in York and was built to endow a chantry in the church of Holy Trinity. The 1316 charter for its construction survives and records that the parishioners agreed to the building of the houses in the cemetery. Several similar charters survive relating to the construction of rows and are often used to date them. However, it appears rows could be built over a protracted period after the charter was granted. This was shown in York during excavations at the end of the surviving part of a row in Newgate. This row was dated by its charter to 1337 and a mid fourteenth-century date for the erection of the row was confirmed by the excavations, although the row at this time only filled part of the area specified in the charter. The row saw about a century of development with the end building having a yard. By the end of the fourteenth or early fifteenth century a brick-lined cesspit was built, but at some point in the fifteenth-century the cesspit was backfilled and the row extended over it.

12 A rare survivor: the small house of an artisan on King's Square. © *The author*

The substantial timber buildings and rows that survive are only part of the medieval building stock. Smaller houses or cottages were excavated in Walmgate and Little Stonegate, and a surviving small house of one-up one-down construction stands at the corner of King's Square and the Shambles. No. 1 Little Shambles is another example of lower-grade properties, but the buildings that once hemmed it in were demolished in the 1950s.

'WHAT HAS THE CORPORATION EVER DONE FOR US?'

Rubbish of all varieties was a serious problem for York, but it can tell us much about the medieval residents. If documents are taken at face value, the Corporation was not very good at dealing with the problem. The most famous indictment of the state of the city comes from 1332 when the mayor and bailiffs are told 'The King [Edward III] detesting the abominable smell abounding in the said city more than any other in the realm from dung and manure and other filth and dirt wherewith the streets and lanes are filled and obstructed … orders them to cause all streets and lanes of the city to be cleansed'.

Complaints were also made by the residents of some parts of the city, such as the parishioners of St John in the Marsh in 1409. They claimed the area around the church was a refuse dump used by the butchers of the Shambles, attracting dogs, and the associated smell meant they were barely able to get through their services. The complaints were apparently not effective, as in 1524 the Marsh and Hungate area became the appointed place to get rid of rubbish. Other areas of the city appear ill-kept, such as the site of the former church of St Benedict, described as 'lying waste and covered with refuse' prior to redevelopment for housing.

Was York as unwholesome as these records would lead us to us believe? The Corporation had measures in place to deal with rubbish as recorded in the Civic Ordinances. The most convenient place for disposing of rubbish was the rivers and from 1300 by-laws were passed forbidding people to use them for this purpose. The paved streets had gutters and in 1301 it was stipulated that they were to be kept free of obstructions. In the sixteenth century it was stated that 'there shal be a dung cart in every ward to take refuse out of the city where it should be layd so that husbands of the contrie may come there to and have it away'.

One of the main problems was rubbish from tradesmen such as butchers, fishmongers and tanners. The Corporation banned the butchers and fishmongers from throwing offal into the river. Washing skins in the same stretch of river 'where water is drawn for brewing or baking' was also banned: 'no refuse of pigs or offal or any noisome stuff shall be thrown in the said water'.

Sewers, known as King's Ditches, were far more prominent than they are today and formed an important part of the topography of the city. They defined property, ward and parish boundaries, and documentary references allow them to be traced across the city. For example, one ran from the Deanery, via Goodramgate to St Andrewgate. There it joined another ditch that started near the Merchant Taylors' Hall and then ran to Colliergate, passing under the road in a culvert, to run between Colliergate and the Shambles. Another defined the parish boundary of St Michael Spurriergate and others are mentioned in Micklegate and Bishophill. Another defined the rear of properties fronting onto Walmgate. Ultimately these ditches discharged into the Ouse or the Foss.

King's Ditches also ran along the inside of the city defences. One is recorded between Bootham Bar and Monk Bar in 1419, in a complaint from the Treasurer of the Minster to the mayor about it being blocked. This ditch continued along the rear of Aldwark and was known as The Werkdyke, King's Ditch or Queen's Ditch. Similar ditches ran around the inside of the defences on the south-west side of the Ouse and part of one was rented to the Guild of Tanners in 1476.

Rubbish disposal changed during the medieval period and was in stark contrast to the Anglo-Scandinavian city with its significant build-ups of rubbish. Through the eleventh to thirteenth centuries the practice of spreading it around or heaping it in the yards behind properties continued. Sequences of rubbish and cesspits, occasionally lined with wicker, are a common feature of excavations of this period and at Coppergate the toilet seat survived in one such pit, having fallen in or been deliberately discarded at the end of the pit's life.

This changed in the fourteenth and fifteenth centuries with the area behind properties being used increasingly for buildings, and a marked reduction or absence of pits. This implies rubbish was being taken away and if there are cesspits they become more substantial structures built of brick or stone allowing regular emptying. This period also

13 Sanitation was simple at first: twelfth-century cess pit and toilet seat from Coppergate.
© *York Archaeological Trust*

sees properties built without access to yards, such as those on the edge of churchyards, which must have had rubbish removed.

Private and religious institutions had higher standards of sanitation and excavations at St Mary's Abbey and St Leonard's Hospital have identified impressive stone drains. Some of the guilds also appear to have had money to spend on drainage, as a stone drain was found at St Anthony's Hall. The effectiveness of the Corporation's measures for dealing with the problem of rubbish comes from the biological and environmental evidence from across the city, which shows a steadily improving standard of hygiene that by the late medieval period was approaching levels comparable with the Roman period.

A supply of water was an important aspect of the well-being of the citizens, but York had no piped water or evidence for a public system of providing water like the public cistern in London. A public well or fountain may have existed off Blake Street, represented by a lane called Fountain Lane (*Funtaynesgale c.*1277). Wells, public or private, and the river were the main source of water. Private wells were located at the rear of properties and are found in archaeological excavations often lined with barrels with the bottoms knocked out, or occasionally with timber, stone or brick linings which supported the sides and acted as a simple filter.

So, levels of squalor are relative and by our modern standards medieval York was far from clean; however it was perhaps not quite as filthy as the documents lead us to believe. This is not to deny the problem that is reflected in the repetition of ordinances. Perhaps documents were couched in terms exaggerating the problems as an incentive to encourage people to keep the city clean.

14 For some, drains could be impressive, such as this stone drain from St Leonard's.
© *York Archaeological Trust*

IN SUBURBIA

Modern York is surrounded by nineteenth-century and later suburbs, but the medieval city also had suburbs. These incorporated areas of housing, pasture, gardens and orchards. Like their successors they developed along the principal approach roads to the city and were characterised by wider streets used for livestock markets and parking for carts queuing to pay tolls at the gates on market days, a situation that may also have encouraged trade free from city tolls. Marketing and transport were key factors in suburban growth.

The majority of the medieval suburbs had their origins in the Anglo-Scandinavian period and land grants of the twelfth century record buildings in Bootham, Fishergate,

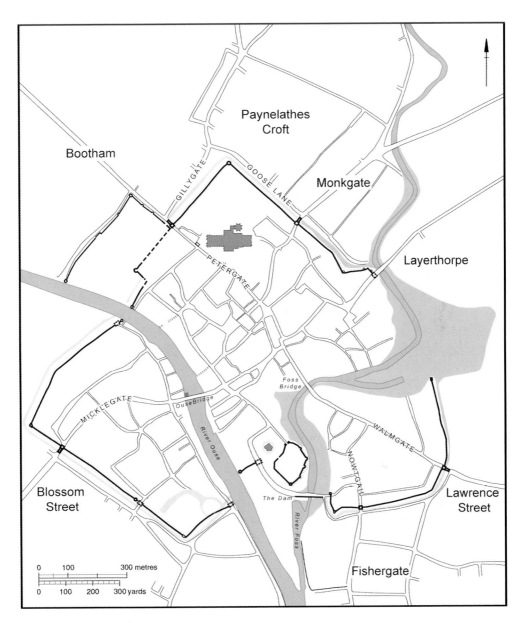

15 The suburbs of medieval York

Gillygate and Marygate. After the Conquest many former suburbs were brought within the defences of the city with the erection of defences that cut cross the Walmgate/Fishergate suburb. Similar defensive realignment occurred in Bristol, Northampton, Nottingham, Hereford and Stamford.

Suburbs were usually home to some of the poorest elements of society that made up a large part of the urban population; in the 1520s up to a quarter of Exeter's population lived in the suburbs. Those living in the suburbs were probably involved in agriculture, working the fields and gardens around the city and perhaps working in or for the hospitals. However, the suburbs were also home to the wealthy who could afford to have large houses close to the city. Hospitals founded before 1300 were located in the suburbs which also had numerous churches and chapels to meet the needs of travellers coming into the city as well as the parishioners. Gallows stood on the approaches to towns at the limits of the city's jurisdiction – St Leonard's had one at Garrow Hill near Green Dykes Lane, St Mary had one near Burton Stone Lane and the city used the Knavesmire.

York's suburbs are not well understood, but the limited excavations shed some light on their development and use. Fishergate had its origins in the Anglian *wic* and by the eleventh century was served by churches dedicated to All Saints, St Andrew (which formed the basis for the Gilbertine Friary) and St Helen. The churches of St George and St Stephen in Fishergate were brought within the city after the construction of the defences. There were also smaller religious houses and a *maison dieu,* though their locations are uncertain. Other than the Gilbertine Priory the area was not heavily built up and Speed's map of 1610 shows it as open land with windmills. Documents record that the area between Fishergate and Walmgate Bar was called the 'Bean Hills' and by the thirteenth century was partly developed with housing. Excavations in the area have identified some evidence for buildings and ditches perhaps defining fields.

The erection of the defences associated with the castle and later the city wall is thought to have resulted in a decline in the suburb by 1436: the parishes of Fishergate were assessed at less that 5s and the Gilbertine Priory was never wealthy. The lack of importance of the suburb is perhaps reflected in the fact that the city felt able to brick up Fishergate Bar in 1489, which suggests that there was not a vast amount of traffic on this side of the city. It was not re-opened until 1827.

On the other hand the creation of the defences does not appear to have had an adverse effect on the suburb of Walmgate. The area outside the defences was known as 'Walmgate Without' and extended along present Lawrence Street as far as the city boundary at Green Dykes Lane where the largest of the York leper hospitals, St Nicholas, stood. As with Fishergate there were several small churches dedicated to St Lawrence, St Michael, St Edward and St Nicholas.

Following the erection of walls around the old suburb of Walmgate, settlement remained focused along the Walmgate street frontage. This is shown on old maps and reflected in the archaeology that suggests intensive use of the street front from the tenth or eleventh century onwards. Maps of the seventeenth century and later show that the plots on the south side of the street respect the course of the King's Ditch, shown as late as the Ordnance Survey map of 1852.

Modern George Street, running off Walmgate, was called Nowtgail which suggests a narrow lane, and the area between the street and the ditch is shown as open land. Speed's plan of 1610 shows buildings near the junction with Walmgate and the bridgemasters record houses near Fishergate Bar. Excavations along George Street have not found evidence for intensive settlement and a similar situation existed to the rear of the north side of Walmgate where excavation also suggests open land. This may have been due to the marginal nature of the land near the Foss/King's Fishpool and the risks of flooding, but may also reflect the relative importance of Walmgate, which allowed road access to the east coast, whereas Fishergate, which ran parallel to the Ouse, lost out to river traffic which had refocused away frm the old *wic* to the area around the King's Staith.

Outside the walls along Lawrence Street excavations have identified buildings fronting the road from the eleventh century, with yards behind used for much the same activities as within the walls. Environmental evidence suggests the suburb was surrounded by farmland. Excavations give clues to activities carried out, such as charred sprouting cereal grains from an oven suggesting it had been used for drying grain as part of the malting process; there is also evidence for light industry. The north side of Lawrence Street towards the Fishpool was the location of tile works during the medieval period.

Blossom Street, the main road running from Micklegate Bar, connected the city to the wider road network giving access to London, Scotland and the west. The present name is a corruption of the medieval *Ploxwaingate* meaning street of the ploughmen. The breadth of the street allowed it to be used as a horse and cattle market. In 1282 it is recorded as having 29 properties, many of which were inns and hostelries.

There were two hospitals along Blossom Street: St Catherine's, a leper hospital, and St Thomas of Canterbury which provided hospitality to travellers and help to the poor. Excavations show that behind the street was farmland, with skeletons in the Roman cemetery found there having been damaged by ploughing. Buildings on the street front had yards and were defined by boundary ditches. Like Lawrence Street there was evidence for corn processing and metalwork.

On the west side of the city, the suburb ran from Bootham Bar to the city boundary at Burton Stone Lane, where the Hospital and Chapel of St Mary Magdalene stood. Control of the Bootham suburb was the cause of much disagreement between the city and St Mary's Abbey. The abbey felt that it had rights there and constrained the area available, and development focused on the opposite side of the road to the abbey precinct wall. In 1354 the abbey and the city agreed that the abbey would maintain a ditch between the abbey wall and the street providing no buildings were erected along its edge. Houses also lined Marygate opposite the abbey walls.

A glimpse of the suburb of Bootham comes in 1298 when Edward I ordered the pavements to be repaired and ruinous houses and pigsties to be pulled down. As in the other suburbs, excavations show a lack of activity away from the street fronts. Gillygate developed probably in association with the foundation of the church of St Giles in the twelfth century. At the end of Gillygate was a large open area known as the Horsefair. Such open areas were a common feature in the medieval period: London had one at Smithfield. Surrounding the Horsefair were several hospitals.

Goose Lane, the modern Lord Mayor's Walk, was largely undeveloped. The area around it was known as Paynelathes Croft, later the Groves, and belonged to St Mary's Abbey. Outside Monk Bar stood St Maurice's Church, of which only the graveyard remains. This served the suburb known as New Biggin and properties have been found near the church dating to the eleventh and twelfth centuries. They were built on material probably cast up from the city ditch which may have also sealed earlier buildings. It is possible that New Biggin was a replanning of an earlier suburb after the Norman Conquest.

Monkgate, Muncegate in 1080, was an extensive suburb and in 1282 had 50 tofts including two occupied by millers, who were perhaps working in the mills that stood near Monk Bridge. On the north side of the bridge stood the leper hospital of St Loy and beyond this lay the road to Heworth village which was in the Forest of Galtres until the twelfth century. Layerthorpe had its origins as a village in the Anglo-Scandinavian period. It had a church dedicated to St Mary and became home to Jewbury, the burial ground of the city's Jewish community. Little has been found of the suburb, but during the rebuilding of Layerthorpe Bridge archaeologists found wattle work and deposits dating to the eleventh and twelfth centuries.

The lay of the land shows the compact nature of the city during the medieval period, surrounded by suburbs that exploited the incoming traffic to the city. It also shows how the natural landscape was modified over time to suit the needs of the city. Within the walls throughout the course of the Middle Ages buildings were to undergo marked improvements, while the Corporation tried to come to terms with the rubbish by generated by the residents. The available evidence may suggest that York was perhaps not as unsanitary as the historical sources suggest.

2

PORTCULLIS AND PALISADE

The defences of York in the late eleventh century were more or less as they still are today. While they still follow a circuit of 2½ miles, previously they would also have been supplemented by the water of the King's Fishpool. A popular depiction of the medieval town shows it surrounded by stone walls and gates, but the castle upon which William might have stood in 1069 when surveying his new town with its encircling defences would have been made of earth and timber. Not until the thirteenth century were York's walls rebuilt in stone. The circuit of walls still retains 34 of its 39 towers, the four principal gates and the earth mounds of two castles, one still topped with its thirteenth-century keep. Nevertheless it is clear that the defences, like the rest of York, are the product of a long process of change.

One of the greatest contributions the Normans made to York was the erection of the castles, perhaps one of the most symbolic and easily recognised features of the period after the Norman Conquest. Equalled only by London in its number of castles, York has two: Baile Hill or the Old Baile, and York Castle, more commonly known as Clifford's Tower. At this point castles were a type of fortification still new to England. Their impact must have been significant particularly in the towns which were among the first to be controlled by this means, a process which can be followed in the narratives of William I's campaigns by William of Poitiers and Orderic Vitalis.

Domesday Book tells us that the creation of the castles destroyed one of the seven shires into which the town had been divided before the Conquest. As potent symbol of the newly established Norman regime, urban castles were also reminders of the conqueror's strength to the indigenous population over whom power was held in the new order. The fact that York had two castles may reflect the strategic importance of the city, its rebellious and independent nature, or both.

The threats of native resistance and foreign invasion were at their greatest in the decade after the Conquest and in York both castles were attacked and partly destroyed before the north finally became settled. The high, raw earth mounds of the castles with their large timber defences were there to impress the citizens as symbols of conquest rather than for their protection. The castles also fulfilled an administrative role, serving as a venue for the new rulers to hold court.

Clearly, complementary castles were considered essential to subjugate a city which was split into two main areas on either side of the Ouse. The castle we know as the Old Baile would have controlled the south-west bank of the Ouse while York Castle controlled the opposite bank of the Ouse, but also the Foss. The two castles together controlled

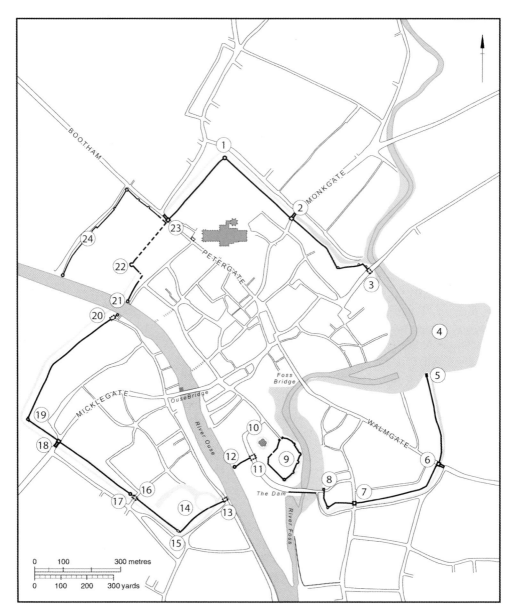

1. Robin Hood Tower
2. Monk Bar
3. Layerthorpe Postern
4. King's Fishpool
5. Red Tower
6. Walmgate Bar
7. Fishergate Bar
8. Fishergate Postern

9. Castle Bailey
10. Clifford's Tower
11. Castlegate Postern
12. Davy Tower
13. Skeldergate Postern
14. Old Baile
15. Bitchdaughter Tower
16. Lounlithgate

17. Sadler Tower
18. Micklegate Bar
19. Tofts Tower
20. Barker Tower/North St Postern
21. Lendal Tower
22. Multangular Tower
23. Bootham Bar
24. St Mary's Abbey Precinct

16 The defences of York at the end of the fourteenth century

movement throughout the Vale of York by dominating the vital intersection of north–south and east–west routes at the river crossings.

Norman castles were often built on the perimeter of the city defences. However, it can no longer be argued, as it was in the past, that the areas chosen in York were undeveloped; in fact they were chosen to exploit naturally commanding positions. The building of York Castle in the angle of the Ouse and Foss led to a reorientation of the routes into and out of the south-east side of the city, shifting them north towards Fishergate with a new route from Castlegate Postern, over a dam across the Foss and skirting the defences to link up with Fishergate.

Throughout the later medieval period, York Castle was the more important of the two and the surviving thirteenth-century keep was known as the King's Tower, Great Tower or the tower by the Castle of York. The name Clifford's Tower was not used until the sixteenth century. The castle was probably at its most developed at the end of the fourteenth century, when it served as a fortress, royal palace, mint, prison, court of justice and administrative centre for the country. Its role as a fortress ended in the sixteenth century; it was not used as a royal palace from the fifteenth century and the mint was moved to the site of St Leonard's Hospital, the present Mint Yard, in 1546.

After the war of succession between Stephen and Matilda and the occasional raids by the Scots there were long periods of peace in England. So why did the towns of medieval England need walls? Walls were not built to impress the residents as they would have been hidden from view by buildings, with the only prominent feature being the gates. The defensive topography of the town was very complex and the walls were an expression of the complementary and competing interests of the residents of the city. They were more significant for the statement they made to travellers visiting the city and those living in the surrounding villages.

York had several competing power bases and it is too easy to underestimate the secular power of the church with its large urban estates, law courts, gaols and gallows exempt from the city tolls. Disputes between the ecclesiastical liberties and the growing independence of the City Corporation in the thirteenth century coincide with periods when these institutions were defining their boundaries with walls that effectively defined space in the city between royal, civic and ecclesiastical authorities

Something of the power play between the Church and city is seen in the development of the precinct walls of St Mary's Abbey; it was stipulated that they could not be built in such a way that could be used to attack the city. The city walls were a political statement, expressing the authority of the city and its independence; this may be why they are shown on the thirteenth-century civic seal.

Access to the city was through the gates, known as bars, which were used as a show of importance, especially after they were rebuilt in stone. They acted as display boards, not only in York, but in other walled towns like Southampton, with the gates and barbicans used to display the city arms, still shown on three of York's bars, emphasising the important rights and privileges of the city. The statues that stand in menacing and watchful poses on three of York's bars are first mentioned in 1603, but may be considerably older and could have been used as a further display of power. The boundary between the city and the castle was marked with stones carved with the city arms.

The bars also proclaimed the legal authority of the city stocks and whipping posts next to them, complementing those in Pavement and the King's Staith. Royal authority was shown through the display of heads and body parts of traitors and rebels on the gates, normally Micklegate. Among the more notable heads displayed were Sir Henry Percy (Hotspur), killed in 1403 at Shrewsbury, whose family was influential in the city and had a town house in Walmgate; Henry, 3rd Lord Scrope of Masham executed in 1415 at Southampton; and Richard Duke of York after his death in the Battle of Wakefield in 1460.

The bars played a significant part in displays of civic authority to important visitors. They were cleaned and decorated as part of lavish ceremonies laid on by the mayor and Corporation. Visitors, such as the king, would be met on the city boundary by the sheriff, gentlemen and yeomen, and escorted, usually to Micklegate Bar. There, to the sound of music being played by the city musicians called the Waits, they were greeted by the mayor, alderman and the twenty-four, who were part of the Council that made up the city's Corporation

These displays could be loaded with symbolic significance, especially if the city wanted something. In 1486 it needed to win the favour of the new king, Henry VII. When he visited York that year he was met by the mayor and York's legendary founder, Eburak, who gave him the keys to the city. According to Geoffrey of Monmouth's *History of the King's of Britain*, Eburak became king on the death of his father, Mempricus, then reigned for nearly 40 years and founded a city 'on the far side of the Humber, which he called Kaereburac [York] in the time when King David ruled Judea'.

York's defences were an integral part of the economy and administration of the city. The bars restricted access, allowing the control of traffic, collection of tolls and imposition of curfews. Manning the defences was the responsibility of the citizens; sections of the walls, called custodies, were allocated to parishes within each of the six wards. The length of wall allocated to each parish varied from 100 to 650 yards and were manned by up to 125 men and a constable. The exception was the area around the Old Baile which was controlled by the Archbishop. The number of wards was reduced in c.1530 to four, each named after one of the bars; these remained in use until 1835.

Each ward had a warden who checked the fabric of the walls and reported areas needing repairs. Documents give a glimpse of the organisation of the walls: the gates were allocated watchmen and in 1327 it was recorded that there were nightly patrols and there was a curfew from 9pm to dawn. In the mid fifteenth century the watchmen, of which there were one or two at each gate during the day, were charged with keeping vagabonds and rogues out and checking for other 'lewd persons likely to disturb the peace'. Outbreaks of plague led to extra watches at the gates and King's Staith to prevent entry of people from infected places such as London or the West Riding.

Licences from the king for *murage*, a tax on goods to pay for defences, were issued from the thirteenth to fifteenth century at a number of towns such as Coventry, Norwich, King's Lynn and Yarmouth. In York a licence was issued from 1251 and *murage* was raised almost continuously until 1449, with the money used for repairs and construction. This was supplemented by tolls collected at the four bars and on the Ouse which had an allowance for annual expenditure on the walls. By the fifteenth century *murage* had become a useful addition to the city finances and in 1445 over £26 was received, but only £4 spent on repairs to the walls.

The defences had a range of uses over the centuries and were exploited to aid the economy of the town. Rooms within the bars were sometimes rented out and rent returns survive for Micklegate Bar, Bootham Bar, Monk Bar and Fishergate Bar. Rooms above the gates were also used as prisons and houses of correction. Barker Tower was let out to the ferrymen, and the city rental for 1376/77 lists several leases for grazing cattle, sheep and herbage on the ramparts.

Pigs were not allowed on the defences and if any were found on the inner or outer rampart they were seized and released once the owner paid a fine of 4d. If the fine wasn't paid the animal was slaughtered and the officer of the walls received the trotters. The city ditches were also leased for grazing. The only section of ditch known to contain water was between Walmgate Bar and Fishergate Bar, as a charter of 1502/03 allowed Thomas del Howe to 'have and hold the said mote and dyke with the fyschyng of the same'.

ARCHAEOLOGY OF THE CITY WALLS

Documents can tell us much about the walls, but in spite of their prominence and influence on the topography of the city the development of the defences is poorly understood. Where excavation has taken place it has shown a complex history of development. The north-east side of the Roman fortress wall was retained and buried by earth ramparts topped with timber palisades, probably in the ninth century, with new external ditches. The defences were extended to the Ouse and Foss, probably in the ninth and tenth century, perhaps driven by growing commercial needs. It is less clear whether the walls around the Micklegate area reflected the Roman defences or not. Parallels for the re-use of Roman defences can be found at London, Lincoln and Canterbury.

The extent to which the Roman defences survived up to the Conquest is open to speculation. Excavations in the Davygate area have shown the south-west wall of the fortress still stood 1m above-ground level in the twelfth century and the south-east fortress wall had become partially buried in rubbish at its south-west end. The northern end of the south-east fortress wall which runs behind St Andrewgate was subject to a concerted effort to rob it of stone in the late eleventh and early twelfth century.

The sections excavated through the ramparts show that they were heightened after the Norman Conquest and again in the fourteenth century, perhaps just before the stone walls were erected. The soil to raise the ramparts probably came from the recutting of the inner and outer ditches, but there is some evidence to suggest that soil may also have been scraped from an area around the walls to supplement the upcast from the ditches. These ditches were substantial features although they are now all but filled in; it is only possible to appreciate their original scale from Lord Mayor's Walk where the ditch is still 40ft wide.

Some stretches of the rampart were difficult to maintain, for example that from the Roman fortress wall to Lendal Tower. This was due to the steep slope to the river and the proximity to the ferry at St Leonard's Landing that saw the defences encroached on by buildings. How this section of defences connected to the existing water gate of St Leonard's Hospital is unclear, as the medieval defences were cleared from this area as early as 1572/3. Excavations in this area in 1914 identified a cobbled road leading to the water gate which may suggest that the area was not covered with a rampart and it may be that there was a small gate through the walls at this point.

17 Excavations have shown the development of the walls from as far back as Roman times in places. © *York Archaeological Trust*

From the water gate of St Leonard's Hospital a section of the Roman fortress wall can still be seen that includes the lower parts of the Multangular Tower. In 1315 and 1505 the Multangular Tower was called *Elrondyng* and its present name only appears in the seventeenth century. It is unusual that this section of Roman wall is not encased in ramparts, but records of St Mary's Abbey suggest there may have been ramparts covering them that were cleared in 1316; the death of five of the workmen during this work was considered an act of divine vengeance. Evidence from inside the wall in the adjoining St Leonard's Hospital showed that the ramparts were levelled to provide space for expansion of the hospital buildings.

Not all of the walls stand on ramparts. Where the defences approach the banks of the Foss and the King's Fishpool they diminish and eventually disappear near the site of Layerthorpe Postern; the same is true of the initial stretch of wall from the edge of the Fishpool in the Walmgate area where the rampart presumably started at the edge of the water. The stretch of wall between Davy Tower and the site of the Castle Postern does not stand on a rampart and is now only 7–10ft high because the ground level has been greatly altered here. However, there may have been a ditch in front of this stretch of wall as a document in 1454 mentions a labourer paid for working in the ditch near the Tower of the Friars Minor (Davy Tower) and there are further references to it in 1569 and later in the seventeenth century.

One of the few sections of the ramparts that have been excavated is near Walmgate Bar. This confirmed the documentary evidence that the defences around the Walmgate area were a creation of the thirteenth century. The excavations beneath the rampart revealed evidence for shallow pits and stakeholes, suggesting earlier occupation, and an old soil horizon had an irregular surface that was thought to be evidence of turf stripping to demarcate the line of the ramparts. There was a wide ditch on the outside and an inner ditch to provide material for the ramparts. The earliest rampart consisted of clay and earth which was sealed by material raising their height in the fourteenth century, probably prior to the construction of the surviving walls.

York's obvious weak points were the rivers. The Foss was defended by the erection of the dam that created the King's Fishpool, but the Ouse was vital to the economy of the town and could not be permanently blocked. The solution was the construction of towers on each bank of the river from which a chain could be raised or lowered. This had the added benefit of helping to control shipping coming into the city and the collection of tolls. A parallel can be seen in Norwich where there are two towers on either side of the River Wensum connected by a chain.

In York there were four towers for use with chains. Downstream, on the south-west bank, was the Crane Tower, adjacent to Skeldergate Postern, from which a chain was stretched across to the Davy Tower or Tower of the Friars Minor on the opposite bank. The site was also the location of a ferry until Skeldergate Bridge was built in 1881. The Davy Tower is first mentioned in 1315 and the wording suggests it originally formed part of an earthwork running from Castlegate to the Ouse along the edge of the ditch at the base of the motte of Clifford's Tower. In 1424 it is described as 'late in the tenure of John Davy'.

Upstream on the south-west bank, next to North Street Postern, is Barker Tower, which dates to the fourteenth century. It is first mentioned in 1376 as 'the tower of the water of Ouse behind the tannery' and in 1380, 1403 and c.1420 as Barker Tower. On the opposite bank is Lendal Tower which was originally circular. It was modified to its present form in the eighteenth century when it was converted to a pump house; the antiquarian John Leland, however, described it as 'a great tower with a chein of yren to caste over the Ouse'. The chain between Lendal Tower and Barker Tower is mentioned in 1315 and the keepers of the chain are recorded in 1380: John de Poynton at Barker Tower and Thomas Smith at St Leonard's (Lendal) Tower.

Although we know *murage* was raised after 1251, the process of wall building at York is not well understood. An impetus for improvement were the Scottish wars of the early fourteenth century – in the records they coincide with the rebuilding of the gates and the addition of barbicans. The walls are built almost exclusively of limestone from Tadcaster, but millstone grit which is also present may have come from re-used Roman material. Building city walls was an expensive and lengthy process and construction often occurred in stages. At Norwich and Newcastle it took around 50 years to complete the circuit of walls.

Documents make it clear that the work at York was not continuous. It seems that the walls on the north-eastern side of the Ouse were completed by 1266. The custody rolls for 1315, however, show that the stone walls had only been partially built in the Micklegate area and that the defences from the Old Baile to Skeldergate Postern, and possibly around Walmgate, still had timber palisades. The stone walls around the Micklegate area were probably complete by *c*.1340 and the Walmgate area by *c*.1345.

An unusual feature of the York defences is that the thirteenth- and fourteenth-century stone walls are not cut back into the earth mounds of the ramparts as they are in other towns, but are built on top of the mounds without substantial foundations. The reason for this is unclear, but it may be that the earth mounds were considered too substantial to alter and it was easier to build the low stone walls across the top of them. As a result the wall is quite low, but nonetheless would still have been a formidable obstacle when the broad, deep ditches in front of the rampart are taken into consideration.

Although the earth ramparts covered the Roman walls on the north-east side of the city, excavations show the medieval stone walls were not built directly over them. From the Multangular Tower to Bootham Bar the medieval wall was built 2–5ft in front of the Roman wall. Interestingly this stretch of medieval wall is also thinner than the other sections perhaps due to the presence of the defences of St Mary's Abbey.

Similarly, from Monk Bar to Layerthorpe Postern the medieval wall is not directly over the Roman line and the sinuous nature of the wall and the presence of several buttresses may suggest it was prone to subsidence. In one section of the wall that forms the extension from the Roman fortress to the Foss near Layerthorpe Postern there is evidence for earlier battlements at a lower level than the present parapet, indicating a remodelling of the wall.

The walls on the south-west side, in the Micklegate area, have been heavily modified due to the arrival of the railways. New arches were cut through the walls first for trains in 1839 and then for a road to serve the new station built outside the walls in 1874 and 1876. Originally there were five interval towers between the Tower of the Tofts and Barker Tower, but none remain and along this stretch of walls the ground dropped steeply towards the River Ouse.

In the Walmgate area the raising of the rampart prior to the construction of the stone wall moved the line of the defences back from their original position. Excavations have revealed that, in contrast to other sections, the wall here was constructed in a substantial foundation trench and after the wall had been built further material was built up against it. It is clear that medieval builders were aware of the possible problems with the ground conditions in this area and built the foundations with arches to help spread the weight of the wall, perhaps because the ground was marshy. These arches would have originally been hidden in the rampart, but can be seen today in the external face of the wall where the rampart has been reduced or slumped.

18 Excavations through the rampart near Walmgate Bar. © *York Archaeological Trust*

An important component of the stone walls are the towers; these were either D-shaped, round, rectangular or polygonal. The towers have all been lowered in height and would once have stood above the level of the wall walk, as they still do on the precinct wall of St Mary's Abbey. Some of the towers have been excavated and it is now known that despite extensive nineteenth-century restoration many retain original medieval fabric. One of the towers facing Lord Mayor's Walk, restored in the 1880s with the upper part totally rebuilt, was shown through excavation originally to have been semi-circular with

19 The Victorian idea of a medieval corner tower: the Robin Hood Tower, where excavations revealed a complex story. © *York Archaeological Trust*

its side walls projecting over 1m beyond the line of the inner face of the wall with the back of the tower open.

Some existing towers were given their present names in the medieval period as we have seen with the Multangular Tower, Davy Tower, Lendal Tower and Barker Tower. The north angle tower behind the Minster was called the Bawing Tower in 1370, the Frost Tower in 1485 and was referred to by its present name, the Robin Hood Tower, in 1622 and 1629. This tower is shown in a variety of forms on maps of the city from the eighteenth century and its original form is far from clear. It was totally rebuilt in 1889 perhaps to form a viewing platform over the gardens to the Minster.

Excavation in the Robin Hood Tower showed that the nineteenth-century modifications had not altered the line of the medieval walls but had completely removed the medieval tower. A curving line of heavily robbed masonry was exposed that may have been the upper part of the Roman wall, just below the nineteenth-century construction point for the present tower, and abutting the external face of this wall were two stubs of limestone walling that may have formed the projections of the original medieval tower. Associated pottery was dated to the thirteenth century.

In the Bishophill area the south corner tower near the Old Baile was called the 'Biche Daughter Tower' in 1566, possibly a corruption of the 'le bydoutre' tower repaired in 1451–52. Another tower near Victoria Bar was called Saddler Tower in 1380 and 1403 and the south-west corner tower of the Micklegate defences was called the 'Tower of the Tofts' in 1380 and 1403. This tower was badly damaged in the Siege of York in 1644, rebuilt in 1645 and further modified in the nineteenth century. Excavation has shown that little of the medieval tower survived, but that the seventeenth-century rebuild had modified the line of the defences.

20 Sometimes excavations of the walls show the effects of centuries of modifications. © *York Archaeological Trust*

In the Walmgate area, the tower of Fishergate Postern at the southern end of the defences was built between 1504 and 1507 as a replacement for an earlier tower called the Talkan Tower, perhaps after the Lord Mayor in 1399, Robert Talkan. At the northern end of the Walmgate defences is the one tower not made of stone but brick, the Red Tower, which owes its present appearance to the restorations of 1857–58.

The tower was built in *c.*1490 by the tilers who had asked for protection after the masons threatened them and one of them was murdered. In 1491 two masons were

21 Fishergate Bar, the most unusual and perhaps the least well understood of the city bars.
© *York Archaeological Trust*

accused but apparently acquitted. The first direct mention of the tower is from 1511 when artillery was assigned to it. The tower is probably not at its full height partly through the raising of the ground level in this area since the mid nineteenth century; it may originally have been closer to 30ft (9m) than the present 16½ft (5m).

Although the bars were important as displays of civic authority they were also an integral part of the defences. Modifications in the late eighteenth and nineteenth centuries, however, mean the gates have lost their original significance in restricting access because large openings have been cut through the ramparts on either side, and a section of wall near Bootham Bar was demolished for the creation of St Leonard's Place in the early 1830s.

The bars were probably originally just arched tunnels through the ramparts with the timber palisades running over the top. This changed during the twelfth and thirteenth centuries when they were rebuilt in stone to a standard form consisting of a central passage closed with wooden gates. Above was a stone tower of two or more storeys that allowed space for raising and lowing a portcullis. The only variant is Fishergate Bar, which is probably a later addition associated with the construction of the Walmgate defences after 1345 and has rectangular flanking towers and three passageways.

The barbicans, added some time in the fourteenth century as part of a rebuild of the bar, also had wooden gates and the passageways through them often needed repaving. In 1380 the gates had locks and later documents mention wicket gates and iron chains and hooks to hold the gates open. The portcullis survives at all four bars, but only Monk Bar's is in working order.

It is not known what the rear façade of the gates looked like in the medieval period; with the exception of Monk Bar's which was always stone, they were probably timber-framed, reinforcing the view that the walls were designed to impress those on the outside. The timber structure survives on the back of Walmgate Bar, dating to the 1580s. At Bootham Bar the rear façade was rebuilt in stone in 1719 and again in the nineteenth century, but before this was timber-framed with three gables. Early illustrations of Micklegate Bar show that until 1827 the inner face resembled Walmgate Bar with a timber building with a crenellated parapet overhanging the rear arch of the gate supported on wooden posts.

One feature of the defences on the north-west side is the proximity of Bootham Bar to the Roman gate. In its present form the bar has late eleventh-century stonework in the outer arch and is first recorded by name around c.1200, although it was also known as Galmanlith. The bar was rebuilt in the thirteenth century and heightened in the fourteenth century to allow the addition of a portcullis. This is when the barbican, removed in 1832, was added; this barbican was 47ft (14.32m) long, 26ft wide and 16ft high, but unusually no provision was made for access to the barbican parapet from the gatehouse as in the other three bars.

The Roman north-east gate (the *porta decumana*), and the twelfth-century Munecagate that replaced it, stood 100 yards (91.44m) north-west of the present Monk Bar. The name Monk Bar first appears in 1370 and the style of the present gate suggests it was built in the fourteenth century; its four-storey gatehouse makes it the tallest of York's bars. The barbican, removed in 1825, projected 44ft (13.40m) from the bar and was 27ft (8.2m) wide.

When access through this stretch of walls was changed is uncertain. The original gate led directly into the Minster Close and may have been closed as part of the defining of the cathedral precinct in the thirteenth century. This definition also involved the closing of a road that ran from Petergate across the east end of the Minster. The position of the Roman and twelfth-century gate is marked by a depression in the ramparts on the line of Chapter House Street. The northern end of Goodramgate was deflected towards the present Monk Bar. The church of St John del Pyke may have derived its name from its proximity to the site of the Roman gate, as it is suggested that the *pyke* element in the name may mean gate. Its name may also be derived from its proximity to one of the gates in the Minster Close.

Micklegate Bar is not on the site of the Roman gate from the *colonia* and excavations have shown that the Roman road runs a little to the south-west of it. The gate may have been moved when the bridge over the Ouse shifted to its present position, but it is first mentioned by name in the twelfth century as Miclelith. The present gate incorporates stonework of the twelfth century, re-used Roman stone and part of a sarcophagus no doubt collected from the extensive Roman cemetery that lined the road immediately beyond the walls.

Micklegate Bar was rebuilt in the thirteenth century and heightened in the fourteenth century to allow the addition of a portcullis, giving the outer façade its present appearance. The barbican was clearly part of the original building of the upper gate of the bar, as two doorways were included which gave access to the parapet of the barbican. The barbican projected 50ft (15.24m) in front of the bar, was 30ft (9.14m) wide and was removed in 1829.

Of all the gates, only Walmgate Bar gives an indication of the imposing nature of the medieval entrances to the city. Walmgate Bar alone retains its barbican, portcullis and inner wooden gates; these probably date from the fifteenth century, are made of oak boards 1¾in thick and are hung on three iron hooks. On the north side is a small wicket gate. The bar is first mentioned in the twelfth century and there is masonry of this date in its inner arch. What form the early gate took is unclear, as the Walmgate area doesn't appear to have been surrounded with ramparts until the thirteenth century. The present bar dates to the fourteenth century when the Walmgate walls were built in stone and the barbican was an integral part of this rebuilding. It is 52ft (15.84m) long and 25ft (7.62m) wide.

As well as the four main gates there were several smaller gates. The appearance of Fishergate Bar in the medieval period is far from clear, but it was certainly of a different design to the other bars. It presumably had a tower above the gate, because a room above the gate was rented as a house in 1440 for 4d. The main arch has a portcullis slot which also suggests there were upper floors to hold winching gear. Drawings from before the late eighteenth century suggest it had rectangular towers that stood above the line of the walls, but by the 1790s the bar looked much as it does now.

During the creation of the modern Victoria Bar in 1838 an earlier gate was found which was probably the medieval 'Lounlith', or secluded gate, mentioned in the twelfth century. It had been blocked with large stones, timber piles and a mound of earth, but when or why this happened is unknown.

There were also a series of posterns probably originally for foot traffic. These were substantial structures and were closed by gates which could be locked. A document tells us that Castlegate, Layerthorpe and Skeldergate Posterns had two gates, but North Street had only one. Two of the smallest were North Street and Fishergate Posterns. North Street Postern, first mentioned in 1315, is next to Barker Tower and was only 9ft high and 4ft wide (2.74 x 1.22m) after it was enlarged in 1577. It was further altered by the insertion of an arch for the railway in 1840.

Fishergate Postern with the adjacent Fishergate Postern Tower survives almost unaltered and is possibly a late addition or alteration associated with the closure of Fishergate Bar. The gate opened inwards and there is a portcullis groove perhaps suggesting the wall above it has been altered. We know it had a portcullis because documents record it being lowered and the gate blocked with earth during the Civil War.

Near York Castle, at the end of the stretch of wall from Davy Tower, was Castlegate Postern. In 1232 a bar below the castle is documented, but the first definite reference to it comes in 1380 when there was a tower adjacent to the postern, three storeys high; this was demolished in 1826. On the opposite side of the river Skeldergate Postern was near the junction of Skeldergate and Cromwell Road. It was known from 1315 as Hyngbrigg and may be the only clear reference to a drawbridge along the defences. It apparently had a pointed arch with a single gate and was demolished in 1808. Layerthorpe Postern or Peasholme Green Postern is first mentioned around 1280 and incorporated a bridge over the Foss. It comprised a large tower with battlements and a central passage, and was demolished in 1829 when the bridge was rebuilt.

THE CASTLES

The areas around both of York's castles has changed considerably since the medieval period, making the reason for their location and their relation to the town difficult to determine. Domesday Book recorded the destruction of a shire for the construction of the castles and there is a growing body of evidence from excavations that there were areas of occupation beneath the castles. Excavations within the precinct of York Castle show this area had formed part of a Roman cemetery focused along the Roman and later route out of the city, perpetuated in the line of Nessgate and Castlegate, which was succeeded by Anglo-Scandinavian occupation.

There is evidence that there may have been a pre-Conquest church beneath York Castle, represented by burials dating to the tenth or eleventh century which are unlikely to be associated with the nearest surviving pre-Conquest church, St Mary Castlegate. Evidence for buildings was represented by slots and other features with quantities of daub, which is not surprising considering the proximity to Coppergate. The evidence points to the continued importance of the area through the Anglo-Scandinavian period.

The impact of Baile Hill on the existing townscape is unclear and it is unknown whether it fell within the area of the Roman *colonia*. However, there is ample evidence for Anglo-Scandinavian occupation in the area of Baile Hill and the Bishophill area had several pre-Conquest churches. Within the area of Baile Hill artefacts found include comb cases, decorated lead and bronze artefacts, and the excavations of 1969 found sherds of Anglo-Scandinavian pottery. In 1802 and 1882 coin hoards of Edward the Confessor and William I were found.

Although slight, the evidence suggests that the destruction of a shire recorded in Domesday included the removal of an Anglo-Scandinavian neighbourhood, reinforcing the view that castles were not additions to, but impositions within towns. This is similar to the picture found by excavations at other urban castles at Bedford, Lincoln, Winchester and Norwich, with earlier streets buried beneath the defensive earthworks of castles.

An unresolved question is which castle is older – York Castle or Baile Hill? It was once argued that the latter was founded first, hence the name 'Old' Baile, but the documentary and archaeological evidence has shown the answer is not so clear-cut. It is also unclear why York Castle was to continue to develop while Old Baille was to fall into disuse. York Castle was an important royal stronghold, always beyond the control of the city, and home to the sheriff of the County of Yorkshire who was answerable only to the king. This independence was confirmed in the charter granting York county status in 1396.

YORK CASTLE

The first castle on the site was erected out of earth and timber with the dam across the Foss in 1068/69. Documents record that the expansion of the castle in 1070 led to the destruction of a house. At its construction the earth ramparts round the bailey were topped with timber palisades and the motte with a timber tower. Much of what we know about the early use and appearance of the castle comes from documentary sources. In the twelfth and thirteenth centuries there are references to the castle gate, the motte, palisades, houses, stables, hall, barn, brew house or smithy and a gaol.

The castle had three bridges, often recorded as in need of repair. The south gate that faced towards the dam was approached by a timber bridge as was the northern gate facing Castlegate. It is likely that the northern gate to the castle was the main entrance, as it was very rare for the principal entrance to an urban castle to face away from the town. The motte was also probably accessed by a bridge across the ditch linking it to the bailey. In 1190 the castle was damaged during the Jewish riots and rebuilt again in timber.

To the south and south-east of the castle stood Castle Mills, St George's Chapel and the dam that retained the water of the Fishpool. Water features associated with castles are often complex and multi-functional, serving social and economic roles as well as defence. York's Fishpool protected the eastern side of the city and was stocked with fish, provided water for the defences and powered mills. Similar pools or ponds associated with castles are recorded at Leeds (Kent), Sauvey (Leicestershire) and Windsor (Berkshire).

Surprisingly little excavation has taken place within the castle; the little that has indicates that the later use of the site has significantly altered ground levels, removing much of the archaeology. There are still deposits, however, that can add to our understanding of the development of the castle.

The Norman castle appears to have consisted of two baileys with the motte in the centre. Major ground clearance seems to have taken place at various times in the area around the castle possibly for the earth for the motte and the defences indicated by the limited evidence for pre-Norman occupation in those areas. Only the kidney-shaped eastern bailey survives, covering about 3 acres, bounded on two sides by the Foss. The early map evidence shows that the other side was marked by a substantial ditch. Evidence for the other bailey was found during excavations which identified a substantial multi-phase ditch on the north-west side of the motte running north-east/south-west.

The earliest ditch was probably V-shaped in section, but was then recut to form a wide flat-bottomed ditch some 20m wide and 5m deep. These phases of the ditch appear to date to the eleventh and twelfth centuries. It was backfilled in the thirteenth century, which may suggest that this is the ditch the Franciscan friars were allowed to enclose when they were given a site on the north side of the castle for their friary in 1268. Defence of the western side of the castle was still clearly a consideration because the friars were allowed to erect an earth mound that was up to 12ft (3.6m) high; the mound could be used by the friars for public preaching, but in times of war had to be used for the defence of the castle. The formation of the castle boundary probably saw the creation of Castle Postern Lane, the predecessor of modern Tower Street, which skirted round the motte.

Something of the earlier defences of York Castle has been identified through excavation. Excavations in 1935 along the line of the eastern bailey walls identified a

22 Clifford's Tower with the outer bailey ditch. © *York Archaeological Trust*

bank of yellow sand and pits containing human bone, but whether ths was related to the Anglo-Scandinavian burial ground or from the prison was unclear. More recent work has identified a clay bank that contained only tenth- and eleventh-century pottery and sealed the Anglo-Scandinavian cemetery. There was also evidence for substantial posts that may have been from the timber palisade and it seems likely that these, along with the bank, are part of the early Norman defences. The absence of evidence for the stone walls of the bailey is probably due to alterations at ground level associated with the construction of the nineteenth-century prison buildings. Excavations within the bailey have not identified with any certainty the location of buildings or the nature of activities carried out, but compact clay and cobbles may suggest yard surfaces.

The motte was investigated in the nineteenth and early twentieth centuries, revealing something of its development. Excavations in 1824 showed the mound comprised layers of earth containing many human bones and timberwork. In 1903 extensive excavations involved cutting a trench 25ft (7.62m) into the motte, showing successive layers of earth, clay and stones which suggested the motte had been raised in four layers consisting of clay and soil that included Roman pottery and disturbed bone. A ditch at least 30ft (9m) wide was exposed, running around the base of the motte.

On the summit, work to consolidate the footings of Clifford's Tower found burnt timbers 13ft (3.9m) below the top of the present mound. These were thought to be parts of the timber tower or palisades that may have been destroyed in the fires of 1190 associated with the Jewish riots. Within the keep a trench 15ft 6in (4.72m) deep suggested that the motte was raised in height by the addition of clayey material sealing the burnt timber prior to the construction of the last phase of timber defences. The rebuilt timber keep was blown down by a winter gale in 1228.

It was in the late twelfth and thirteenth century that the first indications of a programme for replacing the defences in stone appear, although earth ramparts and timber palisades were still in use for much of this period. The Close Rolls of 1225 in the reign of Henry III record a request from the king to Geoffrey de Cumpton, the forester of the Forest of Galtres, for timber to repair the palisades and it was not until the reign of Edward I that the bailey was finally fully enclosed with stone walls made from limestone quarried from Tadcaster.

In 1199/1200, during the reign of King John, documentary sources first refer to the use of stone, possibly for the gates, which were often the first points to be built in stone. It was after a visit by Henry III in 1244 that a definite decision was made to rebuild the keep and perhaps the rest of the castle in stone. The later stone castle is better understood, as it survived intact long enough for something of its appearance to be recorded by artists, and some elements survive even today.

The southern side of the eastern bailey retains nearly 24m of the curtain wall which has been modified over the centuries, but is still 1.2–2.4m thick and 7.5m high. It had a number of towers along it, two of which survive flanking the position of the south gate, and alterations in the stonework suggest the position of another tower.

The south gate was used until 1597, but was blocked by 1660 and mostly demolished by 1735. The footings of the gate were cleared in 1924 and showed that the gate was 12ft wide flanked by quadrant-shaped towers 16ft wide and projecting 16ft in front of the wall. The towers have been reduced in height, but views of the gate before its demolition show it was within a recessed arch, looking similar to gates at Nottingham and Tonbridge Castles. It also appears that the gatehouse was of three storeys. The drawbridge pit has been left exposed and is 12ft deep; it was modified in the fourteenth century.

The approach to the south gate must always have been awkward due to its proximity to the dam and early drawings show there was a water gate into the castle through the outer bailey wall. It was connected to the drum tower of the south gate by a length of wall forming a small outer ward or bailey and may have been used to access the chapel of St George or the castle mills.

The motte appears to have been raised prior to the construction of the stone keep and as it stands is 48ft (14.63m) high and is 220–235ft (67–71m) in diameter. The keep,

Clifford's Tower, is now a roofless shell with walls 10ft thick at the base, narrowing to 9ft thick at the top. It has been reduced in height, but is still an unusual and outstanding piece of medieval engineering. Documents relating to its construction, the Pipe Rolls of 1245–59, show it cost around £2,450 to build. The quatrefoil design of four lobes with a forebuilding is probably due to Henry de Reyns, master mason, and Master Simon, carpenter, who were sent to inspect the castle in March 1245. Parallels for this style of keep can mostly be found in France rather than England.

The forebuilding on the south-east side was the entrance to the keep and the door was made secure with a sliding bar and portcullis. It was of three storeys, with one chamber on the first floor forming a chapel in use by 1245, the room above it housing the winding mechanism for the portcullis. There were garderobes in the tower, with the refuse presumably falling into the surrounding ditch.

It is unclear how the interior of the keep was arranged, but an excavation of 1902 revealed the footings of a central pier which supports the depiction of a roofed keep in early drawings. The space was used for accommodation and documents refer to the chambers on the south side near the chapel as being used by the king and other noble families; the lower floor was probably divided into four rooms.

Many details of the structure and fittings of the castle in the fourteenth and fifteenth centuries are known from records of expenditure. These include the partitions made to the wine cellar in 1327, and the 43,000 nails which were bought in the same year. Bars on the inside of the gate were mentioned in c.1353 and in 1364–65 wall tiles (brick), two stones and iron bars for the hoods of the kitchen fireplaces were bought. In 1451 the building known as the King's Great Hall, which was used by the assize judges and the county court, appears to have been timber-framed, as there is a record for the renovation of its timbers and plaster.

In 1315–16 the winter floods of the Ouse and Foss burst the dam and weakened the motte and part of the curtain wall, which then by 1326 required 14 buttresses. The castle appears to have been in need of some serious repairs throughout the fourteenth century and in 1360 the keep was cracked from top to bottom in two places, the west angle tower had collapsed, the great hall was said to be in a poor state of repair and timber from its tiled roof was taken to repair the dam. The restoration of the castle between 1360 and 1365 cost some £800.

The early fourteenth century saw York at the centre of royal attention due to the wars with the Scots. The king visited the city on numerous occasions although he preferred to lodge in the Franciscan Friary adjacent to the castle. The exchequer and royal courts of justice, however, were housed in the castle from 1298–1392 and on occasions the keep housed the treasury.

The castle was apparently falling into disrepair in the fifteenth century and in 1535 Leland described the castle area as 'of no great importance with five ruinous towers'. Repairs made in 1556 cost £40 and required 30 oak trees, and in 1596 the gaoler Robert Redhead destroyed the outworks around the water gate; at the same time the demolition of Clifford's Tower was contemplated. The work only stopped as it caused unease among the residents of the city who felt it threatened the security of the city. In the post-medieval period the castle developed its role as a prison and home to the assize courts and took its present form after the demolition of the prison buildings in the 1930s.

BAILE HILL

Baile Hill, known as the Old Baile by 1268, is York's less well known, but no less important, castle on the south-west bank of the Ouse. How it fitted into the pre-Conquest defences is unclear. If the Roman and medieval defences are on roughly the same alignment, this probably took advantage of the defensive possibilities. An alternative interpretation is that the castle was built outside the defences which may have run along the line of the north-west limits of the bailey, and the city walls were only extended to enclose it at a later date.

Whatever the answer, Baile Hill had a short life as a castle. It was founded in c.1069, but fell into disuse by the fourteenth century, though it remained an important part of the topography of the city. It appears to have exploited a strong natural position with the steep slope to the Ouse on its north-east side and a natural valley, now followed by Bishopgate Street, on its southern side, perhaps making the only need for substantial fortification on the side facing the town.

Originally the castle appears to have consisted of a motte surrounded by a ditch with a bailey covering an area of 3 acres on the south-west side. We know very little of the buildings associated with this castle, in contrast to York Castle. Today the motte of the castle is flanked by the city walls on two sides and the bailey of the castle has been covered with terraced housing.

The development of the site is not well documented, though it is known that by 1308 it had passed to the archbishops of York. This change from crown to church may have been organised by Archbishop Geoffrey Plantagenet who was sheriff of Yorkshire in 1194 and 1198. The fact that the Baile Hill had passed to the control of the archbishops led to disputes over who should man it in times of war. Eventually, in 1322, the archbishops agreed to the responsibility, providing that the citizens gave assistance if there was a concerted attack on the city. Some work on the defences by the archbishops is recorded; for example, in 1309 Archbishop Greenfield had a ditch cut within the Baile and Archbishop Melton (1317–40) strengthened the fortifications first with wood and then with stone. However friction remained, and in 1423 the city sued the archbishop for failure to maintain the walls beside the Baile. The site was to undergo a further change of hands that brought the disputes to a close in 1466 when Archbishop Bothe granted the Old Baile to the mayor, commonality and their successors.

Under the archbishops the castle site was never developed and was let for grazing. This continued under the city until the eighteenth century. This large open space was also used by the mayor as a place to muster the wardens of the city wards, and for recreation and archery practice. The claim of the city was challenged by the archbishops in 1581, but they did not follow this through and jurisdiction remained with the city.

The comparatively early abandonment of the keep and subsequent limited use of the site has resulted in good preservation of archaeological deposits, but only one large-scale excavation has been carried out. This focused on the motte and its immediate surroundings; the nature of the surviving archaeology within the bailey is less well understood. The trenches within the bailey shed light on the construction of the motte itself. The original ground level at the time of the construction of the motte was identified and it contained quantities of occupation debris and a few sherds of Torksey, Stamford and York type pottery dating to the late eleventh century. On top of this were layers of clayey soil and turves for the construction of the mound. Around the bottom of the motte the defensive ditch, 21m wide, was observed but not excavated to any depth.

Access to the summit of the motte appears to have been via a set of stairs exposed on the side. Although there was modern disturbance around the base of the motte there was tentative evidence for a timber bridge aligned with the stairs and giving access across the ditch. The excavations showed that there had been considerable erosion from the motte into the ditch and the slumps had been sealed by a relict turf line suggesting that the ditch would have been visible as a hollow until it was systematically filled in the nineteenth century by dumps of material to level the ground. The bailey area was heavily disturbed by the construction of two Second World War air-raid shelters.

Excavations at the top of the mound to depths of 1.5m and 2.25m revealed several phases of occupation. Features found at the lowest level, consisting of trenches and posts around the perimeter, were possibly part of a fence or palisade braced on the interior face with lean-to structures. Access to the summit was through a gap in the timber palisade at a point corresponding with the steps and possible position of the bridge.

Near the centre of the mound were traces of occupation in the twelfth or early thirteenth century that were felt to be open to two interpretations. A spread of mortar may have formed a surface covering the top of the motte and there was evidence for timber buildings, perhaps forming two ranges. Alternatively there may have been buildings around the edges facing an internal courtyard. A substantial circular feature was exposed that may have been a latrine or well, possibly timber-lined, which had been filled with soil and limestone rubble. This produced twelfth-century pottery and a cut short cross halfpenny of 1205–08.

The earliest activity was sealed by a layer of cobbles and stone covered with a layer of sand, probably in the fourteenth century. Excavation uncovered no evidence for the abandonment of the site, and it may be that for a while there were still timber buildings or a fence at the top, even though there was no sustained occupation. However, there was clear evidence from the motte for its use as an archery butt.

Clearly York's defences were an important part of the city throughout the medieval period. Archaeology shows that the creation of the castles in 1069 had a physical as well as a psychological impact, confirming the reference in Domesday Book that one shire was destroyed. There is also evidence that there were developed and occupied neighbourhoods in the areas selected for the construction of the two castles.

With the development of the stone walls the defences became a display of the pride and wealth of the city to all those visiting it. Walls also represent the physical manifestation of the boundaries between the developing power blocks separating royal, civic and ecclesiastical space within the city. The walls are still an important symbol of York's past, but there remains much more to learn. Further investigation is needed on both banks of the Ouse to help clarify how they developed from the Roman period to the present day.

3

FOR THE LOVE OF GOD

In the twenty-first century it is difficult to comprehend the influence religion had on the lives of the medieval population. For them the ways of the Church were the norm, the way things were done. The rhythm of daily life was set by the canonical hours – times at which mass was held – determining meeting times, when the city gates were opened or closed and when traders could buy and sell in the marketplace.

The Church had a major impact upon the topography of towns, taking up large amounts of space for buildings and graveyards, many of which have been built over or lost through street widening. The Church had an immense influence on the commercial, architectural, artistic and cultural life of the city. The larger centres exercised influence politically, jurisdictionally and economically and were seen as a threat to the developing civic authority.

An individual living in medieval times was expected to live a good life, as set out in the *Seven Works of Mercy* based on a parable of Christ: to provide food, drink, clothes and hospitality, to care for the sick and visit prisoners. The seventh work was to bury the dead, as suggested in the Book of Tobit. Christ was associated with the poor, which encouraged charitable work and the bequeathing in wills of food and clothes to the poor and sick.

People had to attend regular worship, partake of Holy Communion and attend confession once a year at Easter. On Sundays and feast days parishioners attended mass but did not take part. The separation of congregation from clergy was emphasised by the location of the high altar in the chancel, at a distance from the nave where the people stood.

The year was filled with festivals and saints' days with the highlight being Corpus Christi Day when the craft guilds performed the 48 mystery plays. The following day the consecrated bread, housed in a jewelled and silver-gilt shrine, was carried in procession from Holy Trinity Priory via the Minster to St Leonard's Hospital.

The most important concept in medieval Christianity was purgatory, the waiting place between heaven and hell where individuals were purged (cleansed) of their sins. This led to the development of chantries where prayers were said for the souls of the dead. If you did not found an altar for this purpose you could have services said at existing altars or annual commemorations known as obits. Alternatively you could endow a hospital to pay for the care of a patient, which counted as a charitable act.

Around 140 chantries were founded in York between 1376 and 1400 by artisans, merchants and clergy. From 1425 to 1550 there was a shift to foundations dominated by merchants and the clergy. The Corporation administered some chantries endowed by the commercial elite or associated with craft or religious guilds. Chantries were to affect the appearance and development of churches.

Other ways to reduce time in purgatory was to purchase pardons or indulgences that removed some of your sins. These were sold by pardoners, who, if the *Canterbury Tales* are to be believed, were far from popular. These documents were sealed by papal bullae and are sometimes found with burials.

Throughout the medieval period there was a growing veneration of the Virgin Mary, supplementing the veneration of saints and their relics. Sites or objects associated with them were visited by pilgrims, stimulating the souvenir trade. Evidence for this in York is the ampulla for holy water or oil found at Coppergate. Pilgrimage, saints and relics were an important part of the economy and chandlers would have massed along the approaches to the York Minster selling candles, images and wax limbs that needed healing, as shown in the St William window in the Cathedral.

The Church provided education: in the fourteenth century at St Mary Castlegate and St Martin le Grand Coney Street there was a parish school where reading was taught. Grammar schools were provided by St Leonard's Hospital. The Minster had a school in the thirteenth century and the Augustinian Friary had a *stadium concursorium* suggesting the study of philosophy and theology; the 656 books left to its library by Brother John Erghom in 1372 are remarkable for their range of topics.

Holy wells, which are poorly understood, were often natural springs close to or within churches or their graveyard boundaries. In York there was a Holy Priests' House and Holy Priests' Well associated with chantry priests at the west end of All Saints, Peasholme Green. These were recorded in the will of Roger Dalton, Chaplain, in 1402, although there appear to be other references to it as early as 1386.

During the Middle Ages the Church became increasingly influential in secular affairs and increasingly wealthy as a result of donations and gifts. To many, the Church was also landlord as it was one of the major property owners in York. Property in the city was also held by 39 other Yorkshire religious houses.

JEWS

For a brief period, York's Christian residents were neighbours and business partners with Jews who were brought to England after the Norman Conquest. They were initially established in London and the first reference to Jews in York is made in 1130 when Bertram de Bulmer, sheriff of York, recorded the death of a Jew. By 1290 the estimated Jewish population in England was 2,000–3,000 and even at its peak in the twelfth century probably never exceeded 4,000–5,000. Jews had considerable influence as money lenders, but were also believed by the superstitious public to use spells and magic.

York's Jews appear to have been concentrated around Coney Street. Aaron of York lived near St Martin-le-Grand in 1230 and his neighbour was his nephew Josce le Jovene. It is also possible that the synagogue was in Coney Street. Although Jews held property across the city, only two place names relating to them survive in York. One is Jubbergate, a corruption of Jew Bret Gate, and the other is Jewbury, outside the north-eastern city walls, which was the site of the Jewish cemetery until 1290.

The most notorious event associated with the York Jews was the anti-Jewish riot following the coronation of King Richard I in 1190. The Jews took refuge in York Castle which came under siege for a week, but it is not known how many of the Jews were killed. This riot marked the end of the expansion of Jewish communities and attitudes towards them changed. After 1215 they had to be publicly distinguished by their dress and in 1290 Edward I issued a decree expelling all Jews from England.

'OUR BEAUTIFUL FABRIC' — THE MINSTER

The Minster has altered little in external appearance since 1472, but for much of the Middle Ages it was a building site. Archbishop Thomas's new Minster, built in the 1080s, was aligned east–west in contrast to the prevailing north-east/south-west alignment of the city, a legacy of the Roman fortress it overlay. It appears to have been built to the south of the proposed square enclosure of the pre-Conquest Minster allowing the earlier building to be retained until the new works were finished. In Winchester also the Norman building was constructed beside the earlier church.

Parts of the Norman Minster have been seen since the nineteenth century through excavation and renovation work, but it was the large-scale work of 1966–73 that revealed a large part of Thomas's cathedral. This showed it had massive foundations that consisted of large trenches into which a timber grillage was laid and backfilled with mortar, in a similar way to modern reinforced concrete; these foundations still support parts of the present church.

The surviving fragments of the Norman church show the exterior of the building was covered in plaster with lines drawn in red to represent stone work. The excavations showed the eleventh-century cathedral was not aisled, which made it similar to churches built in Normandy in the 1050s and 1060s, and to English churches in Lincoln and Salisbury (Old Sarum) dating to the 1070s. Under Archbishop Roger de Pont l'Evêque (d. 1181) a new choir was added and the evidence suggests it was the earliest building in the country to use the architectural style called Gothic. He probably added two towers to the west end of the earlier nave, giving it an impressive ceremonial entrance. Roger's choir was perhaps a deliberate statement of the importance of the archbishopric of York to its rival Canterbury.

In addition Roger built the chapel of St Mary and Holy Angels, also known as St Sepulchre's, which stood outside the north side of the nave and it has been suggested that it was a remodelling of a pre-Conquest church dedicated to St Mary. It was built between 1177 and 1181 and was probably accessed through the surviving elaborate blocked door at the west end of the nave. When the nave was rebuilt on a larger scale the chapel must have been modified or rebuilt. Walls associated with it may have been excavated in the nineteenth century and again in 1970.

York needed a saint to keep up with its rival, Canterbury, which had secured the canonisation of Thomas Becket in 1173 and built an elaborate new shrine in 1220. Under Archbishop Walter de Gray efforts were made in York to secure the canonisation of Archbishop William FitzHerbert. Legend had it that on William's return to York, as the crowds crossed Ouse Bridge it gave way and large numbers of people were thrown into the river. William prayed to God and as he made the sign of the cross all were saved. Three weeks later he died, allegedly of poison administered in the chalice during mass, and was buried in a Roman sarcophagus at the east end of the nave. In 1223 the Abbots of Fountains and Rievaulx, with the Bishop of Ely, were instructed to enquire into the alleged miracles occurring at William's tomb and in the same year sweet-smelling oil was said to have flowed from the tomb which was a sign of sanctity. In March 1226 York won its bid to have William declared a saint and a papal indulgence of 40 days was offered to anyone visiting his tomb.

The acquisition of a saint may explain why the new transepts were built (1220–1239) to form a backdrop to St William's tomb at the east end of the nave. Saints were usually placed behind the high altar, but there probably wasn't space in Roger's choir and the aisleless nave was very narrow. The new transepts had aisles and allowed room for the circulation of visitors. The new south transept façade, facing the town and one of the principal gates into the Close, had a wide door to accommodate visitors, in contrast to the west end.

William was finally moved to a new shrine behind the high altar in 1284, in a lavish ceremony paid for by Anthony Bek, Bishop of Durham, attended by King Edward I, his queen, 10 bishops, and numerous barons, with the king helping to carry the coffin. The shrine was behind a large wooden screen against which the high altar had stood. The original tomb was left in the nave and remained a focus for pilgrims. There was also a reliquary containing lesser relics which was carried around the city on the anniversaries of his death and canonisation. The tomb and the main shrine were decked with gifts and wax limbs of those who had received the gift of his help. The St William Window, c.1414, tells the story of his miracles.

St William's shrine was removed during the Reformation, but we know something of its appearance because fragments have been found buried in Precentor's Court. The wooden screen was painted and gilded, and carved with a crucifixion; there was a silver-gilt and jewelled altarpiece, a richly embroidered altar frontal and other statuary, paintings and lights. Niches on three sides gave space for pilgrims to pray. It was carved to a high quality and had many statues including green men and a jester.

The chapter house, similar in size to those of Westminster Abbey and Salisbury Cathedral, is unusual because its roof vault is not supported by a central column. Instead it is supported by a complex timber frame which is one of the masterpieces of medieval carpentry. Dendrochronological dating of the timbers in its roof shows the last timbers used were felled in 1288. It has been suggested that the chapter house occupied the site of the Alma Sophia built in the time of Alcuin. The chapter house is connected to the Minster via an L-shaped passage from the north transept and above it is a room that was used as the masons' tracing floor. Here they scratched onto the mortar floor the shapes that were going to be used in the tracery of several windows of the Minster. This is a rare survival.

The present Minster is the product of a long period of building. The nave was rebuilt from c.1291 to 1360 by enlarging Thomas' nave and reusing the lowest parts of the earlier walls for the foundations of the central passage of the new nave. The choir and east end were also rebuilt from 1360 replacing the work of Roger de Pont l'Evêque. Development of the cult of the Virgin Mary resulted in the addition of the Lady Chapel by 1420. The west front towers were built between 1432/3 and 1445/6. The most striking feature of the east end is the great eastern window which fills most of the wall space. The window was glazed through the funding of Walter Skirlaw, Bishop of Durham, who commissioned the glazer John Thornton of Coventry for the job. It was completed by 1408 and depicted a broad range of themes from the company of heaven through to the biblical stories of the beginning and the end of the world. The central tower collapsed in the winter of 1407, and its rebuilding was well under way by 1420. The Minster was considered finished in 1472.

The Minster stood in a close that formed the heart of the Liberty of St Peter, which was independent from the civic authorities and comprised the Archbishop's holdings within the city. Its residents were subject to the Archbishop's rules and regulations. It changed little until the nineteenth century when buildings were cleared and in 1903 the important route through the Close from Lop Lane, modern Duncombe Place, to Goodramgate was modified to form modern Deangate. The Close was given definite boundaries in 1285 when the Dean and Chapter were given licence to build a stone wall 12ft high with gates that were closed at night. Part of the Close wall may have been seen in excavations, in the form of a length of substantial limestone wall re-used in the 1730s as foundations for one of the properties at the top of Minster Gates.

There were four gates into the Close, but only the timber-framed gateway at the junction of College Street and Goodramgate survives. The positions of the other gates are known but we cannot be certain of their appearance. A gate in the street called Minster Gates was demolished in 1730. As well as the gate there were bollards, known as 'stulpes', mentioned in 1370, to prevent vehicular access. Another gate stood in Ogleforth and was demolished in 1772.

The most important gate led to the west front of the Minster. It stood at the top of Lop Lane at the junction with Petergate and was known as High Minster Gates. Illustrations before its demolition in 1828 show it was a large stone gate with a wide arch for vehicles and a narrower pedestrian gate. It formed part of a range of buildings including the Peter Prison, the gaol of Dean and Chapter, and abutted the corner of the west end of the Minster. The gatehouse had a door connecting it to the Minster through the north-west tower and a second door at ground level set into a buttress.

Much of the area on the north side of the Minster was taken up by the archbishop's palace of which only the chapel of $c.1230$ and part of an arcade survives. The archbishops rarely lived in the palace, preferring the palaces at Bishopthorpe, Southwell, Whitehall or Cawood. Limited excavations near the chapel have identified the remains of walls associated with further ranges of buildings. As well as the chapel, the palace had a great hall, kitchen and several suites of rooms. It was used by Henry III and his queen who had a special privy built next to their bedroom in 1251. In 1327 the palace was altered to house Phillipa of Hainault, future queen of Edward III. They married in York Minster in January 1328.

The Close housed the officers of the posts introduced by Archbishop Thomas: dean, chancellor, precentor, treasurer and prebends. The treasurer was responsible for entertaining nobles and part of the stone buildings that formed a range with two wings linked by a colonnade is built into Gray's Court in Chapter House Street. The present Treasurer's House is built over the north-west wing of the medieval buildings. The surviving medieval walls date to the eleventh and twelfth centuries and renovation work in 1964 showed that part of the outer wall standing to full height was covered externally with plaster. There were also corbels and a string course incised with rosettes; two of the original windows were identified. A section of the original building is visible from the city wall.

On the south side of the Minster was the cemetery, school and the deanery. There are many references to the deanery from the twelfth century describing it as having a hall, cross-wings, a private chapel and kitchens. It stood in its own grounds surrounded

23 A late addition to the Minster Close, St William's College. © *York Archaeological Trust*

by a wall, and early engravings suggest it was demolished and rebuilt in the sixteenth or seventeenth century. A cable trench excavated in this area identified traces of several of the buildings that once filled this side of the close, perhaps including parts of the deanery.

The prebendal houses can be recognised because they are named after the estates assigned to support them such as South Cave and South Newbald on the west side of the Minster. Other houses were outside the Close including Ampleforth, Bramham and five others in Stonegate, two in Petergate and one in Bishophill. The wills of canons show the houses were well equipped with a hall and chapel, buttery, brew house and gateway.

Three parish churches stood within the close: St Michael-le-Belfrey rebuilt in 1525–37, St Mary-ad-Valvas demolished in *c.*1380 and St John-del-Pyke demolished in the sixteenth century. In 1436 St William's College was founded on the north side of modern College Street for 24 priests serving the chantries within the cathedral. The College was first proposed in 1455, but building didn't start until around 1465 by licence of King Edward IV. The site for the College was formed from the site of two prebendal houses, Salton and Husthwaite. The building was constructed around a courtyard with a ground floor of stone and an upper floor of timber framing.

THE COLLEGE OF THE VICARS CHORAL, BEDERN

Some cathedrals were run by monks, but others such as Chichester, Exeter, Salisbury, Wells and York used secular priests called canons or prebends. York Minster needed a large body of staff to carry out all the duties associated with daily services, especially with

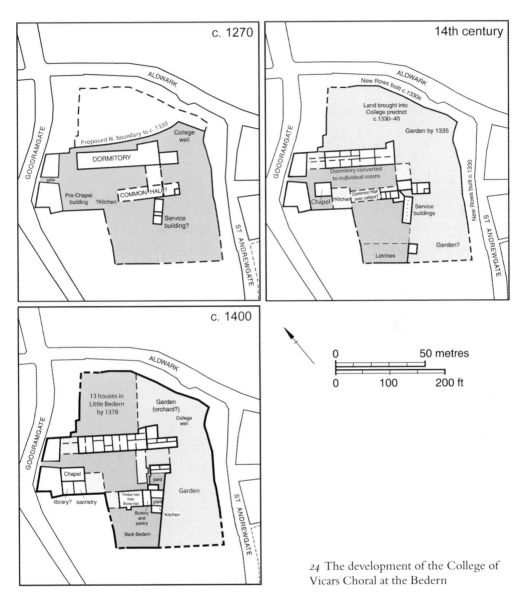

24 The development of the College of Vicars Choral at the Bedern

the increase in chantries. Many canons were non-resident in the city and used deputies, or vicars, to perform their duties for them.

The vicars lived in the College of the Vicars Choral in Bedern, located on the north-west side of Goodramgate. It was founded by John Romeyn, the treasurer from 1241 to 1255, and several of his colleagues. *Bedern* can be translated as 'prayer house' and the Vicars Choral in Ripon and Beverley, minster churches of York, were also located in areas called Bedern. Such institutions were also founded around the same time at the other secular cathedrals like Chichester and Wells.

Until excavations in the 1970s the majority of what was known about the college came from the wealth of documentary sources. Bedern was formed out of prebendary estates in the period between the 1230s and c.1250, and further properties along Aldwark and Goodramgate were acquired in the 1270s. The area known as Little Bedern was not acquired until c.1388. The large urban property estate managed by the Vicars Choral was formed out of Minster property outside the Close along Petergate and Goodramgate and other parts of the city and suburbs.

The acquisition of properties for the college was tied into the wider issue of the Minster wanting to secure its urban estates and gain maximum income. This was because much property had been granted to tenants at perpetual rents that no longer reflected their real value. This was increasingly important after 1290 when national legislation limited the ability of the Church to acquire new land or property.

Individual vicars were often wealthier than their college because as early as 1389/90 some services for the dead set up in perpetuity were no longer observed and the money saved to increase the vicars' pay. Changes in staffing also occurred when the vicars' traditional patrons such as the canons stopped using them in the chantries and started using independent parsons, culminating in the formation of St William's College for chantry priests.

The only college buildings to survive are the gateway into the college off Goodramgate, the chapel and the hall. The present building over the gateway dates to the late sixteenth or early seventeenth century and little is known of its medieval appearance. There is one reference to the gatehouse in 1396 when the vicars applied to the king to build a bridge over Goodramgate from the room above the gatehouse but it is not known whether it was ever built. It was common for institutions to have an imposing gatehouse, such as the College of Vicars Choral at Wells, and Speed's plan of 1610 suggests a tower that may be the more elaborate medieval college gatehouse.

Excavations show the Bedern close was originally built around a central courtyard, and until the mid nineteenth century there was a 50m-long access road through the gate that may reflect the length of the close defined by the late thirteenth or early fourteenth century. This close may have been grassed with a pavement and gutter around the edges and in 1312 there is a record of two men being paid for making a pavement of gravel.

The first buildings around the courtyard consisted of two parallel ranges, probably of two storeys, aligned north-east/south-west and possibly linked by a range at the east end. These buildings were not totally contemporary, but may represent three periods of activity between c.1250 and 1280. The range on the north-east side of the courtyard was a substantial timber-framed structure supported on post pads with the infill between them set on limestone rubble sill walls. The building was at least 50m long and 12m wide, with a latrine block at its south-eastern end. It was probably the communal dormitory for the 36 vicars who made up the College. The other building stood on the south-west side of the courtyard and had an open ground-floor undercroft. This was probably the dining hall, with the original kitchen located at the south-west.

In the fourteenth century there was a move away from communal living and in the 1330s the dormitory undercroft was divided into cubicles or rooms, some provided with their own toilet facilities. The latrine block was also rebuilt at this time, presumably for those not fortunate enough to be in one of the en-suite cubicles. This move towards increased privacy has been recorded at the College of Vicars Choral at Lincoln and in the fourteenth century a street of cottages was built for the Vicars Choral at Wells.

25 The much-altered chapel of the Vicars Choral. © *York Archaeological Trust*

The vicars had a garden on the south-east side of the College near St Andrewgate; this is often mentioned in documents from the fourteenth century. It had raised beds where vegetables and herbs were grown and there was a small vineyard and walled orchard.

In 1340 the vicars built a chapel near the entrance from Goodramgate. Originally it was small and measured only 8 x 6m internally. It was dedicated to the Holy Trinity, the Blessed Virgin and St Katherine, and became the location of a chantry. By the end of the fourteenth century it had rich fittings with high-quality windows and before the end of the century was extended to its present size, reflecting the growing status of the vicars. The chapel as it stands today is much altered: the walls were reduced in height and a new roof added in 1980.

The college underwent a major reorganisation over perhaps 20 years from the 1360s, in two distinct phases of work. The south-east and south-west sides of the courtyard were altered and the common hall moved, making the Close more square than before. The vicars' accommodation in the old dormitory was changed with a partial rebuild in stone, making the earlier divisions into cubicles more permanent; they may even have become small houses between 1360 and 1390, described as having two storeys. Excavations suggest the dormitory block was split into five or possibly eight houses; there may also have been two houses on the south-east side of the courtyard which may have been the houses documented in the fifteenth century in the surviving records of the Vicars Choral.

The space created when the kitchen was moved from the east end of the chapel may also have been filled with houses, making a total of between 13 and 15 properties within the main close. There is also evidence that some of the vicars lived outside the Bedern in a building known as 'Camhall Garth' on the west side of Goodramgate which was rebuilt as a courtyard of houses in *c.*1360. The evidence suggests that the York Bedern was comparable in size to Exeter's and slightly smaller than Chichester's, although much smaller than that of Wells which contained 41 houses.

The dining hall was rebuilt in 1360 using timber together with a half-timber service range at its south-east end. This building appears to have stood for about 10 years before it was rebuilt again in stone, measuring 13.9 x 9.2m (45 x 30ft); this is the building that survives today. The date of the building is based on dendrochronology, which showed that the trees for the roof were felled in 1369/70. The hall was lit by three large windows in each of the long walls. The central window on the north-east side had enough of the tracery surviving to show that it was of an unusual design based on a cross. Perhaps most important is the suggestion that it may have incorporated a very early oriel window.

The half-timber service range was retained and the timbers from this can still be seen in the south-east wall of the hall. It had three doorways, which was a typical arrangement for the junction of a medieval dining hall and its service range. The central door would have led into the corridor that connected with the kitchen, with the flanking doors giving access to the buttery and the pantry.

Archaeology showed that the vicars, individually and collectively, enjoyed a high standard of living in the thirteenth and fourteenth centuries. They had glassware, which was a rarity in this period, including two expensive imported beakers with painted enamel decoration, a stemmed goblet and a rare decorated blue glass bowl. There was also evidence for utilitarian glass vessels for lighting, storage, and distilling alcoholic or perhaps herbal or medicinal diagnosis. The College of Vicars Choral declined through the fifteenth and sixteenth centuries, and after the 1570s it was hardly used and gradually fell into disuse.

PARISH CHURCHES

These private foundations were seen as a threat to the integrity of the Church by the twelfth century and pressure was put on families to hand them over. Some did, such as Walter, son of Fagenulf, who gave two churches to St Leonard's Hospital. Others refused, like Ralph Nuvel, who defended his family claim to All Saints Peasholme Green, and were supported by the citizens of York.

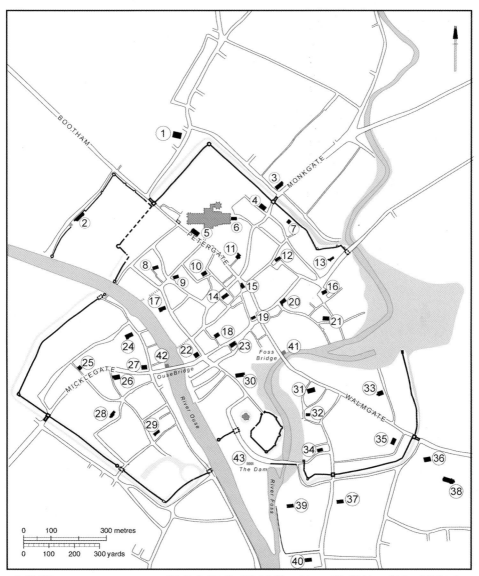

1. St Giles
2. St Olave
3. St Maurice
4. St John del Pyke
5. St Michael le Belfrey
6. St Mary ad Valvas
7. St Helen on the Walls
8. St Wilfrid
9. St Helen
10. St Benet
11. Holy Trinity Goodramgate
12. St Andrew
13. St Cuthbert
14. St Sampson
15. Holy Trinity (Christ Church)
16. All Saints
17. St Martin-le-Grand
18. St Peter the Little
19. St Crux
20. St Saviour
21. St John in the Marsh
22. St Michael Spurriergate
23. All Saints Pavement
24. All Saints North Street
25. St Gregory
26. St Martin (Micklegate)
27. St John the Evangelist
28. St Mary Bishophill Junior
29. St Mary Bishophill Senior
30. St Mary Castlegate
31. St Denys
33. St Margaret
32. St Stephen
34. St George
35. St Peter-in-the-Willows
36. St Michael
37. All Saints
38. St Lawrence
39. St Andrew
40. St Helen
41. St Anne's Chapel
42. St William's Chapel
43. St George's Chapel

26 The parish churches and principal chapels

27 The smallest of York's medieval churches to survive, St Andrew's, St Andrewgate.
© *York Archaeological Trust*

At the end of the eleventh century the number of new churches with dedications to new saints had increased across England, to include Nicholas, Lawrence, Giles, Margaret and Catherine, and is a trend that can also be seen in York. By 1150 parish formation had all but ceased as canon law became stricter, making it more difficult to found new churches. This is why towns founded from the late twelfth century onwards only had one or two churches, for example Hull, Banbury (Oxfordshire) and Boston (Lincolnshire). York had its highest number of churches during the eleventh and twelfth centuries and several were closed in the fourteenth century. These were St Mary's in Walmgate, St Stephen's in Fishergate (modern George Street), St Benet's in Swinegate, St Michael's (Walmgate-Bar-Without) and the church of St Mary-ad-Valvas; the latter was party excavated in 1967.

The plan of churches was driven by changes in religious faith as much as by an expression of wealth of the parish. The majority of York churches were not aligned east–west but north-east/south-west, although in documents they were always described as following liturgical orientation. Although they developed over time, churches were rarely totally rebuilt as the cost would have been prohibitive; they grew by additions or alterations which led to the fabric of the building being a patchwork of different styles and periods. Urban churches had extensive churchyards, but most have been encroached on by buildings or lost to later road widening.

In the eleventh or twelfth century it is probable that at least nine of the churches in the city were rectangular in plan with a single cell. Perhaps going hand-in-hand with changes to the way Mass was celebrated, chancels were added from the late thirteenth century. Aisles were added between the twelfth and fourteenth century, often with a break between their construction. This can be seen at St Mary Bishophill Junior where the north aisle was added in the twelfth century and the south aisle was added in the fourteenth century. Unusually St Martin-cum-Gregory appears to have had both of its aisles added at the same time in the thirteenth century. The development of chantries saw

28 The church of St Crux at the end of the nineteenth century. © *City of York Library*

the addition of a chapel to the south side of the chancel of Holy Trinity, Goodramgate, in the thirteenth century.

Many of the wealthy parish churches were rebuilt in the fourteenth and fifteenth centuries in the latest Perpendicular style, exemplified in the churches of St Crux and St Martin Coney Street. St Michael-le-Belfrey was only completed in 1530. The only surviving church from a poor parish is St Andrew's, St Andrewgate, but even this appears to have been remodelled in the fifteenth-century style. Excavations at its equally poor neighbour, St Helen-on-the-Walls, revealed that it too was rebuilt in the fifteenth or early sixteenth century. The fact that even parishes classed as poor could afford alterations to their churches may suggest the assessment of the wealth of York's parishes is imprecise, especially as late medieval taxation figures are notoriously untrustworthy.

The churches that survive have been altered considerably. St Michael's Spurriergate, for example, was reduced in size as part of the improvements to Ouse Bridge in 1821 and had its tower reduced in height in 1963. Drastic changes were made to St Crux which had dominated the north-eastern end of the Pavement marketplace in one of the wealthiest and most heavily occupied areas of the city. Today its site is occupied by the parish room that retains some fabric from the church and the fifteenth-century doors from the south aisle.

Early paintings, plans and photographs show the grandeur and scale of St Crux. The church was built as a double cube, 104 x 52 x 52ft, with the nave and chancel separated by a screen; it had four chantry chapels. The tower was part of the south aisle and was rebuilt in brick in 1697 in the Italianate style. The church closed in 1881 and there were some plans to restore it. It was demolished, however, despite the protesters who argued against the use of dynamite on the basis that the building was already falling down. All that remains of the medieval St Crux is part of the north wall which at that point stands at 1.5m high and the full height of the west aisle.

Many of the churches that did not survive have been partly relocated through archaeological excavations. Often this is through the discovery of their graveyards, such as St Wilfrid's that stood between Lendal and Blake Street; in 1319 the only mayor of York to die in battle, Nicholas Fleming, was buried there. Other churches located through their graveyards include St Benet's, Swinegate, and St Stephen, Fishergate, both closed in the fourteenth century. In both cases the burials showed that the churches were probably pre-Conquest in origin – St Benet's had wooden coffins made from timber felled between c.890 and 1050. Suburban churches have similarly been identified, such as St Edward's, Walmgate, and All Saints and St Helen's, both in Fishergate.

In some cases fragments of the walls of churches have been recorded. The site of All Saints, Peasholme Green, was located when burials and traces of walls were found in 1853. The site was excavated again in the 1980s, when the north wall of the nave was located. St Peter-in-the-Willows stood just inside Walmgate Bar on the south-west side of the road. Its foundations were exposed in 1827, 1945 and 1973, and it was shown that the church had stood in an extensive graveyard. The suburban St Mary Layerthorpe was located in 1920 during construction work on the south-east side of the road some 50 yards from the Foss.

Only two parish churches have been subject to large-scale excavations. St Mary Bishophill Senior on the south-west side of the river was demolished in 1963. It stood in the angle between the roads Bishophill Senior and Carr or Kirk Lane in a large churchyard on the edge of the steep rise up from Skeldergate. An architectural description of the church made before its demolition suggested it pre-dated the Norman Conquest and had a north aisle and a south door added in the twelfth century. The chancel was added in the early thirteenth century doubling the length of the original church. In 1300 the aisle was widened and in the early fourteenth century two new windows were inserted in the south chancel wall. The fifteenth century saw the aisle rebuilt, two large windows added to the nave wall and the nave reroofed. In 1659 a brick tower was added and the chancel was heightened with brick; in 1860 a large east window was inserted.

29 The fragmentary remains of All Saints, Peasholme Green. © *York Archaeological Trust*

The opportunity to excavate the church added significantly to this description. The early church was positioned on one of the terraces created in the Roman period to exploit the steep slope to the River Ouse. There was evidence that a timber building of uncertain function may have used Roman walls as footings. In the excavations fragments of two stone crosses were found dating to the tenth or eleventh century, one having been re-used in the footings for the later church. There was evidence for an Anglo-Scandinavian burial ground surrounded by a precinct wall enclosing an area 60ft x 54–62ft (18.28 x 16.45–18.89m). Part of this boundary wall runs down the side of Carr Lane where there is evidence for a blocked gateway giving access to the enclosure.

Before the excavation all that was known of the eleventh-century church was the south and west wall. It was shown that the twelfth-century nave arcade followed the line of the north wall, suggesting that the church was a single cell rectangle 41 x 24ft (12.49 x 7.31m). A 6½ft (1.98m) gap in the centre of the west wall implied a doorway. The church had foundations consisting of a trench filled with rubble. The walls of the church varied in thickness, with the end walls narrower than the side walls. Parts of the Roman walls were still standing and were not removed until the church was enlarged in the twelfth century. The eleventh-century west wall was directly over a Roman wall, but the south wall diverged slightly from the Roman line, which may suggest it was a rebuilding of an earlier church wall.

The wall of the twelfth-century north aisle was not located, but the foundations of the arcade piers and the stubs of the east and west end walls showed they consisted of roughly

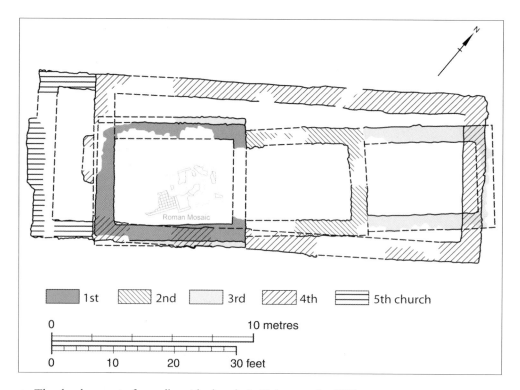

30 The development of a small parish church: St Helen-on-the-Walls

coursed square stones. There was slight evidence for an earlier shorter chancel removed when the site was terraced to accommodate the larger thirteenth-century chancel. Deeper foundations may have indicated the position of a crypt or charnel house under the choir. The chancel was shown to be on a slightly different alignment and may have been built east–west, allowing the old church to function until the two were joined.

The fourteenth-century north aisle wall had slight foundations comprising of a trench filled with rubble and clay. In contrast, the footings for the fifteenth-century west pier of the north choir had a solid masonry foundation of rubble in hard mortar. The west wall of the seventeenth-century tower did not incorporate the west wall of the fourteenth-century aisle but had its own foundation. This was a rare opportunity to combine the evidence from the building with the archaeology and showed the potential of making use of both sources of information.

The other excavated church is St Helen-on-the-Walls which had closed at the end of the sixteenth century and whose site was forgotten. It was not marked on early maps of York such as those of Speed or Horsley (1610 and 1694); Francis Drake in his map from 1736 (copied later by Robert Skaife in 1864) placed the church north-east of the Merchant Taylors' Hall. Medieval documents relating to properties fronting Aldwark suggested that the church was on the south-east side of the Merchant Taylors' Hall and accordingly it was here that the church was discovered in the 1970s.

The excavations found the early phases of the church difficult to date, but suggest that it originated around the mid tenth or early eleventh century as a small rectangular building 7 x 6m with footings that incorporated re-used Roman masonry and a floor of white mortar. In contrast to St Mary Bishophill Senior there was no clear relationship between the early church and an underlying Roman building with a mosaic floor. A chancel 5.8 x 5.3m was added in the twelfth century and had a sequence of mortar and earth floors with footings of limestone and mortar. The chancel was modified in the late thirteenth or early fourteenth century, being extended by some 6m, and the north-west and south-east walls were also thickened with the addition of material to their external faces. The changes of the late fourteenth and early fifteenth century were much more obvious and may relate to the reconsecration of the church in 1434.

This rebuild was a major project in which all but the south-east and north-west walls were demolished. The church was rebuilt as a rectangle measuring 19 x 10m, probably with a door on the south-east side of the chancel and a bell cote or doorway at the south-west end. The final alterations occurred in the late fifteenth or early sixteenth century when the north-west wall was rebuilt and the nave extended by 2m. This church remained in use until 1550 and was still standing in 1580.

More limited archaeological work has been undertaken at All Saints Pavement over the years. Excavations took place in 1963, again in the 1980s and on a larger scale in 1995. The church stands between High Ousegate and Coppergate, dominating the opposite end of the market to St Crux, and was altered in 1778 and 1782 when the chancel and aisles were taken down and an area of the graveyard dug away to widen the road and enlarge the marketplace. The graveyard was reduced when Coppergate was widened again in 1963. The evidence shows it was an important church in the pre-Conquest period and several high-quality floor tiles, similar to those in Canterbury, Coventry, Peterborough, Westminster and Winchester, have been found. Traces of the tenth- or eleventh-century church found in the south aisle in 1995 suggest it consisted of a small rectangular nave and chancel which is unusual at this date in York and perhaps reflects its importance.

After the Conquest, All Saints was the most important medieval church in the city. Not only was it a parish church, but it was also the church used by the guilds and was the civic church of the city; in the fifteenth century council meetings were frequently held there. Furthermore, 43 Lord Mayors were buried in the church, which had at least six chantries by 1311. The church was thought to be cruciform in plan in the late eleventh or twelfth century and excavations may have identified part of the south transept projecting beyond the present south aisle wall, but so far no evidence exists for a north transept. Evidence has also been found for aisles added in the twelfth century. The church was rebuilt again in the fourteenth century as a rectangle; the tower was added in c.1400 and at some point in the following century the crossing arch was removed and a continuous clerestory added.

The excavations in 1963 associated with the removal of the organ chamber (belonging to the 1898 organ) showed that when the fourteenth-century church was rebuilt, the south wall had poor foundations; where it crossed the line of the earlier transepts it was built on a rough arch of stone spanning the space between the old foundations. Several floor levels were found consisting of a series of mortar spreads and appeared to relate to the construction and use of the fourteenth-century aisle.

THE WEALTHIEST ABBEY IN THE NORTH — ST MARY'S ABBEY

St Mary's Abbey did not only rival the Minster in its prominence on the city skyline, but it was also frequently in dispute with the city. It was a Benedictine abbey and occupied an extensive site outside the north-west walls of the city. By 1539 it had an income of £2,000 a year which made it the wealthiest Benedictine monastery in the north of England. The abbey site was given to Abbot Stephen and a group of monks from Whitby by Alan of Brittany with the support of William the Conqueror. The monks moved from a site at Lastingham to York in the 1080s and are recorded in Domesday Book.

The abbey precinct was originally 4 acres in size but was extended to around 12 acres during the twelfth century; from 1266 it was enclosed by a wall nearly three-quarters of a mile long. In 1318 the abbey received permission to raise the height of the precinct wall and crenelate it; this is the wall we see today running along Bootham and Marygate to the River Ouse. At the corner of Marygate and Bootham is St Mary's Tower, which owes its present odd appearance to being blown up in the civil war in 1644. The final alteration to the abbey walls was the construction of a postern gate and tower near Bootham Bar in 1497.

The Abbey also had a wall parallel to the Ouse, but whether it was part of the original walls built in 1266 is unclear, as the earliest reference to it is in 1354. It appears on Speed's map of the city in 1610 but had been demolished by the eighteenth century. Francis Drake included in his *Eboracum* a drawing of the river wall with an archway; he also refers to the removal of quantities of ashlar stone for use at Lendal Landing. Part of this wall was exposed during the construction of flood defences in 1985 which identified a 14m stretch of the river wall with areas of ashlar stone work still surviving; this was a little over 1m wide. There was also evidence for buildings along the inside of the wall.

The gatehouse to the abbey from Marygate, and its adjacent lodge, formed part of a range of buildings that connected with the church of St Olave which may have stood on the site of the church founded by Earl Siward in 1050 and was connected to the gaatehouse b a chapel dedicated to St Mary. St Olave's and part of the gatehouse survive, and in their present form are mostly of fifteenth century, although work on the chapel and gatehouse was begun before 1314 and completed by 1320.

The abbey site comprises an elevated area with a steep slope to the river that may have been terraced to accommodate the abbey buildings. The church is not aligned east–west but north-east/south-west probably due to the constrictions of the space available. It is dedicated to St Mary and its foundation stone was laid by William Rufus in 1088 at a ceremony attended by Alan of Brittany, Odo of Bayeux and Archbishop Thomas Bayeux. The footings for this church were first exposed in the excavations of Charles Wellbeloved in 1827. This showed that the chancel ended in a large semi-circular apse which housed the high altar. It was flanked by aisles that also terminated in apses although they were square externally. The Norman nave and transepts corresponded in size to their replacements, probably due to the limited space.

Rebuilding began in 1270 when the foundation stone was laid by Abbot Simon de Warwick. What is unusual is that the work was done fairly quickly in one unified campaign. This is the church whose ruins we still see today. By 1277 the outer walls were complete, but the rebuilding of the east end was more difficult as the work caused cracking in the tower. Despite this the east end appears to have been completed by 1283

31 The river wall of St Mary's Abbey. © *York Archaeological Trust*

when the Archbishop of York dedicated six altars in the aisles of the chancel and the transepts. The tower was complete by 1294 and was to remain largely unaltered except for a campaign of repair after the steeple was struck by lightning in 1377; this work was still in progress in 1391.

The abbey cloister lay on the south-east side of the church; parts of the lower walls of its east, south and west sides were excavated in 1827–29, but were buried when the Yorkshire Museum was built. The only remains of the buildings around the cloister are part of the chapter house vestibule, built between 1298 and 1307, and roofed over in 1911–12 when the Tempest Anderson Hall lecture theatre was built. The chapter house entrance was richly carved and stood 2m high when it was exposed in 1827. In contrast to the entrance, the chapter house itself, where the monks assembled each morning, was demolished to its foundations some time after the Reformation; its appearance is not clear but its stone vault rose from 12 supports that incorporated life-size statues of the Apostles and 12 prophets which were colourfully painted.

The abbey precincts are poorly understood and little excavation has been carried out. The historical records mention granaries, barns, stables, a brew house, bake house, fish house, mill and tailor's workshop which were located in the lower areas near the river. The only surviving building in this part of the precinct is now called the *Hospitium* and was probably built around 1300, forming part of a range of service buildings with a water gate. Its upper storey is probably the oldest timber-framed structure in York.

The excavations in the 1820s identified part of a range thought to be part of the school house and dormitory of *c.*1310. It was re-excavated in the 1990s, exposing a section of wall still standing 1.5m high with a pillar to support the vaulting of the roof. There was a doorway into the building, and it had a tiled floor.

32 The only precinct building to survive, the *hospitium* of St Mary's Abbey. © *York Archaeological Trust*

The abbey had an extensive and complex system of drains which were found during excavations. These were made of limestone blocks and could be up to 1m high. Some of them were re-used by the Victorians when they built the Museum. Examination of the abbey drain showed that its roof was largely arched but in some places was flat and this was thought to indicate where it passed under buildings.

The abbot's house was built in 1483. It survived because it became the headquarters of Council of the North in 1539 and is now known as the King's Manor. It has been rebuilt and extended over the years. Its scale and the fact that it was constructed of brick which was becoming increasingly fashionable, testify to the grand lifestyle of the abbot.

HOLY TRINITY — YORK'S RESIDENT ALIENS

Holy Trinity was York's other Benedictine monastic house and is the only surviving monastic church still in use in the city. It survived because the nave was used throughout the medieval period as the parish church of St Nicholas. Before 1682 the nave walls were reduced in height and the north and south arcades and western crossing arch were walled up to create a smaller space. The church achieved its present appearance in the late nineteenth century when a south aisle and chancel were added. The gateway into the priory survived until the 1850s when it was destroyed to create Priory Street.

The site was important before the Norman Conquest and in 1089 it was held by Ralph Pagnell. He endowed the monks with large landholdings and then gave Holy Trinity to the abbey of Marmoutier near Tours in France. As a result the priory appears in the documents as the Alien Benedictines because it was under foreign (alien) control.

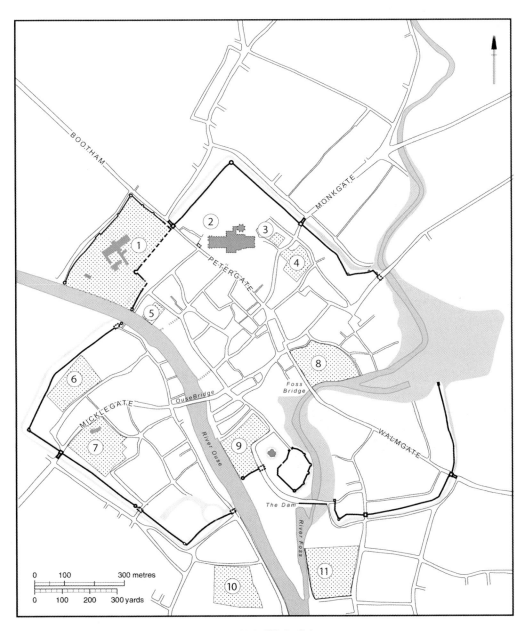

1. St Mary's Abbey (Benedictine)
2. The Minster
3. St William's College
4. Vicars Choral (The Bedern)
5. Augustinian Friary
6. Dominican Friary

7. Holy Trinity Priory
8. Carmelite Friary
9. Franciscan Friary
10. Clementhorpe Nunnery
11. St Andrew's Priory (Gilbertine)

33 The religious houses of York

Unlike St Mary's Abbey it had close ties with its local community and was a small foundation of 10 or a dozen monks. Many were drawn from the close vicinity and the last prior was Richard Speght, son of Henry and Margaret Speght of Micklegate. He had been ordained into the priory in 1510 and was probably born in the parish. Despite its small size it was very powerful and was a source of annoyance to the archbishop of York and the crown from the twelfth to the fifteenth century, as they had no control over it. It was not until 1426 that it was granted non-alien status, and consequential independence from its continental parent.

Most of what we know of the priory comes from documents, the surviving buildings, and the small-scale excavations that were carried out by the York architect and antiquary Walter Harvey Brook between 1892 and 1911. The remains of the priory church comprise the partial nave and the surviving south and east walls of the choir, some of which are incorporated into surrounding properties. This shows that the medieval church was considerably larger. The north wall of the choir has not been located, but the excavations showed it had a floor of red, undecorated tiles. The choir is a large rectangle and its date of construction is uncertain, though there are references to alterations made between 1446 and c.1470. This work appears to have generated the stone used in the surviving north-west tower built in 1453 by the parishioners of St Nicholas; the tower also includes reset windows from the twelfth century. Combined with the details from the excavations and the surviving architectural fragments this suggests the choir which was standing at the start of the fifteenth century was built c.1170–1190s and may have had a parallel in the rectangular choir at Byland Abbey built c.1165–75. It appears, based on the architectural fragments, that it was inspired by the building work carried out by Roger Pont l'Evêque at the Minster, since very similar styles and designs were used.

This is possibly supported by the surviving crossing piers between the nave, choir and transepts. The piers are undecorated on the side that faces into the crossing because the stalls of the Benedictine churches extended up the last bay of the nave. The appearance of the tower of the church is uncertain as it collapsed during a storm in 1551, but it was referred to as a campanile or bell tower. The fact the nave is undamaged and that the choir may have disappeared by the 1560s suggests that the tower fell on the choir making it unusable.

A second phase of building saw the construction of the present nave, west front (restored 1904–06) and possibly the cloister and cloister arcade from about 1200. The style of architecture of the west front suggests the work was completed by the 1240s. Again there is evidence in the stonework to suggest that it was heavily influenced by the Minster. An unusual feature of the nave before the construction of the tower in 1453 is that there appears to have been a chamber at the upper level. This has tentatively been interpreted as an elevated chapel, probably dedicated St Michael, which would have parallels at Much Wenlock and Brinkburn priories.

THE FRIARS

Only Boston, Bristol, Cambridge, King's Lynn, Lincoln, London, Newcastle-upon-Tyne, Northampton, Norwich, Oxford, Stamford, Winchester and York were home to all four of the major orders of friars. York was also home briefly to the Friars of the Sac. Some of the friars were identifiable from the colours of their habits: the Franciscans or Friars Minor (grey friars), Dominicans (black), Carmelites (white).

The Dominicans arrived in England and established themselves at first in Canterbury in 1221 and the Franciscans arrived in 1224. The Carmelites arrived in England in the 1240s with the Augustinian Friars slightly later. The subsequent decades saw a rapid expansion with friaries found in most major towns by the 1250s, with the foundations often aided by royal patronage. The friars moved away from the monastic ideals of isolation and contemplation. Instead they worked in the towns amongst the poor. They came to dominate the highest levels of English academic and intellectual life, as is seen by the example of Franciscan Roger Bacon who saw the spectrum of white light 400 years before Newton. Despite this we know very little of their daily routine and communal life.

The simplicity of their orders had the effect of making them popular because they were seen as very pious. Friaries were a favoured place for burial, judging by the evidence from York's will makers. The location of the York friaries were recorded by the antiquary John Leland: 'The Gray freres not far from the castle; nor far from Michelgate a house of Blake Freres; the White freres near Layerthorpe gate; the Augustine bytwixt the toure on the Ouse … and Owse Bridge'.

The Dominicans were first to arrive in York and may have established themselves in Goodramgate initially; in 1228 Henry III gave them the former Royal Free Chapel dedicated to St Mary Magdalene and an adjacent block of land off Tanner Row. The precinct had two gates: one on the west side faced Toft Green and the other faced the Ouse. The friary church was opposite modern Barker Lane (medieval Gregory Lane).

The Franciscans arrived c.1230 and Henry III gave them timber for building works in 1236, but the original location of their house is unknown. In 1243, they moved to the west side of York Castle which was the former outer bailey and probably a royal gift. Like their brethren in Oxford, they expanded their holdings by encroaching on existing defences, by gaining permission to fill in the ditch of the outer bailey. The precinct wall formed part of the western defences of the castle, ran along Castlegate, along a line close to modern Friargate (Hertergate) to the Ouse. The Franciscan precinct was cut through by Clifford Street in the 1890s. The river wall is still visible up to the Davy Tower where the city wall up to Castlegate Postern completed the boundary. The friary gate, with the church just inside, opened into Castlegate near to St Mary Castlegate. The friary was used by the king for accommodation when he visited York and there was a king's chamber within the precinct.

The Carmelites were originally established outside the walls on the edge of the Horsefair at the north-east end of Gillygate in around 1250. Henry III gave them oaks from the Forest of Galtres for the building of their church in 1253 and 1255. Excavations in Union Terrace identified late twelfth- or thirteenth-century buildings that may be the chapel or church, based on their east–west alignment and fine stone construction. In 1295 William Vescy gave the Carmelites a site off Stonebow Lane, close to the centre of the city. Their precinct covered an area between Stonebow Lane (lost when the present Stonebow was created) and the Fishpool in the south, and from Fossgate in the east to a street called the Mersk in the west. The friary church was under construction by 1300 and was consecrated in 1304. The church probably stood in the western part of the precinct as it was within the parish of St Saviour's.

The friary gradually expanded its holdings through the fourteenth century until they covered a block of land up to Hungate and towards the Foss where their landing stage may have been identified. The gateway was in Fossgate near the junction with Pavement and there was a chapel over the gate with an image of the Virgin Mary. This was a popular place for prayers and gifts, but it fell within the parish of St Crux and became the subject of disputes as the latter claimed the chapel was taking away some of its custom.

The Austin Friars (Augustinians) according to tradition had come from the friary in Tickhill (Doncaster). They bought seven houses along Old Coney Street (modern Lendal) in which to found their friary, probably around 1270. They were certainly in the city by 1272 when Henry III granted them protection. They expanded their original site through bequests of land and their precinct was walled with a gate onto the Old Coney Street.

One order failed, not only in York, but also across Europe – the Sac Friars, or the Brothers of the Penance of Jesus Christ. The order was founded around 1256 and was abolished by papal edict at the Council of Lyon in 1274. They were called the Sac Friars because they wore sackcloth over a tunic of better quality material. They arrived in England in the mid thirteenth century and had twelve foundations, the first of which was in Oxford; they arrived in York around 1260. Their precinct can be located through documents and was on the west side of Spen Lane, the boundary running around the corner of the friary towards St Andrew's Church. After the order was disbanded the York friars were allowed to continue their life together and there were three brothers left in 1300 when Edward I gave them alms. Presumably the end came when the last of them died around 1310 and the lands passed to the king.

With the exception of the Carmelite site in the Horesfair, none of the York friaries have been excavated. Those outside York that have, such as those in Oxford and London, and the surviving friary churches such as Norwich, Chichester and Coventry, give an impression of what may have been found in York. The main characteristic was the large nave, narrow choir, central tower, and a cloister. The spire of All Saints, North Street, may well have been influenced by the spire of the nearby Dominicans.

GET THEE TO A NUNNERY

Clementhorpe was the city's only nunnery and the first post-Conquest religious house for women in Yorkshire. The nunnery site had been home to a Roman building with a mosaic floor, but little is known about the use of the site until the Anglo-Scandinavian period when there may have been a church dedicated to St Clement, who was popular with the Danish; some possible evidence for this was uncovered during excavations in 1976–77. The site was marked on maps until the nineteenth century before being covered with terraced housing. The foundation and early history are poorly recorded, but references increase from the thirteenth century and show that it held estates within the city in Bootham, Bishopthorpe, Layerthorpe and Middlethorpe as well as further afield. The church also served as the parish church for the Clementhorpe area.

The nunnery was Benedictine and was established between 1125 and 1133 by Archbishop Thurstan. The nunnery and its estates were run by the prioress. The first known is Alice in 1192 and prioresses were likely to have been of high status; Constance Basy, elected to the post in 1315, was daughter of the prominent York citizen Roger Basy who represented the city in parliament in 1295.

The nunnery was on the east side of Bishopthorpe Road close to the city walls and had a staithe (landing stage) on the Ouse. This staithe was recorded by Francis Drake who reported seeing large limestone blocks dug out of the banks of the Ouse around 1730 to make it more navigable.

When the nunnery was excavated there were no clearly defined buildings because they had been comprehensively taken apart in the sixteenth century, as shown by the presence of limekilns. The archaeological evidence consisted of floors represented by mortar spreads and areas of heavily worn unglazed floor tiles; one floor consisted of much-repaired glazed and unglazed tiles. Another floor was represented by a spread of mortar with the impression of tiles. Fragmentary remains of walls showed they were made of limestone and there was one example of faced stone ashlar. It was thought these remains formed part of the nunnery church especially as there were discrete clusters of burials perhaps reflecting a distribution in the nave, aisles and side chapels.

The nunnery had a large graveyard and many burials have been found in the streets surrounding the area of the nunnery. Requests for burial at the nunnery in wills show there was a statue or image of the Virgin Mary in the nun's choir and in the cloister there was an altar to St Catherine along with images of St Mary and St William. Gifts left to the nunnery included silver spoons, a bed cover, and a chest for church ornaments; Elizabeth Conyers provided an altar frontal, an altar cloth of two ells (7ft 6in), a rack and a towel.

The majority of the nuns at Clementhorpe lived quietly although a few appear to have had colourful lives. In 1300, the assizes record men arriving at the nunnery gate, leading a saddled horse. They were met by a nun, Cecily, who threw off her habit and rode off to Darlington to live with Gregory Thornton. Perhaps the most interesting was Joanna of Leeds, who in 1318 left the nunnery and fabricated her death and funeral in Beverley with the aid of accomplices. She was caught and Archbishop Melton was lenient and directed the dean of Beverley to tell her to recant her sins so she could return to Clementhorpe.

ST ANDREW'S, THE GILBERTINE PRIORY

The Gilbertine priory, excavated in 1985, was established outside the walls in the area of the Anglian *wic*. In the tenth to twelfth centuries the site was part of the small suburb along Fishergate served by a small wooden church dedicated to St Andrew, which was later replaced in stone, within a large cemetery. The priory was founded in 1195 by Hugh Murdac, prebendary of Driffield, to house 12 canons and was one of four Gilbertine houses in the diocese of York. The precincts of the priory are shown on the first Ordnance Survey map as Stone Wall Close.

The Gilbertine order was established in the mid twelfth century by St Gilbert of Sempringham and there were two types of priories: double houses for nuns and canons and single houses for canons. The order followed the Rule of St Benedict, but was heavily influenced by the Cistercians, on whom they based their buildings, and their institutional and spiritual life. The main priory in Yorkshire was Watton which was a double house.

The York priory occupied a 5-acre site, with the main area consisting of the priory and gardens and covering about 1 acre; additionally there were 4 acres of pasture and an orchard. The course of the modern Fishergate cuts through the site of the priory and is first shown on maps from 1682. Medieval Fishergate ran along the line of modern Fawcett Street that leads directly to Fishergate Bar.

The priory, according to an inquest of c.1230, had retained the property associated with the earlier church as well as the land granted by its founder, including money rents and property in and around York. The buildings within the precinct are known from the surveys carried out at the Dissolution and show that the church had a clock and there was a kitchen, brew house, granary, buttery, kiln house, prior's chamber, guest chamber and parlour. The demolition horizons showed the priory buildings used limestone from the Tadcaster area and there was evidence for stone working on site through spreads of limestone chippings. The buildings were roofed with tile and stone, though the cloister may have been roofed with lead. On the Foss near the dam was the priory landing, St Andrew's Landing.

After the priory was founded a layer of imported earth was spread across the site to form a level building platform. Excavations identified the late twelfth-century cruciform church that probably had a low central tower, with north and south transepts with eastern chapels, a presbytery and an aisleless nave.

Associated with the church were the chapter house, eastern dormitory, latrines block and refectory around the cloister. This conformed to the general layout found at other monastic sites. The appearance of the early church was suggested through the simply carved architectural fragments and an extensive assemblage of colourful and highly decorated window glass. Minor alterations were made to the church and the cloister arcade through the late thirteenth or early fourteenth century. In the fourteenth century a major campaign of rebuilding or alteration was undertaken with the church made a smaller, simple rectangle with no structural variation between nave and chancel, and it was given a new south entrance. The new church was provided with a tiled floor and some of the earlier windows were re-used. As part of the rebuilding there was a general rearrangement of door positions and access routes throughout the priory. The east range was also rebuilt on a smaller scale and used low arches to bridge soft areas in the foundations, and the chapter house was reduced in size. The undercroft in the north range was altered, perhaps from a storage area, to a ground-floor refectory or domestic accommodation.

Despite their smaller size, these buildings were of lavish construction and the changes may reflect changes in religious practice, with a shift towards private prayer and a move away from communal eating and sleeping arrangements. They may also reflect the insignificance of Fishergate as a route in and out of the city, with the priory unable to rely on the support of passing traffic. They may also be associated with the priory's external patron, the Bishop of Lincoln, Henry Burghersh, who may have financed the documented building work which corresponds with the excavated evidence for changes to the priory. He had quarters within the precinct that he used when parliament was in York in 1330s and this might explain the modifications to the north range.

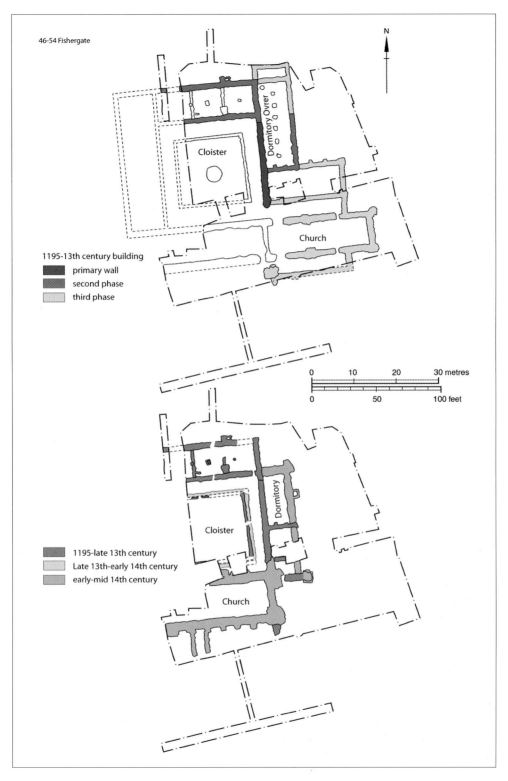

46-54 Fishergate

Dormitory Over

Cloister

Church

1195-13th century building

■ primary wall
■ second phase
□ third phase

N

0   10   20   30 metres

0   50   100 feet

Dormitory

Cloister

Church

■ 1195-late 13th century
□ Late 13th-early 14th century
■ early-mid 14th century

34 The development of the Gilbertine Priory

There was very little evidence relating to the everyday life of the priory; presumably rubbish was regularly disposed of in the convenient River Ouse. Despite this some artefacts were found associated with manuscripts and books suggesting the presence of library/ scriptorium which was usually associated with the dormitory on the east side of the cloister.

Minor alterations and adaptations were carried out during the fifteenth century and the priory was still functioning on the eve of the Reformation. After the priory was dissolved it was demolished and limekilns were built in the cloister garth using elements of the cloister arcade. The building was comprehensively robbed of stone and lead. The northern range of buildings appears to have been used as stables or stores during the demolition of the priory.

CHAPELS

As well as the parish churches and large religious houses there were numerous chapels in and around the city which are often mentioned in documents. For example, a chapel was erected at Clementhorpe in 1405 to commemorate Archbishop Scrope, executed for rebelling against Henry IV. Others lay close to the city boundaries, such as St Catherine's which was near Green Dykes Lane and stood within a garden surrounded by a wall and a ditch.

Ouse Bridge had a chapel, built in c.1170 as the King's Free Chapel. In 1228 it was rededicated to St William of York and was adjacent to the council chamber. It was an important part of the city's ceremonial infrastructure. It had a gold and silver Corpus Christi shrine that had been moved from Holy Trinity and was shown to visiting dignitaries by the Lord Mayor. Foss Bridge had a chapel dedicated to St Anne that housed altars for masses for the souls of the royal family, the mayor and the citizens and was managed by the Corporation.

Outside the south-east side of York Castle stood the Chapel of St George established in the twelfth century. It stood close to the banks of the Foss and gave its name to the area – St George's Field. The chapel was at first granted to the Knights Templar in 1246, but on their suppression in 1311 it became a Royal Free Chapel. In 1447 it passed to the Guild of St Christopher and St George and was suppressed in 1547. The chapel passed to the Corporation and was largely demolished in 1566 for the rebuilding of Ouse Bridge; the last traces were demolished in 1856. Excavations of the chapel in 1990 identified some of the walls which were 0.7m wide and survived to a height of 1.3m. The north wall consisted of coursed limestone with a rubble core and there was evidence for several floor surfaces and episodes of ground-raising within the chapel.

The Mount used to be St James's Hill and was renamed in the mid seventeenth century. The name came from the chapel founded by Roger the Priest, which stood on the south side of the road. In 1134–35 King Stephen granted this chapel to Holy Trinity, Micklegate, and in 1150–54 he granted them the land where the thieves' gallows stood with bodies to be buried at the chapel. According to the statutes of the Minster, new archbishops were met at St James's Chapel. The archbishop then walked barefoot to the Minster in procession. The chapel was a prominent landmark often mentioned in documents and according to Francis Drake it was removed in 1736 for road widening.

1 York's oldest row: Our Lady Row, Goodramgate. © *York Archaeological Trust*

2 Shady on a summer's day: the Shambles. © *The author*

3 The old and the new: water gates in the river wall along the Ouse. © *York Archaeological Trust*

4 Bootham Bar, the northern entrance to the medieval city. © *York Archaeological Trust*

5 York's tallest gate, Monk Bar. © *The author*

6 A cause for murder? The Red Tower in York. © *York Archaeological Trust*

7 York's most complete gate, Walmgate Bar. © *York Archaeological Trust*

8 Fishergate Postern tower, formerly on the banks of the Foss. © *York Archaeological Trust*

9 The imposing east bailey walls of York Castle. © *York Archaeological Trust*

10 The city walls from the Saddler Tower to Micklegate: a statement of medieval pride.
© *York Archaeological Trust*

11 The principal entrance to the city, Micklegate Bar. © *York Archaeological Trust*

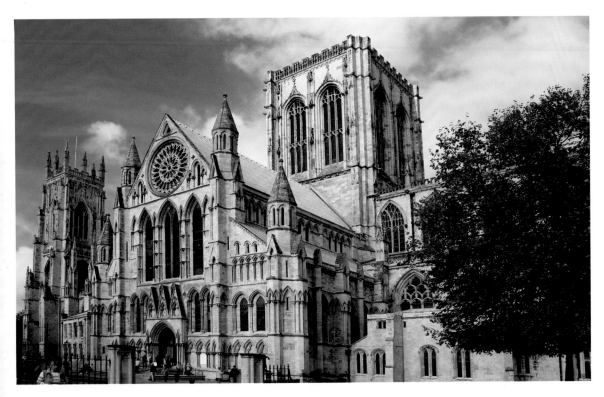

12 York Minster still dominates the city. © *York Archaeological Trust*

13 The Gilbertine Priory: the poor religious house. © *York Archaeological Trust*

14 'The wealthiest religious house', St Mary's Abbey. © *The author*

15 The hall of the wealthiest and most powerful guild, the Merchant Adventurers.
© *York Archaeological Trust*

16 The rivals: the Merchant Taylors' Hall. © *York Archaeological Trust*

17 A hall for all, St Anthony's. © *York Archaeological Trust*

18 In the balance: a steelyard, stamped with the three royal lions, used to check the weight of goods. © *York Archaeological Trust*

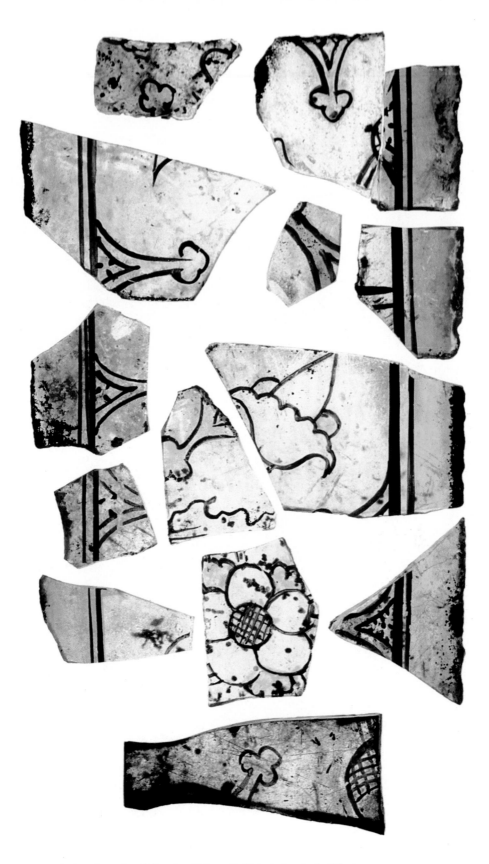

19 Stained glass from the Gilbertine Priory. © *York Archaeological Trust*

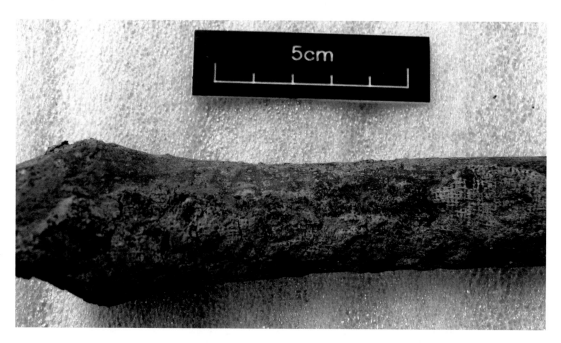

20 A rare survival: fragments of shroud from a burial in Silver Street. © *York Archaeological Trust*

21 Part of a decorated blue glass bowl from the Bedern. © *York Archaeological Trust*

22 An inlaid knife: evidence of the skill of the medieval metalworkers, but also a sign of status.
© *York Archaeological Trust*

23 Someone's prized possession? A gold wire brooch. © *York Archaeological Trust*

24 Feasting medieval style: a banquet held at Barley Hall. © *York Archaeological Trust*

St Martin's Chapel in Aldwark was recorded in a charter of St Leonard's Hospital in 1272. In 1389 John de Kyghlay, glover, mentions in his will a garden opposite the chapel of St Martin in the place called Hikenyld and Hakenhyld. The chapel priest in 1432, John Ravensthrope, had a dwelling and a servant, and in his will in 1432 asked to be buried at St Saviour's, leaving vestments to the chapel if it continued to stand. In 1447 the site of the chapel was given to the Guild of St Anthony. Their new guildhall still stands and during renovation in 2006–07 parts of this chapel, consisting of robber cuts for walls and floor levels, were exposed, having been sealed by a layer of mortar and limestone chipping associated with the construction of the hall.

IN SICKNESS AND IN HEALTH

The church also cared for the sick and York had about 30 hospitals by the sixteenth century. Medieval hospitals were very diverse with different hospitals serving different functions. They often focused on easing pain and suffering of the sick rather than attempting a cure, which some saw as interfering with the natural will of God. Some hospitals were outside the walls close to the city boundaries, such as St Mary Magdalene at the northern end of Bootham near Burton Stone Lane.

Some hospitals cared for orphans or foundlings like St Leonard's, while others sheltered the poor and provided hospitality for travellers, especially pilgrims, such as St Thomas's Hospital outside Micklegate Bar. Caring for the sick or needy was seen as a charitable act, so there was a shift from the foundation of hospitals by religious institutions in the eleventh to early thirteenth centuries to foundation by wealthy secular institutions from the fourteenth to sixteenth centuries. Guilds occasionally cared for the aged or infirm of their own guild. The foundations of the fourteenth to sixteenth centuries were called *maisons dieu* (houses of God) and York had over 20 of these, an example being the one founded in St Andrewgate by Cecilia Plater in the fourteenth century. The Corporation had its own *maison dieu* on Ouse Bridge which was refounded in 1302, standing opposite St William's Chapel.

Hospitals are hard to detect archaeologically, with the associated artefacts predominantly domestic or religious in character. *Maisons dieu* could be within a standard house converted for the purpose and thus undetectable. Healing was based on traditional medicine supplemented or modified by books in the library and probably included minor surgery. Herbs were regularly purchased to make medicines. Some idea of the use of herbs comes from a book called the *Macer Floridus de Viribus Herbarum* which offered recipes for cures for all parts of the body. One recipe involved cumin soaked in vinegar that had been dried on a hot iron, mixed with pepper, then ground together with honey. This was good for aches in the breast, sides, liver and kidneys, destroyed cholera, comforted the stomach and improved digestion!

The oldest and largest hospital in York was St Leonard's, standing in the western angle of the Roman fortress within a precinct of 4 acres. It had two main gates, one opposite Blake Street and the other accessing a lane to St Leonard's Landing. The hospital was originally called St Peter's but was rededicated to St Leonard when King Stephen funded the rebuilding of the church in the 1130s.

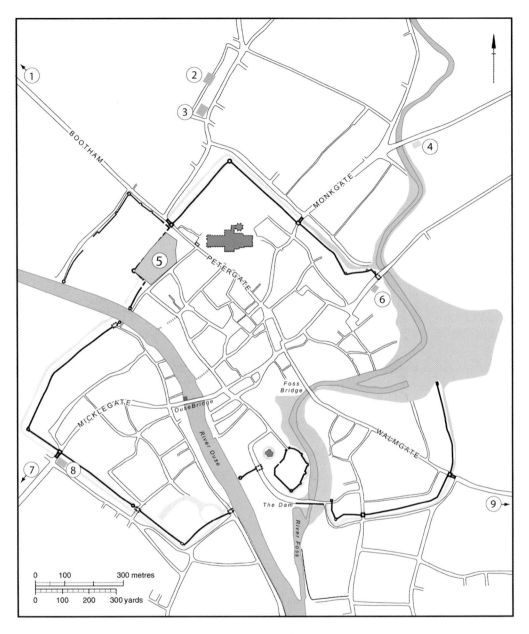

1. St Mary Magdalene
2. St Anthony-in-the-Horsefair
3. St Mary-in-the-Horsefair
4. St Loy (or St Leonard), Monkgate
5. St Leonard's Hospital

6. Maison Dieu
7. St Katherine
8. St Thomas
9. St Nicholas

35 Some of the hospitals in medieval York

36 The vaulted
undercroft
leading to
St Leonard's
Hospital.
© *The author*

The hospital's water gate with its vaulted passage and part of the infirmary and chapel survive. These were probably built with the funding of the Minster Treasurer, John Romeyn, in the middle of the thirteenth century. There is also an undercroft, beneath the Theatre Royal, which was more extensive until 1901. One of the boundary walls with a blocked gate with cruciform arrow slits has been built into the theatre. Many of the buildings within the precinct are known from documents that list the infirmary, orphanage, domestic offices, master's house, cloister and church with a tower.

St Leonard's followed the rule of St Augustine and had thirteen brothers and eight sisters. The sisters were probably responsible for the care of the patients while the brothers dealt with the religious services. Little is known about treatments, but there are references to *medica*, doctors, and in 1287 the hospital owed Adam the apothecary (who sold and collected herbs) money. St Leonard's cared for over 200 *cremetts* (poor people) as well as

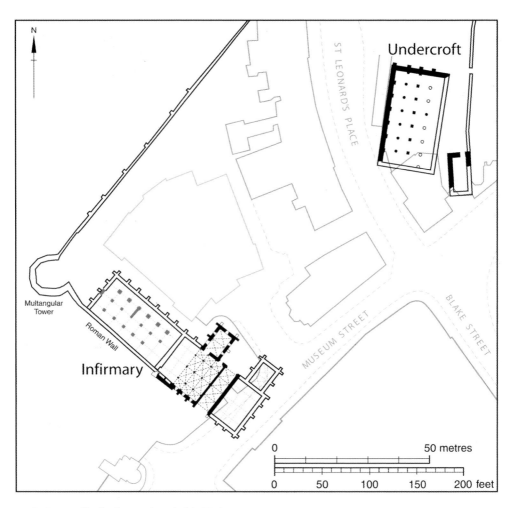

37 St Leonard's, the largest hospital in York

corrodians, holders of *corrodies* (a type of allowance), a function of which allowed them to retire into the house as boarders to live out their final days. Corrodies were often purchased for cash or a donation of land or property but were also given as an expression of the hospital's gratitude for services done. Outpatients, called livery holders, lived in the city and were provided with money or food.

Excavations have been carried out at the hospital in the area of the infirmary. These showed the massive earth ramparts of the city walls were a serious obstruction to the construction of the hospital buildings. The solution was to dig away the top 3m of the rampart and redeposit it at the base of the rampart to form a level surface for the construction of the infirmary buildings which incorporated the newly re-exposed Roman walls.

The infirmary buildings were extended in the thirteenth century up to the north-east wall of the defences, increasing the length of the building to almost 50m. It was a two-storey building and excavations identified the line of the demolished north-east wall

38 The complex walls and features of St Mary-in-the-Horsefair. © *York Archaeological Trust*

consisting of a robbed-out foundation of mortared rubble 2.4m wide and at least 1.2m deep. Associated with the construction of this wall was a large drain made of massive limestone blocks capped with stone.

The upper floor of the infirmary was supported by a vaulted undercroft. Six of the column bases have been investigated and were built of massive limestone blocks which were set in small pits. Two column bases with a different construction of larger pits filled with mortared rubble were thought to suggest that the north-west part of the infirmary was older and dated to the eleventh or twelfth century. Something of the appearance of the medieval hospital can be surmised from decorated ridge tiles, glazed floor tiles, some of which were decorated, and fragments of decorated window glass found in demolition layers.

On a smaller scale was St Mary's Hospital that took over the buildings of the Carmelites in the Horsefair. The Horsefair had another hospital, dedicated to St Anthony, but its location is uncertain. St Mary's originated as a chantry and the associated chapel is recorded in 1315. It was enlarged into a hospital in 1318 for a master and six infirm and aged chaplains.

Excavations in 1972 traced the change in the use of the building in the early fourteenth century to a hospital with the rearrangement of the interior. One area was subdivided into four rooms with sills for timber partitions to form the infirmary hall. A second entrance was inserted into the north wall opposite an existing south door to form a cross passage. The Carmelite chapel continued in use as the hospital chapel, with other buildings converted to form a latrine. In the mid fifteenth to mid sixteenth century a

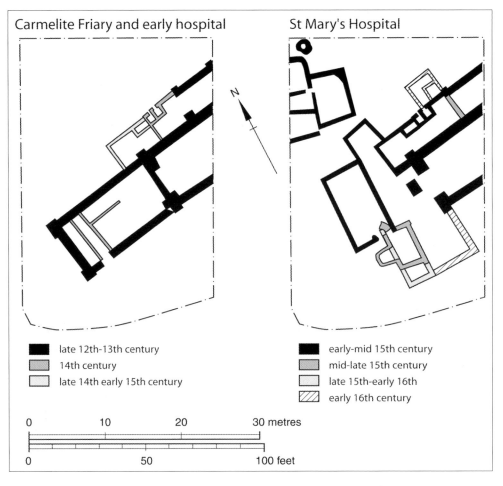

39 From Carmelites to hospital, the development of St Mary in the Horsefair

domestic range was constructed that may have had a timber superstructure; part of it was used as kitchens and there was a cellared room built in stone. The redesign made the hospital quadrangular in plan with a move away from communal living. The hospital closed during the Reformation, but was described in 1556 as having a pond, orchards, gardens, a mansion, lodging chamber and chapel.

UNCLEAN — YORK'S LEPER HOSPITALS

The majority of leper hospitals were founded in the twelfth and earlier thirteenth centuries. The church legislated against the disease in the twelfth century, segregating lepers from the rest of society. The disease could have unpleasant effects depending on where it occurred in the body and was believed to be contagious. The stigma associated with it derived from the bible, however, particularly the passage in *Leviticus* stating it was an unclean disease and a punishment for a sin.

Only one individual with leprosy has been unearthed in the city, from the burial ground of St Stephen's Fishergate. Even so York had four leper hospitals to deal with the disease and these were located in the city suburbs. On the north-east side of Monk Bridge stood the hospital of St Loy and excavations in this area have identified a massive boundary ditch that contained twelfth-century pottery and was recut in the fifteenth century. The gatehouse of the hospital was incorporated in a later building demolished in 1925.

On the Mount was St Catherine's, first mentioned in 1333. It consisted of a small group of buildings surrounded by a wall with separate accommodation for men and women. By 1648 the buildings were in ruin and it was rebuilt before being demolished in 1835. In Fishergate was the hospital of St Helen's, which may have been associated with the church of St Helen and was demolished in the seventeenth century.

The largest leper hospital was St Nicholas's near the city boundary at the northern end of Lawrence Street. It may have been founded in the twelfth century as grants of land were given to the hospital in 1132 and 1161. By the late thirteenth century the inmates were all women. The church also acted as a parish church and survived the Reformation, but was destroyed at the end of the English Civil War. The doorway at St Margaret's, Walmgate, showing the signs of the zodiac, was said to have come from St Nicholas's Church.

Excavations in the area of the hospital identified a series of well-preserved buildings dating from the eleventh or twelfth century to the fifteenth century. The late twelfth-century buildings were substantial, consisting of a rectangular structure with a series of chamfered padstones for timber posts. This aisled building was some 20m long and 10m wide. It had a large central aisle with a large square tile hearth that had been rebuilt several times. The northern end of the building was divided into cubicles with hearths. The associated sequence of floors suggested it was in use for over a hundred years. In the fourteenth century the building was reduced in size with the abandonment of the north and south aisles. Brick walls were constructed linking the padstones. An extension to the northern end of the building had a sequence of circular hearths which may have been ovens for a kitchen.

AND IN THE END

In the 1530s religion was to enter the forefront of national politics. The Church had been challenged before at the end of the fourteenth century by John Wycliff, and the same arguments were raised again in the sixteenth century by people such as the German preacher Martin Luther – that salvation could come directly through Christ rather than through the saints, good works and masses for the dead.

The changes to the Church came about through Henry VIII's need to secure a divorce from Catherine of Aragon. The pope had refused this so the Archbishop of Canterbury, Thomas Cranmer, annulled the marriage in 1533. This was the start of the break with Rome and in 1534 the Act of Supremacy was passed recognising the king not the pope as head of the Church in England.

The crown also needed money and the Church was an obvious target. The survey of the monastic houses, the Valor Ecclesiasticus, formed the basis for the 1536 Act permitting the confiscation of all monasteries with revenues of less than £200. In the summer of that year Richard Speght and his community surrendered Holy Trinity Priory and the Prioress Isabel Ward surrendered Clementhorpe Nunnery.

The closures sparked dissent in York, with a riot in August 1536 and a serious quarrel in the Merchant Adventurers' Hall in September. The unrest peaked in the East Riding under Robert Aske and this rebellion came to be known as the Pilgrimage of Grace. The city joined the rebels and on 16 October Robert Aske marched to the Minster and posted an order restoring the monks and nuns to their houses. The rebellion ended after a meeting at Pontefract, but a second revolt, not joined by the city, saw Aske sent to London for trial after which he was sent to York for execution.

The monastic closures resumed in 1538. The Dominican, Franciscan, Carmelite and Austin Friaries closed in November, as did St Andrew's Priory. In November 1539 St Mary's Abbey closed and the end of an era was marked when St Leonard's closed on 1 December. In all some 150 monks, friars and nuns were without a home, though some found a role in the parish churches in York and on their houses' former estates across the country. The priors, abbot and prioress were all given pensions.

The closure of the hospitals left a gap in provision for the sick and of education. The topography of the town was radically changed, with the large religious precincts and all their property made available for sale. With the exception of St Mary's Abbey that was retained by the crown until the nineteenth century, religious property was sold off to the local gentry like Ralph Beckwith who acquired the Carmelite Friary. It was not only the gentry in York who benefited; in 1545 Sir Richard Gresham, a London financier, paid £1,200 for about a quarter of the York housing stock previously in Church ownership and then began selling it to local men with the remainder to be sold on his death.

Chantry chapels were untouched until the reign of Edward VI. York's Corporation had already secured an Act of Parliament in 1536 to close municipal chantries which were no longer financially viable, but Edward's commissioners arrived to oversee the closure of around a hundred chantries in 1548, divided between the Minster and the parish churches.

The parish churches did not escape the effects of the Reformation: walls were limewashed to cover over the paintings; interiors were reorganised with the removal of rood screens and images of saints, reflecting changes in the liturgy. Even after the closures of the fourteenth century, York was over-churched by the Reformation; in 1535 York had twice as many churches as Exeter even though the cities were of similar size. Through the Act of the Union of Parishes in 1547 the Corporation reduced the number of parish churches to 25. The Corporation argued that many were too poor to support themselves, but the motives behind the closures were probably more complex. In addition to the effects of a declining population and economy, the closures may also have been influenced by changing patterns of faith.

By the 1560s the infrastructure of the medieval Christian Church in York had been either swept away or changed irrevocably, but the deeply rooted beliefs and traditions of the people were not changed in a single generation.

4

MERCHANT, BUTCHER
AND CANDLESTICK-MAKER

The trade of its residents was the lifeblood of medieval York. The goods made and sold in the city provided it with the wealth that found expression through buildings such as the guildhalls, the city walls and parish churches. Much of what is known of the medieval economy is derived from documentary sources which often focus on the wealthy merchants; little is known about the hundreds of craftsmen, known as artisans, with their specialised skills. It is through archaeology that we can learn much more about the activities of the city's artisans.

The regulation of York's economy initially fell to the sheriff of the county, but as the city slowly gained independence this responsibility passed to the mayor and council. They were expected to enforce the ordinances (decrees) issued by central government. Not all artisans fell under the control of the Corporation, notably those living near the Minster and in the other city liberties. Within the city, freemen were the registered artisans. Achieving the status of freeman was seen as a mark of success and the person was classed as a burgess or citizen. Freemen could trade goods without incurring penalties.

The enforcement of regulations is perhaps reflected in the presence of balances and weights found in excavations across the city. A late thirteenth-/early fourteenth-century steel yard weight was recovered from Coffee Yard. Steel yards were balances with unequal arms, the longer measuring arm having the weight attached; this was moved along until the arms balanced. The Coffee Yard weight is made of lead alloy cast in one piece with a hole for hanging. It bears the royal coat of arms of Edward I, c.1290–1300, implying the enforcement of royal control.

Some traders were outside the franchise (foreigners) and paid the fines or annual licences permitting them to trade. In 1425 and 1482 the city encouraged country butchers to sell meat in the city in order to bring down the price of meat. Concern over ale prices saw the city brewers threatened with 'foreign competition' if they did not amend their prices. Throughout the medieval period the main concern for the Corporation was to ensure the city had adequate supplies to feed and clothe its residents.

There has been much debate over the economy of York during the medieval period. It is difficult to reach firm conclusions about its state after the Conquest, but it has been argued that by the thirteenth and fourteenth centuries the city was at its wealthiest. From the fifteenth century to the mid sixteenth century the city is generally viewed as suffering a period of decline until managing a recovery in the 1560s. The causes and effects of urban decline merit further study.

IMPORTS AND EXPORTS

The city needed money to meet its financial obligations to the crown. It had to pay an annual sum (the 'fee farm') fixed at £100 in 1086. The crown also raised money from cases in the city courts and from numerous taxes. These royal burdens were enforced by the king's representative, the sheriff of Yorkshire, and his assistants. With the growing independence of the city this responsibility fell to its Corporation, which also needed money to fund its own civic life of feasting, processions and pageants. Changes in the national economy due to war and disease also affected the city. This was especially the case with the infamous Black Death of 1348–50 and its subsequent outbreaks; however by the sixteenth century York was to suffer less from the plague than other cities.

York had been a major trading centre since the Anglian period, supplying a wide range of goods to the surrounding region through its markets. These contacts were maintained and expanded after the Conquest, with a shift in focus towards the European markets, which reflected the origins of the new rulers. Trade was one of the principal ways the city funded itself: through goods brought into York, and taxes, tolls and fines which were collected at the city gates, bridges and quayside.

The developing trade was controlled by the merchants, but their activities in the eleventh and twelfth centuries are not well recorded. William of Malmesbury commented on Irish and German ships in York in the twelfth century and by the thirteenth century documents tell us that Flemings, Bretons, Frenchmen and Italians were trading in the city. Archaeologically the evidence for this trade is reflected in the presence of German lava quern stones and pottery; the continuation of old contacts with Norway represented by sharpening stones of ragstone and phyllite.

Evidence of York's growing trade is the establishment of the Merchant Guild in 1130, although it may have had its origins in the late eleventh century. We do not know how it operated, but its members probably paid for privileges such as the exclusive right to buy or sell in the town, which was a precursor to the later rights of the freemen. The powerful merchant families such as Lefwin, Nuvel, Tickhill and Selby were the driving force behind the city slowly gaining a degree of independence from the crown. The city gradually gained administrative and financial privileges from the reign of Henry II (1154–58) onwards and the earliest seal of the city is dated to 1191x1206.

In 1212 King John gave the citizens the right to organise the fee farm and pay it to the crown rather than the sheriff, and to appoint a mayor. The first recorded mayor is Hugh Selby in 1217, a merchant who exported wool to the Low Countries and imported wine from Anjou. Initially the city government was made up of the mayor and three bailiffs. Other offices developed and by end of the century the city had its own coroners and chamberlains who were responsible for the city finances. By 1256 this corporate elite had a guildhall or common hall built on the site of a stone house that had been acquired or left to the Merchant Guild, and this was the site of the present guildhall. The culmination of these privileges was the granting of independent county status by Richard II in 1393 that gave the city autonomy from the sheriff in the castles; two sheriffs of the city were elected by the ruling citizens.

The Ouse was the centre of commercial activity and from the thirteenth century more and more warehouses were constructed along its banks. The port of Hull, founded in

1299, was useful to the city as it could accommodate the larger ships of the late medieval period. Goods were then transhipped on smaller craft up the Ouse to York. From the fourteenth century York was dealing with merchants from Holland, France, Italy, the Low Countries, Spain, Portugal, Germany, Iceland and the Baltic.

The charges recorded for using the common crane show the range of goods brought into the city along the Ouse: wine from Gascony, Greece and Spain; oil, raisins, preserved ginger and spices from India and the Mediterranean; woad from France; iron from Spain and Sweden; alum from Greece; and sea coal from Newcastle. Other imports included glass, pewter, wooden vessels, boots, shoes, cloth, linen, furs, madder, grain, salt, wax, steel and lead. In return the city exported a range of finished goods, including wool, cloth and lead. Archaeology has shown changes in the trading contacts of the York merchants during the fourteenth and fifteenth centuries, with the appearance of red wares from the Low Countries – cooking wares such as dripping pans, pipkins and skillets – and German stonewares. The Minster imported window glass from Hesse, Burgundy and Lorraine from Hansea merchants.

York was also at times a staple town, where specific goods such as wool could be exported or imported, and at the end of the Middle Ages the city sought to make itself a staple for Richmondshire lead. This meant that the city had a monopoly on these products and could generate significant income from the associated tolls. Trade was not just international, but also national and regional. York was a natural focus for the exchange of goods from the north of England, handling products such as East Riding wool, Dales butter, Kendal cloth and grain from Holderness and Lincolnshire. The city was well served by the river and road network.

Regional trade was perhaps of the greatest importance to the city. People from nearby towns and villages bought and sold products at the weekly markets, and made use of the city's services. The importance of York as a food market is reflected in the tolls on horses, cattle, sheep, pigs and goats, which in 1226 helped pay for work on the city defences. Lardiners (kitchen workers) drew some income from butchers, bakers, corn merchants and the Foss Bridge fishmongers. York served as the centre of distribution for towns and villages in Yorkshire, and its markets and specialist fairs were in great demand.

THE WORKERS

With its wide range of crafts York needed a large body of workers both skilled and unskilled. Some workers have left little or no documentary evidence, such as the lawyers and clerks employed in religious houses, secular administration and ecclesiastical and secular courts. They were beyond the jurisdiction of the civic authority and yet must have been a significant group. The courts generated important traffic of their own, drawing in a wide variety of individuals with business in the Church, city and county courts.

Most of what we know about the city workers comes from the Register of Freemen that started in 1272. Becoming Freemen allowed residents to exploit the growing autonomy of the city as it allowed them to set up shops and trade in the city, exempt from the tolls levied on non free traders. The Register lists the trade and initially place of origin of some of the residents and at first the freedom was purchased, but soon other ways to acquire the freedom of the city developed. This included apprenticeships and inheritance (the son of a freeman became a freeman) and before 1300 being a freeman was probably more of a privilege than a necessity; by the fifteenth century it was an obligation imposed as part of the control of fiscal power by the urban elite.

The artisans were a distinct class in their own right and were active in distinguishing themselves from the unskilled labourers. A definition of an artisan household might be one where a significant proportion of their income was gained from manufacture or processing of goods for sale. The merchants' influence over artisans may have manifested itself in the encouragement of the formation of guilds from the twelfth century, which allowed the ruling elite to keep a check on the workers. The guilds, however, gave the workers a sense of unity which they could use to challenge authority. The average artisan did not always confine himself to a single craft and most households derived income from a variety of sources, taking on piece work or wage labour to supplement their income, and their wives were often involved in tasks such as brewing. Other residents of medieval York included the self-employed, the wage labourers and the servants.

The workers in the city were not all native to York. Before the development of fixed surnames, people were often named after their place of origin and the Register of Freemen gives an idea of where people working in the city came from. This is of course biased, as women were excluded from the Register and may have had a different migratory pattern. Similarly it does not include non-franchised males, paupers or vagrants. York drew most of its immigrants from the surroundings rural villages, with many others coming from Lincolnshire, Cumbria, Lancashire, Northumberland and Durham. A very few came from other parts of the country such as Oxfordshire, Somerset, Wales and London. There were also a few foreigners in the city who had come from Brittany, Flanders, France and Germany. There was clearly a link between the areas with which the city traded and the people who came to settle and work in York.

THE GUILDHALLS

The role of the guilds changed and developed during the medieval period. Initially there was the Merchant Guild, a grouping of the mercantile elite which developed into the city council. The various crafts grouped themselves into associations called crafts or mysteries throughout Europe in the tenth to twelfth centuries; some were associated early on with religious fraternities. One of the earliest guilds in York was the guild of the weavers who acquired a charter in 1163 granting them the regional monopoly of production of cloth in return for an annual payment. At this early stage the guild doesn't appear to be concerned with regulating workshops, but rather with protecting trade.

Craft guilds were not formed by all crafts and did not represent all household producers since women and servants were excluded. Although some of the wealthier guilds were able to build guildhalls, sometimes using properties donated to them, others met in one of the many parish churches, the friaries or private houses. Why some chose to build halls and others did not is far from clear. One problem is that few records survive for many of the guilds and study has often focused on the well-recorded, wealthy and influential Merchant Adventurers and the Corpus Christi Guild; these do not accurately reflect the smaller guilds.

The development of the guilds, both craft and religious guilds, was significant for the city's developing political and economic functions, but they were not always imposed by the ruling merchant oligarchy. They had a political role and gave a sense of unity to workers; they were also a source of pride, which is seen in the investment by the members in the annual mystery plays. Guilds were also a social support system, giving professional identity, but also providing for the burial of members and prayers for their souls which might otherwise have been unaffordable.

The number of guilds increased in the years after the Black Death, possibly as an attempt to help regulate a fluid labour market and the resultant shifts in social hierarchy as people sought to exploit opportunities left by the dead. A key official of the guilds was the searcher, responsible for overseeing the quality of goods both produced in the city and brought to York for sale at the markets.

Guilds were not always craft-based, but could also be religious groupings known as fraternities. Despite this apparent distinction, their activities were not always that different. The fluid nature of religion and craft can be seen by the fact that the Merchant Adventurers' Hall had its origins as the guildhall of the Fraternity and Guild of Our Lord Jesus Christ and the Blessed Virgin Mary in 1357–61. All guilds had a religious function, though this was suppressed during the Reformation in the sixteenth century.

The guildhalls built in the city were the manifestation of the wealth and social standing of the various groups that built them. The clearest surviving statement of civic pride is the Guildhall, or Common Hall, in Coney Street. In the medieval period it was not the main meeting house for the Corporation, which held the most of its meetings in the council chamber first mentioned in 1376, adjacent to St William's Chapel on Ouse Bridge. The common hall was in existence by the reign of Henry III (1207–72) and may have been on the site of an earlier property. The hall was almost destroyed during an air raid in 1942, but has been carefully restored.

No excavation has taken place at the Common Hall, but we can recreate much of its appearance from the tenement rentals for the properties near the gate to the hall. A lane running under the hall was a common lane giving access to the river. The lane, known as both Stonegate Landing and Common Hall Lane, still survives and marked the boundary of the Augustinian Friary. Leading to a staithe, the lane was originally accessed from Coney Street and was closed with a door or gate at night. The churchwardens of St Martin Coney Street paid 2d a year for the privilege of locking the door at night.

The decision to rebuild this guildhall was taken in 1433–34 and building materials began to be stockpiled. The new Common Hall was a joint venture between the mayor, the commonality and the Guild of St Christopher, which joined with the Guild of St George soon after the building was complete. Construction began in 1449 and the hall was largely complete by 1453–54; it is typical of medieval design with aisles and a dais at the west end. The chamber behind the dais survived the bombing and retains much if its fifteenth-century carving.

The medieval entrance to the guildhall must have been quite imposing and was flanked by properties rented out on one side and a chapel to St Christopher on the other, probably where the present passage is. The chapel belonged to the Guild of St Christopher and St George, which also owned St George's Chapel near the castle. The present entrance

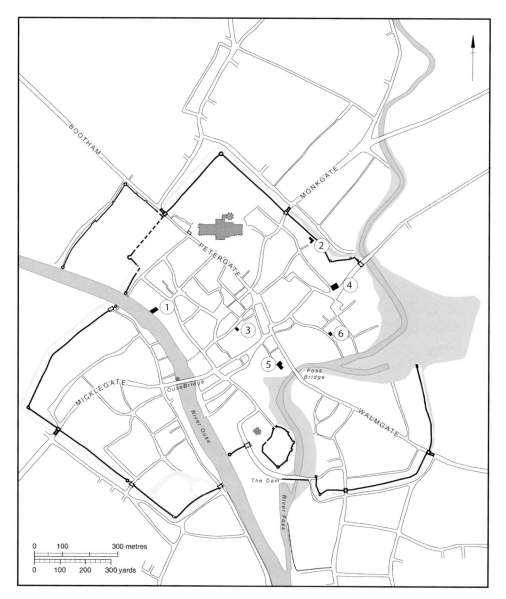

1. Guildhall / Common Hall
2. Merchant Taylors' Hall
3. Butchers' Hall
4. St Anthony's Hall
5. Merchant Adventurers' Hall
6. Cordwainers' Hall

40 The guildhalls of York

was constructed along with the Mansion House in the eighteenth century. In 1502 a statue of York's legendry founder, Eburak, was moved from the corner of St Saviourgate to the guildhall, perhaps as a statement of civic pride.

41 A statement of civic pride? The Common Hall in Coney Street. © *York Archaeological Trust*

The open area in front of the Guildhall was part of the original building agreement and was called the Common Hall Yard; on one side was a garden. Ancillary buildings on either side of the hall included a buttery and a pantry which were also used to detain prisoners; there was also a kitchen and a stable. Although the hall was not used for regular council meetings it was used by the Guild of St Christopher. Other functions held there included the city assize courts where the mayor, coroner, bailiffs, sheriffs and other officials exercised jurisdiction over disputes affecting property, criminal offences and trade. It was also used for civic and ceremonial occasions such as the election of sheriffs and the swearing in of the mayor.

Only three other guildhalls survive in York: the Merchant Adventurers' Hall, the Hall of the Merchant Taylors and St Anthony's Hall. Other guildhalls may have existed, but have subsequently been demolished, such as the Butchers' Hall that stood near the Shambles. Of the surviving guildhalls, Trinity Hall, the home of the Merchant Adventurers, is perhaps the most studied.

The area around the hall has been considerably altered, largely through the creation of Piccadilly in 1912. Originally the hall was bounded on one side by the Foss and on another by a series of small lanes with the principal entrance probably off Fossgate, through the passage incorporated into a later range that now stands on the street frontage. A lease of 1312 refers to a passage and a lane called *trichourgail* and *bacusgail*. During excavations in 1995 a lane was found with a cobbled surface that ran along the south-west side of the hall and may be the medieval *bacusgail*. Between the hall and Castlegate were the properties that ran down to the river from Coppergate and Pavement, York's second principal market.

Trinity Hall was therefore located in what could be classed as York's commercial sector, home to prosperous merchants, mercers and drapers within the parish of St Crux which was the church of the guild that originally built the hall, the Fraternity of Our Lord Jesus Christ and the Blessed Virgin Mary. The land with a building which formed the site for the hall, was acquired in 1356 from William Percehay (Percy). The guild was formerly incorporated in 1357 and in 1371–72 it gained permission to found a hospital in the undercroft. By 1430 the guild was dominated by merchants and acquired the name Merchant Adventurers. The religious link was kept in their seal, which showed the Holy Trinity flanked by sailing ships.

The standing building suggests that it is of three principal phases of construction: late fourteenth-century undercroft and first floor hall; early fifteenth-century chapel; and early seventeenth-century north-east range. The fourteenth-century hall was heavily restored with many timbers replaced in the early twentieth century, though most of the principal timbers are original. These have been dated by dendrochronology to 1338–55. The hall is a double-aisled eight-bay structure arranged in the typical medieval plan of dais or high end to the south-east, with the low end having a buttery and pantry. The presence of a central hearth is suggested by references to louver strings in the fourteenth-century accounts rolls.

The hall had a chapel, possibly built in 1368 and associated with the undercroft hospital which was founded in 1371–72. The present chapel is a replacement built in 1411 and contains a large quantity of older, re-used architectural fragments. Excavations in the chapel exposed foundations thought to represent the base of an altar. Work near the south-eastern side of the chapel suggested that it had been extended shortly after its construction. The original fifteenth-century window was wider than its replacement, and parts of it have been incorporated in the garden of the hall as an ornamental structure.

Excavations in the gardens in 1995 showed how the Foss influenced building campaigns on the site. Environmental evidence indicated a sequence of encroachment onto the river bank associated with episodes of silting, which represented periods of flooding throughout the medieval period, probably made worse after the creation of the Fishpool. To combat the problems of flooding the ground level around the hall had been raised through the deliberate dumping of large amounts of soil, gravel and rubbish in the fourteenth century.

A trench against the external wall of the hall showed that further changes in ground level had led to the windows of the undercroft being made smaller, as the earlier sill was found 0.95m below the present ground level. The exposed brickwork of the hall undercroft was shown to have been built on five courses of fourteenth-century limestone masonry. The fourteenth-century stonework had been constructed on nine courses of high-quality ashlar limestone walling; similar walling was exposed in 1949–50 and probably represents parts of the building left to the guild in 1356. The quality of the twelfth-century masonry indicated the status and prestige of the building.

Internally, excavations in 1925 exposed the bases of three fourteenth-century posts in the south-west wall suggesting an original floor level 1m lower than the present surface. In 1995 excavations identified floor levels 0.6m below the present floor level, with divisions defined by brick walls forming the footings for timber and plaster walls. These floors with their brick divisions probably date from the sixteenth century since medieval hospitals had undivided open spaces and the 1411 licence for the hall makes it clear that the inmates were able to witness the culmination of the Mass which would have been impossible with subdivisions.

42 How the Merchant Adventurers' Hall may have looked in the medieval period.
© *York Archaeological Trust*

The hall of the Merchant Taylors stands in Aldwark and is known as St John the Baptist's Hall. The number of tailors in the city increased between 1326 and 1350, with their ordinances registered with the city in 1386. Very little is known about the early life of the Guild of Taylors, as their pre-sixteenth-century records do not survive. The association with St John the Baptist is also unclear, but two tailors left bequests to a guild of St John the Baptist in the late fourteenth century. It may be that there was an informal association between the tailors and this guild, perhaps similar to the link between the mercers and the Fraternity of Our Lord Jesus Christ and the Blessed Virgin Mary. In 1415 the site of the hall was leased to four tailors, rather than to the Master of the John the Baptist Fraternity. The two bodies were only formally joined in 1452–53 in a royal grant to 15 tailors to found a guild in honour of St John the Baptist. Documents also imply that the hall had a hospital, or *maison dieu,* and a chapel.

The building was originally timber-framed, but much of this is now hidden by the later brick facing of the hall. The framing suggests a date in the fourteenth or fifteenth century. Dendrochronology suggested a felling date of *c.*1413/14 which accords well with the lease of the site and proposed date for the construction of the building. The tailors' hall originally had a gatehouse range and was not open to the street as it is today. The medieval gatehouse was probably demolished in the eighteenth century, though a range of buildings with a gate still stood on the Aldwark street front until the 1950s. The only excavations of the site that are well recorded did not expose levels earlier than the sixteenth or seventeenth centuries. These exposed part of a north-west range associated with the hall that is shown on early maps and may have represented a rebuild of an earlier structure. There are still many questions relating to the development of the hall.

At the north-eastern end of Aldwark stands St Anthony's Hall, which was built on the site of the chapel of St Martin. The hall was the result of the amalgamation of the religious Fraternity of St Anthony and the unlicensed guild of the Holy Trinity and the Paternoster Guild. A charter of incorporation was given in 1446 by Henry VI confirming a grant to them consisting of the site of the chapel and an adjoining garden. The Paternoster Guild had originally met in a room in the house of Bridlington Priory in Aldwark.

Until recently the majority of what was known about the hall came from the standing building. The hall is aligned north-east/south-west, but there were differing opinions on how the building was constructed and its internal arrangement of space. Some believed the hall had been built from north-east to south-west, but later work suggested it had been constructed in the opposite direction.

The hall has an undercroft which contained the chapel and a hospital. The chapel, which was consecrated in 1450, was probably located at the south-west end of the building which has a large window and high-quality carving on the timber framing. There is also evidence to suggest a grand ceremonial entrance from Aldwark flanked by images, which have been recarved, showing St Martin and the Virgin Mary. Above was the great hall, the roof of which is irregular as it is partly crown-post roof and partly arch-braced roof. This was thought to indicate different phases of construction or perhaps use in the hall.

Archaeological work during the renovation of the hall during 2005–07 revealed a wealth of archaeological deposits under the hall and resolved many of the issues relating to its construction, although the analysis of the work is yet to be completed. Two phases of construction were indicated for the hall which supported the interpretation that the hall was built from south-west to north-east.

The south-west façade to Peasholme Green was constructed first, cut back into the natural slope still visible in modern Aldwark. The ground sloped to the north-east so the foundations had to compensate, with one end built directly on the clay sub-soil, the other on substantial cobble, clay and timber pile foundations. Built into the foundations was a stone drain. The second phase of construction was the north-east wall built in a broad foundation trench, which was not tied into the south-west wall. Internal work reducing floor levels exposed features relating to the hall and earlier chapel. Re-exposed medieval timber-framing showed it had been cut back to respect inserted seventeenth- or eighteenth-century walls, although their limestone padstones survived.

CRAFT AND INDUSTRY

Craft and industry were both vital parts of York's economy in the medieval period. It is not easy to draw a distinction between the two as some trades could fall into both categories. A craft comprised small-scale manufacturing, such as bone working and some forms of textile production, carried out at the home of the artisan. Industry on the other hand involved the production of goods on a larger scale, using fixed equipment such as hearths or water tanks in workshops that were not necessarily the residence of the workers. So the process of tanning could be classed as an industry, but the process of making gloves was a craft because it was carried out in the home.

The majority of production in the city was practised in a semi-domestic setting, by a household consisting of husband, wife and one or more servants or apprentices. Some of those involved in manufacture owned a workshop, others were paid for the work they did either in the form of a daily wage or as piece work. A fundamental change occurring in the late eleventh or early twelfth century was the move away from the Anglo-Scandinavian material-based work to product-based crafts. The common factor was that both craft and industry used skilled manufacturers to produce goods for sale; throughout the medieval period there was a fine distinction between manufacturing and retailing.

Unlike towns such as Wakefield and Rotherham which were dominated by textiles, clothing and mercantile activities in the fourteenth century, York had a wide range of craft and industries. These can be grouped into six broad categories: merchants, builders, cloth workers, leather workers, victuallers and metalworkers. These main groups were in turn divided into smaller specialist groups. The most important groups were the leather, textile, clothing and metal trades, whose importance stemmed from the fact that they produced goods not easily made by householders at home. Non-artisan workers included water carriers, laundresses, gardeners and prostitutes. Victuallers formed the largest group in the city, as will be shown in the next chapter, supplying the city with the food and drink it needed.

Craft and industry leave variable traces of their activities on the city's archaeological record. The principal group, the mercers or merchants, leave little direct evidence for their activities in trade at regional, national or international levels. The majority of information for them comes through the few imported goods, predominantly pottery, that have survived and the documentary records for the tolls collected. This evidence shows that they were usually very wealthy and dealt with a wide range of goods and were vital to the governance and economic vitality of the city, but also held posts in national government.

WE BUILT THIS CITY

Builders included stonemasons, carpenters, plasterers, tilers and pavers, and some of their handiwork survives to this day. The materials they worked with, such as stone and wood, were imported from the area immediately around the city or further afield, such as Balkan forests. Tools associated with the building trades have been found, including plumb bobs and trowels. Carpenters' tools include spoon bits for making holes in timber, a saw, which wasn't often used in the medieval period, and carpenters' axes and knives

43 The skills of a range of York's craftsmen: the bucket and barrel (coopers) and the chain (metalworkers). © *York Archaeological Trust*

for shaping timber. Other than building, the wood workers made bowls, cups, plates and buckets, showing the range of wooden artefacts in use. They also made barrels, some of which survive as well linings.

Tiles and bricks were made in the areas around the city which were rich in natural clay. The Vicars Choral owned two tile houses and the products of these kilns are often found in excavations; however, no evidence for the kilns themselves has yet been found. Tiles were increasingly important in the city from the twelfth century and references to tilers appearing in the city's Register of Freemen show that not all of them were men. In 1327 Constance Tiler supplied tiles at 10*s* a thousand in York. Bricks, initially called wall tiles, were used as the infill for timber framing and sill walls at first. By the late fourteenth century they were used for walls themselves. Roof tiles changed in form and style from those used by the Romans to peg or nib tiles from the thirteenth century, with the more elaborate ridge tiles made by potters.

THE FABRIC OF THE CITY

The textile industry in York shifted emphasis in the course of the medieval period from production to finishing of cloth. The textile workers in towns were among the first to form guilds, with weavers' guilds formed in York, London, Winchester, Oxford, Huntingdon and Nottingham from the mid twelfth century. At first the guilds paid the king for a monopoly of their craft, but later began holding meetings and regulating techniques and apprenticeship. The urban textile industry faced competition in the thirteenth and fourteenth centuries with the rise of textile centres such as Wakefield.

Linen, made through the processing of flax and hemp plant stems, is not well documented. Although there is evidence that cotton was imported in the thirteenth and fourteenth centuries it was not used for clothing but for candle wicks and as padding for garments. Silk was also imported at considerable expense from Italy and Spain and was a luxury item. A cheaper alternative was half silk, a combination of linen and silk made in Spanish and Venetian workshops from the mid fourteenth century.

The major wool producers were the monastic houses. Fountains and Byland Abbeys had wool houses in the village of Clifton, a mile north of York – probably trying to avoid the tolls of the city – until the fourteenth century. Direct evidence for the wool trade comes from the discovery of wooden bale pins at Coppergate from the twelfth and thirteenth centuries and at Piccadilly from the fifteenth and sixteenth centuries; these were used in the handling and packing of raw wool. Bale pins have also been found in other towns like Oxford, London and Hull. Wool wasn't only used for cloth – it could also be made into felt, and from the twelfth century was it used for felt hats and hat brims.

Evidence for the processing of wool, flax and hemp is found in the archaeological record in the form of iron teeth from combs used to work the fibres. At Coppergate, wool carders were found dating from the twelfth or thirteenth to the sixteenth century. Flax and hemp processing was more labour intensive. First the seed heads had to be removed – a wooden tool for this was found at Coppergate. The next stage was to soak the stems to soften them. They were then dried, beaten and scraped with knives, and the plant fibre drawn through combs called heckles. Environmental evidence from the Bedern College and the Bedern Foundry identified seeds of the flax plant in the Anglo-Norman period suggesting processing for linen manufacture. Iron teeth from heckles have been found at Bedern, Piccadilly, Fishergate and Coppergate.

Spinning wool or linen ready for weaving was carried out with a distaff, but the process was greatly speeded up with the introduction of the spinning wheel from the fourteenth century. After spinning, yarn was washed and dyed. Importing dyes was an important business, with woad (blue) imported from Gascony and later the Azores, Picardy and Languedoc. Kermes, orchil and brazil wood, for deeper reds and purples, and indigo (violet/blue) were imported from the mid thirteenth century. The medieval dyer also used madder (red), weld and woadwaxen (yellow). The importance of the quality of dyes is reflected in the woad assayers (checkers) set up at Exeter, Winchester and York.

Once the yarn was dyed it was 'fixed' with alum imported from Asia Minor or the Greek Islands to prevent it washing out. Woad didn't need fixing, but potash made it soluble; potash came primarily from wood ash. Evidence for York's dyers has come from Piccadilly where environmental analysis of a well backfill of the fifteenth/sixteenth century identified woad, greenweed and bran (used to ferment the dye to make it soluble). This supports documentary references to dyers living in the parish of St Denys from the late fourteenth century.

Whorls for spinning, made from stone, pottery, wood and bone, are rarely found in the medieval city. The major change in weaving was the introduction of the horizontal loom from the eleventh century which allowed the production of wider cloth. Tools associated with small looms used by tapiters, who made hangings, rugs and coverlets, have been found at Coppergate and include a weft beater and a pin beater.

Linen, once weaved, would be washed and laid out to bleach in the sun. Woollen cloth was washed in water and fullers' earth, a naturally occurring clay, to remove grease and matt the fibres, a process called felting. Glass slick stones were found at Coppergate; these were used to smooth garments after laundering. For the basic woollen cloth this marked the end of the process, but for higher-quality broadcloth further processing was necessary to give it a smooth velvety texture. Finished cloth would be checked by the guild searchers and the evidence from London suggests that from the fourteenth century the bales of cloth were marked with a lead seal showing their weight, place of origin and size.

Surviving textiles range from coarse sackcloth, wool clothing, household linen and prestigious silks and half silks, providing valuable information on changing fashions and styles. Sacking was coarse material used to wrap merchandise and occasionally for burials as a sign of penitence. From the mid fourteenth century York specialised in the production of rays, cloth with bands of colour within the weave, a design which originated in Flemish cloth traded in the thirteenth and fourteenth centuries. It may be that weavers from the Low Countries who settled in the city during the fourteenth century introduced this type of cloth.

Needles found in excavations show a shift away from the use of copper alloy towards iron during the medieval period, and their size and shape reflect a variety of uses from leather to silk work. Thimbles made of copper alloy have been found at the Gilbertine Priory, the Bedern Foundry and the College of Vicars Choral. The late thirteenth- or early fourteenth-century thimble from the Foundry is a tailor's thimble and one of the earliest surviving examples in England; the thimble from the priory, dating to the fifteenth/sixteenth century, had a detachable leather lining. Iron shears and a very rare set of fourteenth-century scissors found at the Bedern may have been used for all sorts of tasks including cloth manufacture.

Knitted goods reached Europe with the Arabs in the fourteenth century and were initially made of silk. By the end of the fourteenth century wool was being used and it was a well-established home industry by the mid sixteenth century. The first direct evidence for English knitters appears in a fifteenth-century document with 'cappe knyters' in Ripon (1465) and Nottingham (1478). Objects which may be knitting needles of the fourteenth century have been found within the floor deposits of a house in Aldwark.

ANY OLD IRON?

Evidence for the metalworking industry is prominent in the archaeological record. Some 800 individuals worked in the metalworking industry during the fourteenth and fifteenth centuries according to the Freemen's Register. Metalworking was carried out in workshops situated at the rear of properties and opened onto streets such as Swinegate,

Petergate, Goodramgate and Walmgate. The industry was divided according to whether workers used iron, steel, non-ferrous metals or precious metals.

Medieval metalworking was done through hammering and casting. Hammering involves sheets of metal being beaten into shape on anvils when the metal is cold. Casting involves pouring the molten metal or alloy into moulds made of stone or clay. Large-scale production of small artefacts such as buckles was achieved by making large stacks of moulds and casting them in a single operation. Some moulds were reusable, such as those from the Bedern Foundry made of chalk quarried from the Yorkshire Wolds. These formed part of a multi-piece mould and were used for decorative discs, perhaps counters of lead or pewter. Another may have been for making metal beads, as were found in London.

More delicate shapes were made in clay moulds using the lost wax method. In this process a wax model of the item to be made is wrapped in clay which is then heated so the clay hardens and the wax melts out leaving a hollow mould into which the metal is poured. In this process each mould can only be used once. Making moulds for casting metal objects was a separate trade and the Register of Freemen records four mould-makers between 1351/52 and 1409/10.

Metalworkers' hearths could be at ground level or elevated to waist height. They used anvils, though these rarely survive. Excavations at Bedern Foundry have recovered other tools including tongs dating to the mid fourteenth or early fifteenth century and hammer heads from the late thirteenth and mid to late fifteenth century. Punches of varying size and form as well as a metalworking file were also found at the same site.

Metalworking freemen were allowed up to three apprentices, but were also actively helped by their wives who were expected to work the bellows and stoke the hearth. As a result women were assumed to be part of the guild as soon as their fathers or husbands were masters. Some women were even entered into the Register of Freemen in their own name, for example Juliana Fosse, daughter of Johannes Fosse.

Ironworkers listed in the Register of Freemen include ironmongers, lorimers, locksmiths, pinners, ferrours, furbours, wiredrawers, armourers, cutler, nailers, bladesmiths and arrowsmiths. The term ironworker only appears at the end of the fourteenth century and blacksmith at the end of the fifteenth century. The ironworkers were of great importance as they provided many of the tools and equipment for the other crafts.

Iron ore was found in England, but was also imported from France, Germany and Sweden (where it was called 'osmund' iron). Iron had to be prepared through the addition of charcoal in bloomeries before it could be used or further processed to make steel through the addition of more carbon. Steel was vital for giving a good, sharp edge to tools and weapons, but production was a slow process. As a result iron and steel were often combined in an item, like a knife, to give it a steel tip. Steel was sometimes wrapped in iron so the steel protruded like the lead from a pencil. Some knives were ornate and decorated, and several such examples were found at the College of Vicars Choral.

The bronze casters were called potters in the late thirteenth to sixteenth centuries, but other names for the same workers included founders, mentioned from 1367/68, and brasiers in 1472/73. Medieval bronze was not the same as modern bronze, but rather a combination of modern bronze and brass. Higher-quality products used an alloy called latten, similar to brass and made of copper, zinc, tin and lead.

44 Buckles and other objects made by the copper alloy workers of York. © *York Archaeological Trust*

The potters made functional items and there was a growing market for metal domestic utensils in the fourteenth and fifteenth centuries. These included cooking pots, cauldrons, kettles and skillets, but potters also made candlesticks, taps and spouts, buckles, badges and ornamental fastenings. Most prestigious were the bell founders. In the fourteenth century Richard Tunnock, bell founder but also city mayor and member of parliament, funded the glazing of the bell founder's window in the Minster.

The majority of excavated metal waste consists of slag, failed castings, offcuts, strips, bars, rods and wires. Finished goods include knives, locks, keys and structural fittings like nails. A clearly industrial building was the Bedern Foundry that stood on the south-west side of the College of Vicars Choral, accessed from a narrow lane off Goodramgate. A sequence of timber workshops was exposed during excavation which had undergone many changes and rebuilds between the mid to late thirteenth century and the early sixteenth century. Within these buildings were a series of hearths and pits associated with founding or casting of copper-alloy objects including cauldrons and other domestic vessels.

Archaeology shows that workers using copper alloy and iron often operated on the same sites. There is evidence for metalworking workshops at St Andrewgate from the late fourteenth to sixteenth centuries, and at Low Petergate in the fourteenth and fifteenth centuries. Evidence for metalworking consisted of blank iron sheets, mould fragments and tile hearths, at both ground level and waist height. Hammerscale indicated the working of metal on anvils, and another feature may have been quenching pits. These workshops were producing goods ranging from strap guides to copper-alloy pots, an everyday cooking utensil.

45 Industrial archaeology: the walls of the workshops of the Bedern foundry. © *York Archaeological Trust*

Evidence for extensive metalworking was also found at 41–49 Walmgate. A sequence of buildings underwent numerous modifications from the fourteenth to sixteenth centuries and the evidence suggests iron and copper-alloy working were practised in different rooms within the same building. There were crucibles, sequences of hearths and a possible furnace, as well as evidence that copper-alloy workers were recycling miscast or broken items.

York had armourers and bladesmiths making swords, many of whom were German immigrants. There is evidence from excavations for chain mail being made in the city

46 A metalworking furnace, Low Petergate. © *York Archaeological Trust*

from iron and copper wire created by drawing heated bars through plates punched with holes, called draw plates, to give the required thickness. This process was often carried out by women such as Agnes Herche, who was left the instruments for mail work by her father in 1403. Two female armourers, children of freemen, were granted freedom: Margareta Langshawe in 1436 and Johanna Armourer in 1488.

Specialist metalworking also included the manufacture of monumental brasses from the late thirteenth to the sixteenth century; these brasses were attached to the grave slabs, often of Purbeck marble. Study of the surviving brasses shows close parallels to the depictions of people in stained glass windows across the city suggesting either the same artists were at work or the same patterns were being used. Less well represented in the archaeological record of the city is the work of pewterers, the first of whom to be recorded is William de Orddesdale in 1348. Pewter was cast in clay moulds and finished on a lathe, and fragments of moulds that may have been used with pewter have been found in the city.

The highest quality metalwork was carried out by the goldsmiths, who also worked silver. Between 1272 and 1399 a total of 83 goldsmiths were admitted to the freedom of York and another 105 between 1399 and 1509. Unfortunately, archaeology has added little to our knowledge of their activities. Gold and silver were often recycled or imported mostly in the form of coins from Byzantium, Moslem Spain or North Africa in the twelfth and thirteenth centuries, and from Germany in the late fifteenth century. Silver was also imported from Germany in the eleventh century and from Bohemia and Hungary in the fifteenth century.

Goldsmiths made objects like vessels and dishes by forging with a hammer, and cast decorative items in moulds using the loss wax method. In the medieval period London

47 Hearth and casting pits at Low Petergate. © *York Archaeological Trust*

and York were the major centres for goldsmiths. Both supported associated smaller groups like *finers* (refiners of precious metals), gold beaters, gold wire drawers, burnishers, gilders, *selers* (makers of seal matrices) and jewellers. Silver or gold wire was made in the same way as iron or copper alloy wire.

Gold and silver were used for gilding items made of base metals, wood and stone. Gold leaf was used on manuscripts. Some idea of a goldsmith's workshop comes from the inventory of John Collan, perhaps a German immigrant, in 1440. He had a variety of hammers, anvils and tongs; equipment for enamelling, punches and stamps; and raw materials including tin and book gold (gold leaf). The presence of tin suggests he was making goods for a church, since goldsmiths were banned from using base metals except for church plate. Enamelling, which involved the application of coloured glass, suggests decorative work on his products.

The term jeweller is hard to define in the medieval period and could include those who sold the products of the goldsmiths, those who purchased, sold or assessed gemstones, and even the workers who set stones. Rubies, sapphires and diamonds were imported from as far away as India or Burma, as were less precious stones like garnets. The Mediterranean was a source of coral and pearls and the Baltic supplied amber. Pearls were collected from freshwater mussels in Wales, Cumberland and Scotland. Jet found at Whitby was worked in York from Roman times. Jewellery was worn by both sexes, sometimes in association with clothing such as brooches, and sometimes as a statement of wealth and social standing in the form of rings for example. Jewellery gives us clues to changing tastes in fashion otherwise unrecorded.

Goldsmiths were subject to royal control and the London goldsmiths were the first to receive a royal charter. In 1238 the king ordered the mayor of London to appoint an overseer to check the quality of the goldsmiths' work and if it passed it was stamped with a leopard's head. These regulations spread and other towns with goldsmiths had to send a representative to London to ensure they were familiar with the regulations. Two York goldsmiths were appointed by the London Goldsmiths' Company in 1330 to ensure the regulations were adhered to in the city and in 1410 a city ordinance mentions the city mark, half a leopard head and a fleur-de-lys, as well as an assay office.

Some goldsmiths produced seals. The York goldsmith, Hugh 'le Seler', made a silver seal for the see of Durham in 1333 and Richard de Grimsby worked for Edward III. The use of seals increased between the eleventh and fifteenth centuries and cheaper seals were often cast from copper alloy or carved from jet, bone and ivory. In York personal seal matrices have been found, such as that of Thomas of Swin, stonemason. Another, found at the College of Vicars Choral, shows a squirrel surrounded by the inscription 'I crake notis' (I crack nuts). One seal found in the city belonged to Snarrus, the toll keeper, and is dated to the twelfth century; it shows a man holding a bag into which coins are dropped.

One seal in the city belonged to a very unusual craftsman, a clockmaker. Found during excavations in Petergate, the seal shows a wheel surrounded by text that translates as 'the seal of Robert the clockmaker'. It dates to around 1300. Mechanical clocks were only just coming into use, to replace water clocks. Clocks were important to the clergy in regulating their services and mechanical clocks are recorded in English monastic and collegiate records by the early fourteenth century. The most likely place to employ a clockmaker would be the Minster, although we do not have any record for a clock there at this date.

TOUGH AS OLD BOOTS

The leather industry has a long history and was one of the earliest to form guilds in towns such as Wallingford, Winchester, Oxford, London and York by the end of the twelfth century. Considering the size of the tanning industry in York, it is surprising that we have no direct evidence for the industrial side of the process, only the material derived from the finishing process and the final products made. The leather working industry consisted of small specialist groups such as those that prepared hides, the glovers, girdlers, saddlers and trunk-makers.

The recovery of skins for tanning was part of the butchery process, with the cow slaughtered and the by-products of horns and hides sold to the horners and the tanners.

48 York's least known trade? The seal of a clockmaker found at Petergate. © *York Archaeological Trust*

The hide would usually have the foot bones attached which would be deposited in an area where hides were prepared. Such a site may have been identified at the Bedern Foundry where large numbers of sheep foot bones were recovered dating to the fourteenth and late fifteenth century. Smaller animals provide skins and at the Bedern there was a fourteenth-century pit with evidence for the skinning of a squirrel, perhaps indicating the use of squirrel pelts brought into the city with the feet attached.

Curing the hides for use was divided into two main processes: tanning (red leather) and tawing (white leather). Tanned leather was passed to the curriers who worked the leather into a useable product by shaving the skins to the required fineness, and applying oil and tallow to make it supple. This type of leather was durable and was used by belt-makers, purse-makers, sheathers, harness-makers and bottle-makers. Other crafts also used leather in their products, for example scabbard-makers, saddlers, bookbinders and cofferers who made travelling trunks.

Tawing used the skins of sheep, goats, calves and deer which were the skins used by glovers and parchment-makers. There are few mentions of tawing in the city records, but we know something of the range of goods made by the glovers from the inventory of John Grene, who died in 1525. His stock included a number of gloves, eight bags and

49 In need of a cobbler? Fragments of a leather shoe. © *York Archaeological Trust*

18 purses. There was a fine dividing line between manufacturer and mercer – Grene also had a packing house with weights and scales, and a stable with five horses and four pack saddles. One woman is recorded as a master glover, Anne de Kepewyk. Parchment-makers were also occasionally female and Isabella de Morland is one of four listed in the late fourteenth century.

Iron tools associated with leather working have been found in excavations, such as the blade unearthed in late fourteenth/early fifteenth-century levels at the Bedern Foundry. Called a 'slicker' it was used during tanning to force out the hair retained under the roots and shave the flesh side of the skin until it was smooth. Knives used by curriers were found at Coppergate; they dated to the eleventh and twelfth century, with a few from the fifteenth to sixteenth centuries. Many of the metal awls used for piercing holes may have been used in the leather trade as well as in other crafts such as woodworking or bone working. Likewise some of the shears, often associated with textile working, may also have been used for cutting leather.

The offcuts from leather working consist of primary waste from the trimming of hides to remove unusable parts of the skin or hide, following tanning and currying; secondary waste from cutting out pattern pieces; and tertiary waste from the finishing of a product. The finished products included shoes, boots, scabbards and straps used as belts or handles. Excavations across the city have found evidence for the working of finished leather usually in the form of shoes made by the cordwainers (named after high-quality Cordovan Spanish leather) or repaired by the cobblers. The surviving leather artefacts show changes

50 The fine workmanship of a leather worker on a scabbard. © *York Archaeological Trust*

in styles, fashion and decoration during the medieval period and details of how they were made. A major influence of the guilds is perhaps seen in the standardisation of goods, such as shoes, from the twelfth century, in the materials and the regulations for manufacture.

MINOR CRAFTS

A wide range of trades was practised in the city, though some may have left no record if their practitioners did not gain freedom across the city or operated only within the liberties. Glass working in the city for beads can be traced back into the Anglo-Scandinavian period, but later it was the production of stained glass that was important. The York glazers formed a guild in 1278 and the church of St Helen at the end of Stonegate was their guild church. York dominated the northern markets for glass, but other centres of production included Bath, Canterbury, Chester, Coventry, Lincoln, London and Norwich. By 1463–64 the York glaziers consisted of small groups of inter-related family firms – the Chambers, Pettys, Shirleys and Inglishes. Wills of members of these families give an insight into the business. Windows were set out using books of drawings, passed through the family, such as that of Thomas Shirley (d.1458) who left his son Robert his drawings, and Robert Petty (d.1528) who obtained his drawings from his elder brother John. These pattern books may have been borrowed by the funerary brass workers.

Glass was either coloured or plain. White glass was made in England, with coloured glass being imported from Normandy, the Rhine area, Burgundy and Lorraine; it was brought into Hull by Hanse merchants. A change occurred in the fourteenth century with the development of stained glass. The design was painted on using pigments either of silver nitrate or copper or iron oxide; powdered glass; wine, urine or vinegar; and gum Arabic which made the pigment adhere to the glass during firing. Once fired, the glass was laid out for leading with cames and the individual pieces were held together with nails and fitted to the window.

Evidence for a glazer was found in excavations in 1972 at the rear of Blake Street and Stonegate. Over 2,500 fragments of glass were found in a pit dating to the late fifteenth/early sixteenth century, ranging in colour from shades of dark red and pink to white. The glass fragments included both muff glass, produced from glass blown in cylindrical form then cut down one side and flattened, and bull's eye glass, formed by spinning molten glass on the end of an iron implement so that centrifugal force draws out circular sheets of glass.

Pottery was not made extensively in the city; the only known kilns were in Walmgate and outside the walls in Fishergate. Most of the pottery used in York came from the surrounding countryside or elsewhere in the country. In the post-Conquest period there were three main types: Thetford, Stamford and St Neots ware. In the thirteenth and fourteenth centuries there were regional variations and pottery became more colourful through the use of variegated glazes using lead, copper (deep green) and iron (black). Other changes included the development of decoration and puzzle jugs.

York's pottery was initially drawn from the workshops to the north of the city in the Howardian Hills, but in the later fourteenth and fifteenth centuries pottery came

51 Pottery, not a big business in York, although the most common artefact found. © *York Archaeological Trust*

from the Humber Basin. The decline in coarse wares for items like cooking vessels may reflect the increased use of metal wares and may be the reason why metal forms were imitated by the potters. Some pottery was also imported from abroad, particularly the Low Countries, in the fourteenth and fifteenth century.

A craft associated with the Church was the carving of alabaster figures and panels for tombs. Alabaster is a form of gypsum and was easy to carve; it was most valuable if it was pure white as it could be polished to resemble marble. York became a regional centre for alabaster work and several 'alabastermen' were admitted to the freedom of the city.

The working of bone and horn continued from the Anglo-Scandinavian period. After the Conquest, however, composite combs, using bone and antler, ceased to be made, perhaps because of a decline in the availability of antler, in turn as a result of stricter forest laws. Items made out of bone in the medieval period ranged from gaming counters, knife handles, styli for writing like those recovered from the Gilbertine Priory and Bedern, and tuning pegs for stringed instruments found at the College of the Vicars Choral. At Coppergate more simple instruments made of bone included whistles.

York is the only city outside London with documentary evidence for horners, but the point at which their guild was founded is unknown. Horn is the exterior material, something like fingernails, around a bony core and was collected from goats and cattle. The removal of the exterior horn material produces a malleable and versatile material that was put to multiple uses such as buttons, drinking vessels, spoons, knife handles, and also panes for lanterns and windows, and was the 'plastic' of the medieval period. Horn does not survive well in the ground and so the cores are often the key indicator for its use. The most conclusive evidence for horners in York was found near Hornpot Lane off Petergate. Horn working evidence from rubbish pits and a possible soaking pit to separate the horn from the core has been found dating from the fourteenth century. The concentrations of goat horncores suggest these were primarily used by the York horners; they have also been found in Aldwark and along Skeldergate.

52 The waste from the medieval plastics industry, horn cores. © *York Archaeological Trust*

Vestment-makers do not appear in the Register of Freemen until the sixteenth century, probably as a consequence of pressure from the Corporation, at that time increasing its regulation of trade. We know that Thomas Setter worked for the Minster in 1371 and there is no doubt that vestments were constantly needed by the clergy throughout the medieval period; many sumptuous vestments are listed in church inventories.

Another group of craftsmen that have left little trace are the chandlers or candle-makers, though indirect evidence for their activity comes from the many candle holders and other light fittings found in excavations in the city. The chandlers made wax candles, with the low-quality tallow candles made from animal fat being undertaken by other groups such as sauce-makers. In the fifteenth century York became the fourth English town with a printing press, established by Fredericus Freez, probably a Dutchman.

ZONING

It might be expected that crafts would be concentrated on the edges of the town because of the problems of noise, noxious fumes and risk of fire. Documentary and archaeological evidence, however, shows that industries were located in the middle of the city, perhaps influenced by the fact that many were interdependent. An example of this relationship may be seen at Petergate where three adjoining tenements housed metalworkers, leather workers and horn workers. They all produced items that could be used together and perhaps one of the shops on the Petergate frontage was home to a cutler making knives from the blades produced by the smiths, handles produced by the horners and sheaths by the leather workers.

Information for the zoning of craft and industry comes from the street names, although York has fewer such names than for example Beverley, Nottingham or London. York street names, recorded from the eleventh century onwards, probably had older origins. For some, the name remained after the craft or industry had gone. The name Coppergate, for example, the cup-makers' street, was first recorded in *c.*1120, but after the Norman Conquest the area shifted away from manufacturing and became home to some of the city's wealthiest residents.

Street names reflect the importance of some the food trades: Shambles (butchers), Ketmongergate (flesh-sellers), Fishergate (fishermen), Swinegate (swine street) and Noutgeil (a cattle lane, now known as George Street). Other street names relate to the cloth or clothing trades such as Fetter Lane (felters), Glovergeil (glove-makers/sellers), Girdlergate (girdler-makers/sellers) and Hosier Lane (hosiery-makers/sellers). Several streets relate to other industries: Barkergate (tanners), Colliergate (charcoal sellers), Nedlergate (needle-makers), Sadler Lane (saddle-makers) and Haymongergate (hay-seller). This shows that many of the trades associated with the provision of food, and crafts reliant on the by-products of butchery, were found in or near the central area of the city.

Some idea of occupational zones can be gained from the poll taxes of the fourteenth century and the wills of the wealthier citizens recorded by the Dean and Chapter. Butchers focused in the central area around King's Court, with a smaller group on the south-west bank of the Ouse. Trades needing water, like the dyers, were located on the river edges, predominantly in the North Street area on the south-west side of the Ouse in the twelfth and fourteenth century, and in the Walmgate area by the later fifteenth century. The tanners were concentrated around North Street, a feature reflected in the names Tanners Row, Barker Tower and Tanners Moat. Girdlers and glovers were based around Holy Trinity, King's Court, St Sampson and St Crux. Parchment-makers appear to have been based around Holy Trinity Goodramgate and skinners in the parishes of St Martin Coney Street, St Michael Spurriergate and St Peter the Little. Saddlers, lorimers and armourers lived in the parishes around Coney Street and Spurriergate. The cordwainers, like bakers, cooks, innkeepers and smiths, who were in regular demand were found in most parishes.

Merchants, mercers and drapers were concentrated in the area around Fossgate, where the merchants had their guildhall. Metalworking is poorly represented in wills from the fourteenth and fifteenth centuries, but archaeological evidence suggests it was concentrated in the parishes between Petergate and Coney Street. There is little evidence for textile workers, but they appear to have been concentrated in the central area and Walmgate. Goldsmiths, pewterers, glass-makers and booksellers were based in the area around Stonegate and the glazier's parish church was St Helen's Stonegate.

THE FIFTEENTH AND SIXTEENTH CENTURIES: BOOM OR BUST?

York's prosperity was due to its role as a regional capital and a trading, distribution and manufacturing centre. Between the Conquest (or possibly before) and the fourteenth century the economy grew, as did the population. This pattern was broken between 1310 and 1375 by famine and the Black Death. Grain prices and rents fell, although there was a modest rise in wages, with a recovery from the late fourteenth into the fifteenth century. The growth of the economy came to an end in the late fifteenth century with the towns, particularly those in the north and eastern coastal areas of England, entering a period of decline which lasted until the mid sixteenth century.

York's decline came about in part through a fall in overseas trade, reflecting a general trend in trade becoming focused on London. York and other northern ports resisted London merchants' attempts to dominate trade with the Netherlands in 1478 with limited success. Disputes with the Hanseatic ports saw a reduction in trade with the Baltic ports. In addition to this, changes in the cloth and wool trade in the West Riding adversely affected the city.

The main evidence for decline comes from comparing evidence for population in the poll taxes of 1377, 1379 and 1380–81 and the lay subsidy of 1524–25. However, interpretation of this data is fraught with problems, partly because of the disparity in time between the compared dates and partly because of the different methods of assessment used. All figures need to be inflated to allow for children, women and evasion. In 1380–81 York seems to have been under-assessed to a greater extent than other towns and the 1524–25 subsidy was assessed on a different basis in the north to the south. As a result northern towns have impossibly low numbers of taxpayers. It may be that the wealthy were avoiding taking up civic posts in order to avoid the financial burden of office.

This evidence cannot be taken at face value since the same material has been used to argue that the lowest point in the fortunes of towns came in the late fourteenth and early fifteenth century when the population was still recovering from the Black Death, with the late fifteenth and early sixteenth centuries being a period of economic growth. By the 1530s, and probably earlier, the population was rising and so were agricultural prices.

Key questions have to be asked when considering the issues of decline, such as how wealth was measured; was it the increase per capita of small groups of artisans or merchants or the corporate wealth of the city? The terms decay and decline used in medieval documents are problematic. Decline implies a loss, either of wealth or population, in comparison with an earlier period, other towns or the countryside. Decay consists of the changes to the physical environment, such as the lack of maintenance of buildings. But is decline the same as decay and to what extent does the evidence for one imply the other?

Evidence for tax evasion, and the differences between personal and corporate wealth can be found in the documents. In 1535 Alderman John North, William Holme and John Lewes were reported for buying corn in Lincolnshire and Holderness to enhance the price in York. They had assessed themselves in the lay subsidy at under £20 but Holme alone bought corn to the value of £100! In 1537 seven former chamberlains subscribed £70 to the city coffers to help balance the books, while 20 elected chamberlains offered 200 marks between them. There is no evidence for widespread abandonment of civic duties, with plenty of wealthy individuals willing to take up posts; the city continued to pay for two members of parliament on the grounds of the city's county status.

A straightforward reading of the pleas for relief from the fee farm to the crown by towns between c.1420 and 1560 could indicate that towns were in decline. It may, however, suggest that towns were simply exploiting the weak nature of the monarchy during the War of the Roses. One of York's main issues with the fee farm was that the payment went to William Roos as a gift from Edward II, but his descendants, the Earls of Rutland, were also keen to claim the payments. This involved the city in long disputes with the exchequer, which saw the end of the payments in the 1530s.

Rebuilding is taken as a sign of economic vitality; a drop in construction and falling rent values is seen as an indicator of decline. Urban rents, however, are complex and changes may be associated with a wide range of factors such as fluctuations in demand for particular housing stock. Excavations contribute to the debate, but identifying stagnation or decay is not easy. From the fourteenth century there seems to have been an increased concentration upon durable building stock and improved living conditions, with the latter involving the replacement of open halls with multiple floors and smaller rooms with heating. As a consequence there is less evidence for complete rebuilding, but this does not necessarily point to economic stagnation.

Archaeology offers an opportunity to survey streets within the city for evidence of decline, stability or prosperity. A rapid overview shows that across the city there is evidence for rebuilding and structural alteration of residential and industrial buildings throughout the fifteenth and sixteenth centuries. Some areas within the town were no doubt in decline, but the same cannot be said of the whole city. The same situation can be seen in a walk around the modern city, with thriving businesses adjacent to empty properties. But who would argue that the modern city is in decline?

Apparent contradictions can be found in excavations of a single area. For example, in Aldwark, excavations in the area behind properties on one side of the road suggested limited activity in the fifteenth and sixteenth centuries. On the opposite side of the road, excavations within buildings on the street frontage showed a complex sequence of alterations and rebuilding in the fifteenth and sixteenth centuries. Bedern Foundry continued in use during the sixteenth century, the major change being a shift from metalworking to bread making. This may reflect a trend seen in other cities, with industry increasingly marginalised at the edges of towns in the sixteenth century.

At 41–49 Walmgate, excavations showed the continued alteration and modification of buildings used for industrial purposes throughout the sixteenth century. Even along the river fronts excavations have shown continual activity during the fifteenth and sixteenth centuries. Rebuilding may not always be associated with economic vitality and researchers need to examine whether wealth could be expressed through material culture such as furnishings, decorations and personal jewellery, defining an individual's place in the social order of the fifteenth and sixteenth centuries.

The late fifteenth and early sixteenth century saw changes in the organisation of the established hierarchy of towns. As in the fourteenth century governance of the city was by a closed group, excluding certain crafts, but in the sixteenth century there was a deliberate attempt to maintain order against the rise of the artisan class, the post-medieval middle class, who had a level of wealth not seen before. The infrastructure of the Corporation, formalised through the charter of 1396 with councils of 12, 24 and 48, was changed by the influence of tradesmen such as tailors instead of simply the merchants.

Too much emphasis has been put on York's involvement in the cloth industry as an argument for decline. In response to the rise of the West Riding centres, York began to work finished cloth, transported long distances to the city by the merchants, instead of actually producing cloth. The city merchants diversified into other products and in 1511 the Merchant Adventurers wrote that 'lead is our principal commodity'. There is evidence for trade with Germany, the Baltic area and the Netherlands, and throughout this period York used Hull as its port; it was not until the seventeenth century that Hull started to assert itself through its own merchants.

The Register of Freemen shows changes in admissions to the freedom of the city, with fewer entrants buying their freedom; by the Elizabethan period the city was dominated by a few leading York families who had inherited their freedom rights. The fact that freemen were entered on the basis of specialising in a particular trade obscures the fact that craftsmen often practised more than one craft and merchants sold a variety of goods. Another major change was that craftsmen such as drapers, goldsmiths, skinners and tailors both bought and sold goods, effectively becoming guilds of merchants.

The Register of Freemen provides evidence for the range of goods and services but also shows that manufacture was relatively stable from 1500 to 1650. The food and drink, leather and distribution trades accounted for over 50 per cent of entries and, while textile production was reduced, the numbers of tailors, cordwainers, glovers and haberdashers all increased. There is no major change to the city trades other than that seen in the decline of the fisheries, which may be associated with the changes in religious practice.

The supposed upturn in the mid sixteenth century may have had as much to do with the arrival of the Council of the North and the Ecclesiastical Commission becoming based in the city as with changes in the economy. These new bodies provided a potential new market and increases in the number of freemen may relate to opportunistic people seeking to exploit the situation. For example, there were 12 innkeepers in 1500 but by 1596 there were 68 innkeepers in the city, with one inn alone having stabling for 266 horses! This rise was to cater for the people bringing their cases to the courts and also transacting business in the city.

If evidence for decline in York is to be sought, it is perhaps to the periods before and after the English Civil War we should look. After the war York lost its importance as an administrative centre, with the loss of the Council of the North and the Ecclesiastical Commission. The Register of Freemen shows fundamental changes to the organisation of the city trades in the seventeenth century. Mercantile trade peaked in 1625–49 but then the number of merchants falls and a similar pattern is seen with innkeepers and the clothing trades, which declined after 1650. The biggest change is the emergence of labourers, skilled or unskilled people working for a wage, who first appear after 1625, and who top the number of entries in the Register of Freemen in 1699.

A sign of decline may be seen in the fact that parts of the river front along Skeldergate were given over to gardens in the seventeenth century, and that in Coppergate one of the more substantial houses of the medieval period is divided into multiple tenancies for poorer families in the 1620s. The evidence suggests that York needed to find a new role for itself in the late seventeenth and early eighteenth century. Indeed it became a centre for the gentry, and this is reflected in the new crafts and the loss of older established trades.

5

EATING, DRINKING AND SHOPPING

Having taken a look at York's corporate, craft and industrial infrastructure, and how the medieval city fitted into the wider economy, the question remains as to how the medieval residents fed themselves, and bought and sold goods within the city. These issues are more closely related to the experience of living in the medieval city than anything we have dealt with so far.

The medieval diet naturally had an effect upon the health of York's residents. Medicine in the Middle Ages was based on the idea of the four humours; imbalances in these were thought to be caused by foods people ate. Surprisingly, towns had a strong element of self-sufficiency, giving an impression of the medieval 'good life'. The provision of food for sale in the towns was predominantly carried out locally.

Markets were established before the Norman Conquest: Domesday records 50, and two fairs. The number of markets increased rapidly during the twelfth and thirteenth centuries, although many were ultimately forced out of business by the markets in the large towns like York, Southampton, Bristol and London. Markets were the outlets for the merchants, both freemen and non-freemen, who controlled the sale of more prestigious goods such as spices, fruit and wine. The medieval domestic market is not well understood, but the cities were vital for redistributing goods, especially luxuries, and for providing services unavailable elsewhere.

The medieval economy needed excellent communication routes, and rivers such as the Ouse were the principal method of transport, though some bulky goods, usually relatively cheap commodities like grain, herring, animal fodder, fuel and building materials, were moved by road. Most medieval highways are believed to have been in disrepair and impossible to travel along. This opinion is partly due to the growth in heavier traffic in the eighteenth century and the 'spin' of the turnpike trusts trying to gain funds for new roads. Medieval roads were in fact surfaced and a great deal of effort was put into maintaining them. Money was often left in wills for the maintenance of roads and bridges.

A FOOD FOR ALL SEASONS

Foodstuffs were always in high demand in towns and the diet of the residents of medieval York reflected social standing. From documents and archaeology we know about the meat, dairy produce and other foods they ate and also how diet changed after the Conquest and again after the Black Death. The medieval diet was seasonal and fluctuated according to the weather, but was also affected by issues of storage and distribution.

An important influence on what people ate was the Church calendar, creating weekly fasts (on Wednesdays, Fridays and Saturdays), and feasts throughout the year such as Advent, Christmas, Lent, Easter and numerous saints' days. Restrictions on diet did not apply to the young, pregnant, sick or old.

Merchants imported a range of foods including the exotic: between 1453 and 1471, ginger, cloves, mace, pepper and a range of nuts including almonds were brought into the city. Locally York relied on its own county, the Ainsty, and access to the Forest of Galtres. The main providers of food were the victuallers although the residents supplemented their diet through the exploitation of land at the rear of their tenements, if it had not been developed for housing or other purposes. In this space they could have grown vegetables and kept chickens or pigs although this practice may have declined during the fourteenth and fifteenth centuries. More food could have been grown in gardens within the town and the surrounding area.

Information on food can be found in the probate inventories of the wealthy; these often mention brewing equipment, animals and crops alongside household items. Other information comes from documented feasts: food consumed at William Garton's funeral in 1430 included bread, ale, spices, beef and veal, capons, doves, pullets, fruit, milk and mustard. Food was purchased from the markets or the shops and its quality was determined by its length of time in transit and how it had been stored.

The increase in environmental archaeology, the study of plant, animal and insect remains, has added considerably to our understanding of what was eaten in the medieval period. Animal bone is the predominant evidence, but is biased due to the easier collection and better survival of larger bones such as those from cattle. Smaller bones from fish and birds can be missed unless deposits are sieved, which leads to certain species being underrepresented. The comparison of data from many sites, however, allows us to trace broad trends of what was eaten.

Bread was the principal food bought by householders, and also bequeathed for funeral meals, eaten at civic and guild feasts, and given as dole to the poor and prisoners. The importance of bread was reflected in the Assize of Bread and Ale in 1267, which laid our standards for bakers and brewers. Wheat was used for the best bread while rye was used for cheaper loaves; a variety of grains have been found in environmental samples from York. The Corporation controlled the activities of the bakers who provided bread at prices and quality according to the requirements of the Assize.

The bakers' monopoly on bread was often challenged and at various times innkeepers and millers were banned from making bread. Housewives were able to make flat breads at home on baking stones or beneath cooking pots. Bakers were concentrated in the area around Pavement, although they could be found across the city. In 1337 Robert de Sutton, a baker, rented property in Coppergate from a merchant; other tenements in Coppergate, owned by the Corporation, were let: one to a baker in 1322 and another to a cook in 1440. Evidence for the Coppergate bakers and cooks has been found in excavations. A twelfth-century building, located in an open area at the base of the slope from the Coppergate street frontage near the Foss, was thought to be a bakery. It had

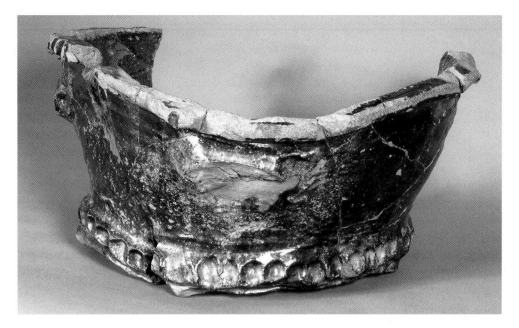

53 Medieval plant pot from the Bedern. © *York Archaeological Trust*

been rebuilt several times, given new ovens each time, and both quern stones and charred cereal grain were found.

Gardens are often overlooked but contemporary records suggest their importance; some archaeological evidence for gardening comes from the discovery of plant pots. Growing vegetables and fruit trees, and keeping domestic fowl and a pig or two, were commonplace urban activities which supplemented the diet of the poor. Gardens could also be used for beehives for honey and to grow dye plants. Monastic communities had gardens as did the Vicars Choral, but other gardens within the city are recorded in the bridgemasters' accounts, such as the one inside the city walls near Fishergate Bar that was apparently walled or fenced and had a gate.

The environmental evidence from cesspits is directly related to what was consumed; plant remains are preserved through waterlogging or mineralization. Seeds from fruits, nuts and herbs have all survived. As a result we know that people were eating things like apple, fig, plum, cherry and hazelnuts. The herbs available to flavour dishes included dill, fennel, coriander, celery, black mustard and opium poppy. Preserved skins from either from leeks or onions have been found in York.

Fish was an important part of the diet. As well as sea fish, the Fishpool and the rivers were also exploited. Complaints were often made about fishing with wicker and timber structures that caused problems for shipping on the Ouse. By the late fifteenth century many of the fisheries were owned by the Church, with the worst culprit on the Ouse being St Mary's Abbey. Before the Conquest, river and estuarine/inshore fishing was the most important, but later there was a distinct shift towards deeper sea fishing. Cod appears in the archaeological record from the eleventh century in eastern England in places like York, Norwich and London.

54 Evidence for diet: plant and seed remains under a microscope. © *York Archaeological Trust*

The consumption of fish was associated with the tightening of Church regulations relating to periods of fasting from the late eleventh century. Fish could be eaten during fasts as it was not classed as meat, but there appears to have been a decline in the amount of fish eaten in the fifteenth century and this trend was exacerbated by the Reformation of the 1530s.

Fish bones show the range of marine and river fish that was available in the city. Unsurprisingly the religious sites such as the College of Vicars Choral and the Gilbertine Priory provide evidence for a wide variety of fish. The residents of the priory ate marine fish including ray, dogfish, herring, grayling and sturgeon, and river fish such as pike, carp, perch and eels. The Vicars Choral seem to have eaten few freshwater fish, but did consume species not otherwise found in York, such as gurnard and sole.

In York changes in fish consumption can be seen, with herring becoming more popular from the eleventh century and cod from the twelfth century. At the Bedern Foundry evidence for roach, cod, haddock, ling and halibut was found and in Coppergate the residents were eating a range of fish that included salmon, carp, eel, cod, herrings, whiting, saithe and ling. Away from the city centre in Walmgate, environmental evidence shows that a similar range of fish was eaten.

Meat came from a variety of sources, but residents of York predominantly ate beef, followed by mutton and pork. Most of the animal bones are not associated with particular joints of meat, a specific family, house or event, but are found in anonymous dumps or rubbish pits. A wider range of foods was available at feasts, such as those held by the guilds.

Animal bone provides information on animal husbandry before beasts were brought into the city for slaughter, and also on the processes undertaken to convert the carcasses into food and other commodities. Some bones were separated from the carcass during initial butchering and disposed of immediately; others were disposed of after consumption. Inedible animal parts such as horn and bone were used for craft or industrial processes, and hooves were used for glue. Unusable parts were deposited in rubbish pits.

A factor to bear in mind when considering the supply of meat is that many of the city's residents had fields outside York for fattening stock, which was then brought into the city for slaughter. Changes in butchery during the medieval period show that before the thirteenth century carcasses were dealt with locally on a small scale, but after this butchery became more organised allowing the maximum recovery of parts for meat. This is shown by consistent patterns of knife marks and sizes of bone fragments. Most of the evidence for butchery comes from cattle, although there is evidence for sheep and pigs being dismembered by axe, cleaver or knife.

The slaughtered animals provide information on farming practices around the city, suggesting that the cattle and sheep slaughtered for food were older animals that had previously served other purposes. Cattle would have been used on the farm as a source of power and sheep for the production of wool. Pigs, perhaps because they were kept within the city, were killed young for their meat. In 1498 butchers and other citizens were banned from keeping their pigs in the city or the suburbs and ordinances often stressed that pigs should not be allowed to run in the streets. Butchers also sold suet, fat and marrow bones for enriching dishes, and probably sold or used the blood to make black puddings.

Domestic fowl such as geese and chicken were eaten and hens also provided eggs. Evidence for game birds such as peacock, partridge, red grouse, pheasant and capercaillie was found at the College of Vicars Choral and this reflects an element of social difference. Sea birds such as guillemot, razorbill and wader may also have been eaten. Not all birds found in excavations were eaten – some may represent wildlife on the site. Rabbit appears in the archaeological record from the mid fourteenth century.

Dairy products would have been important in the medieval diet, but these leave only indirect evidence in the archaeological record. A dairy herd consists of female cattle, with most males killed off young and a few kept for breeding. Excavations at the College of Vicars Choral found evidence for a concentration of younger animals amongst the older cattle, a pattern not seen elsewhere in the city until the sixteenth century; this was thought to suggest a dairy herd.

For those who could afford them there was a range of spices available to flavour dishes, sold from the shops of the spicers, a small guild. One shop where these could be brought belonged to the chandler Thomas Grysthorpe; in 1446 he had raisins, cloves, mace, galingale, ginger, cinnamon, sugar and saffron for sale. He could also provide his customers with knives, caps, purses and cloth!

THE COOK'S TALE

Food was cooked at home or by professional cooks and was also sold in the streets. In 1301 cooks were ordered to charge no more than 2*d* for roast chicken or chicken in bread and no more than 4*d* for roast goose; the same order mentions the sale of other meat in bread.

Kitchens are hard to identify archaeologically and hearths rarely provide evidence of what they were used for. For example, a building, possibly a kitchen, adjacent to a building in Walmgate contained a large hearth. There was associated food waste, but there was also metalworking waste, so it may have been used for craft/industrial activities. Other ovens identified during excavation contained charred cereal grains; these have been interpreted as ovens for drying corn.

Probate inventories of wealthy citizens and the clergy show they had kitchens and other food preparation areas such as brew houses and bolting houses for sifting flour. There are examples of well-equipped kitchens belonging to wealthy citizens like Robert de Crakall, mason of St Michael-le-Belfrey parish, who in 1395 had brass vessels, stone mortars, pans, pewter dishes and spits, implying open fires for roasting.

Hearths and ovens are rarely mentioned in inventories unless something valuable stood near them. They would have been made of stone or brick, heated with firewood, then the ashes swept out and the food to be baked placed inside. Bread was cooked first as it needed the highest temperature and as the temperature dropped other foods such as pastries could be cooked. Kitchen furniture recorded includes wooden stools, tables and cupboards. The majority of city residents used the hearth in the hall (living room) or the parlour for cooking. This is inferred from the inventories of Thomas Peerson and John Brown whose families cooked in the hall and William Coltmans whose cooked in the parlour. At the other extreme was Richard Bishop, who lived in one room above his shop.

Evidence for the preparation of herbs and spices comes in the form of pestles and mortars, usually made of stone. Pottery was used for a variety of purposes including cooking pots, jugs, bowls, strainers or colanders, although these may have been made of metal in wealthier households. Much of what was used in the kitchen would have been made of horn, wood or leather which don't survive well in the archaeological record. From the fourteenth century pottery use diminished and many domestic utensils became made of metal, including cauldrons, brass pots and pans as well as plates and cups of pewter.

Many of the knives found in excavations may have been used for cooking or eating. Knives were the main tools used at the table for eating food, although spoons made of horn were sometimes used; in wealthy households silver spoons might be used. Knives were of various types depending on their purpose. There were chopping knives, dressing knives and leeching knives for slicing food; wooden boards were used for chopping.

The use of pottery vessels in cooking suggests that for much of the population stews or pottage were cooked slowly over open fires. This form of slow cooking worked well with vegetables, cereals and meat and could also be done in metal cauldrons. It was not the only form of cooking and for those that could afford it roasting in an oven was an option. Ceramic posnets, small pans with handles like modern saucepans, were also used. Frying over the open fire, cooking slices of meat or making pancakes was done in long-handled iron frying pans. Charcoal was used to heat small amounts of food or sauces in chafing dishes. Ceramic chafing dishes are often found in excavations although more expensive versions may have been made of bronze or iron. Fuel for cooking came in forms other than wood: inventories show that Richard de Crackall had peat turfs, sea coal, kindling and faggots in his kitchen. Poor people without ovens could take food they had prepared to a cook or baker to cook it for them.

55 This jug from the Bedern would have been used in the kitchen or the dining room. © *York Archaeological Trust*

Food was served in wooden bowls, pottery or pewter dishes. The wealthier households had a wide range of serving dishes and inventories of the archbishops' palace show they had silver platters and chargers for joints of meat. Food was also served in trenchers made of hard bread although these could also be made of wood or pewter. More elaborate were the glass goblets and bowls found at the College of Vicars Choral and at Coppergate, imported from France, Germany or Italy and used for drinking wine.

SEASONALITY AND PRESERVATION

An important consideration in the days before refrigeration was how food could be preserved. Salt, usually evaporated from seawater imported from the Bay of Biscay, was used to preserve beef, pork and mutton. Alternatively, meat could be smoked or dried.

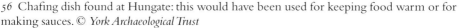

56 Chafing dish found at Hungate: this would have been used for keeping food warm or for making sauces. © *York Archaeological Trust*

Meat products could also be preserved as puddings or rendered for fats, and in autumn pigs were butchered and made into sausages; this also made use of offal.

Seasonality of meat was also a factor in the supply of food to the medieval city. Birds like pigeon were available from April to November and partridge and swan from October to March, although capons and chickens were available all year. Beef consumption peaked in December and January, with calves available from April to July and again from December to February because cows birth in both spring and summer. Lamb was available from April to July and mutton from June to August.

Milk was made into butter and cheese in the summer months by women. Cheese was a compact storable product which would have year-round value and was both imported and exported.

Fresh fruit and vegetables were eaten in accordance with the seasons although some, like onions, were harvested in the summer and stored for the winter. Apples and pears were eaten fresh in the autumn with some stored for the winter. Religious festivals also influenced food; in Lent, for example, no poultry or animal products were eaten for six weeks. In contrast, Easter and Christmas and other holy days were times of feasting. Preserved fruits such as dried dates, figs, currants and raisins along with nuts like almonds were often eaten at Christmas.

Fish was preserved, partly to help with transportation of sea fish from the coast to the inland markets. The availability of fish was also dictated by the season, with mackerel in plentiful supply in early summer. Fish like herring could be preserved in various ways: if smoked it was known as red fish; if steeped in brine or salted it was known as white fish. Fish in the cod family, including saithe, ling, haddock and hake, were preserved either as salt fish or stock fish (wind-dried).

SO WHO ATE WHAT?

The varieties of food available in different parts of the city reflect the complex patterns of social organisation: what you ate said much about where you stood in society. The reasons why beef dominates urban assemblages are complex, but it may reflect the more diverse range of people living in towns than in the country. The fact that a cattle carcass provided a large quantity of meat of varying quality of cuts allowed distribution to different types of household.

Food waste found during excavations at 41–49 Walmgate, a home to metalworkers, shows that in the late twelfth to fourteenth centuries food consisted of chicken, cod, figs, oats, barley, rye and hazelnuts. There was a change in the early to mid fourteenth century with a far more diverse range of food available including ling and cod, shellfish, crab, sheep or goat, cow, pig, fallow deer, chicken, goose, crane, wheat/rye bran, fig, apple and blackberry. For the later periods the information is patchier, reflecting a change in rubbish disposal as there were fewer food remains spread around the site or in rubbish pits, with material being taken out of the city or to other areas such as Hungate for disposal. What survived included shellfish, fish, sheep or goat, cow, pig, chicken, barnacle goose and duck.

At Coppergate, despite the area being home to some of the more affluent inhabitants of York, a similar range of food was eaten: a high proportion of cattle followed in quantity by sheep, pig and fowl. This may suggest that in this case status was expressed through means other than types of food. The small numbers of fowl were mainly adult hens, implying egg production, whereas geese were seen as a source of meat. There was also evidence for improved cleanliness at the site, with the dumping of rubbish in pits decreasing after the fourteenth century and a reduction in surface waste by the sixteenth. This may have coincided with the end of cultivation in the backyards, which were increasingly surfaced with cobbles or other material.

The upper class generally used food as a mark of status: they could afford the finest white bread, more meat and access to elaborate, spiced foods and wine. Such foods were eaten from silver dishes and wine drunk from glass goblets. These foods also featured in the monastic diet. Copying aspects of this lifestyle was a sign of social mobility among the aspiring artisan classes. The majority of the urban population ate beef, pig and mutton, but probably consumed a higher proportion of vegetables and cereal grains. Herring was cheap enough to be brought by most people.

Clear evidence for a different supply of food was seen at the college in Bedern where the animal bone, which contained a higher number of calves, suggested that the vicars had access to specialised dairy herds. Thirteenth-century sites across the city were dominated by cattle that were at least 7–8 years old at the time of slaughter and it was not until the sixteenth/seventeenth century when young calves commonly appear more generally across the city as a source of food. It also seems that at Bedern they were carrying out their own butchery, with an absence of skulls suggesting they had been taken away for the horn cores. The differences in butchery patterns of sheep at Bedern may also suggest that the College had access to different herds from the rest of the city; there was also evidence for an unusually wide range of birds that were presumably eaten.

The religious houses and hospitals would also have had a different diet from the residents of the town, but only the Gilbertine Priory has been studied in detail. This showed that the priors, like the rest of the citizens of York, ate a lot of beef. Whether this was a deliberate choice of the institution or reflected its comparative low status is unclear, as is whether they sourced their meat through the city or from their own rural estates. The priory was unusual, however, in the range of fish consumed, a large proportion of which being freshwater fish. In the few environmental samples sieved at the Bedern a similar pattern of fish bone was seen, which suggests an association between ecclesiastical sites and a higher consumption of fish.

Excavations at Baille Hill might also have been expected to expose patterns of diet different from those of the rest of the city. The excavated animal bone dating predominantly to the twelfth and thirteenth centuries consisted of sheep and goat, pig, fish and bird; it did not reflect aristocratic dietary preferences or functional differences between the top of the motte and the bailey. This may suggest that while building the castle was a statement of the ruling elite, those who lived at the castle had close links with the local economy in terms of food supply.

DRINK AND BE MERRY

Although water was available from wells and rivers, the residents of York also drank ale. Ale was brewed from grain and water, and fermented with yeast. Brewing was initially a home business in towns, carried out by women, and probably made a valuable contribution to the economy of many city households. Legislation in 1301 stated that people shouldn't be prevented from brewing at home. Ale was important because it provided a healthier alternative to the well or river water that carried a wide variety of diseases that were reduced through the boiling and fermenting processes associated with brewing. It was brewed to varying strengths and was drunk by both children and adults. The Assize of Ale (1267) regulated the price of ale; it was strictly maintained and was a useful way of raising money from brewers who broke the rules.

Brewing remained a small-scale trade and it had no guild. In 1450/51 out of the 221 persons fined for violating the Assize of Ale, only seven were recorded in the Register of Freemen as brewers. Home brewing is suggested in probate inventories such as Emma Stayngate's. She was a saddler's widow who died in 1370 and left brewing equipment to Agnes Paponham for a year on the condition that she gave four gallons to the poor.

The move away from a home industry started with the introduction of hops from the Low Countries. This made beer possible and brewing became increasingly professional during the fifteenth century. An alternative, for those that could afford it, was wine. This was drunk mainly by wealthy merchants and the aristocracy; it was also used by the Church for the celebration of mass. There were no controls on the quality of wine sold, until the Assize of Wine was introduced in 1330.

While ale and wine could be consumed in the home, there were also alehouses, taverns and inns. Some of these also provided food and were an important part of the medieval townscape. Despite their prominence, they are almost impossible to detect archaeologically, as their foundations would be similar to other houses and the associated artefacts would be domestic.

The Assize of Bread and Ale makes it clear that there was a distinction between inns, taverns and alehouses. Hostellers (innkeepers) provided accommodation for travellers, wine was sold by taverners, who became known as vintners in the fifteenth century, and ale was probably sold from alehouses. Women often ran alehouses, taverns and inns. Robert de Selby, a York merchant, sold wine in a Selby tavern through his cousin Joanna Palfrayman.

Alehouses had a reputation for being unruly and in 1393 countrywide legislation ordered that a sign must be exhibited at all alehouses and hostels so they could be easily identified, not just by patrons, but also the authorities. The standard sign was a garland of foliage attached to a projecting pole called an ale-stake and these are mentioned by contemporary authors like Chaucer. To help distinguish themselves the many alehouses, taverns and hostels in the city started to use painted signs. The earliest recorded is *The George,* mentioned in a will of 1455. In 1459 the Corporation ordered that 'all aliens coming from foreign parts shall be lodged within the said city, within the liberties, or suburbs thereof, but only in the Inn of the Mayor and Commonality, at the sign of *The Bull* in Conyng Street'. Others listed are based on heraldic devices like *The Crowned Lion* (1483), *The Dragon* (1484) and *The White Swan* (1487). Religious symbolism also appears, such as *The Three Kings* in Micklegate run by John Ellis in 1475.

Hostelries are not easy to find in records, as the occupation was not considered socially acceptable. They only begin to appear more frequently in the records from the fifteenth century, although a certain William the innkeeper is mentioned in the 1250s. Hosteller and innkeeper were the same, with the former name used until the fifteenth century; they dealt with the streams of people visiting the city for social, administrative, political and religious reasons.

Women were often innkeepers and in 1301, of 45 hostellers, 11 women were accused of overcharging, but no innkeepers at all appear in the Register of Freemen before 1396. Inns could be large establishments and the number of people and horses that could be accommodated in York was considerable. The Corporation took an active interest, to ensure guests were well served with food, drink and stabling.

Keeping an inn was also a service offered by the owners of large houses. In 1304 Alice Manner ran one in the house of William Fader, but the rates charged were also subject to council control. Three of the 13 hostellers listed in the poll tax of 1381 were mercers who presumably used their wives or servants to run the inns. In 1526 Agnes Johnson, widow of

William Brigges a tailor, became a freeman as an innkeeper. Of the four innkeepers who made wills in the sixteenth century, none gained the freedom of the city as innkeepers: William Penyngton was a haberdasher, Richard Tourner a smith and haberdasher, Gilbert Walron a mercer and John Ellis a chandler.

The best information for an inn in York comes from the 1450 inventory of John Stubbes, who became a freeman as a barber in 1441. He used his large house for guests and it had two halls, six bedchambers and a servants' room. In the rooms he had seven feather beds, 18 other beds, 10 mattresses with bolsters, and a quantity of linen. He also had a gyle house where vinegar was made; a bolting house where flour was sifted and where he stacked away another mattress with 16 pairs of sheets; a kitchen and a brewery; a granary with a large quantity of grain; a hay store, stable horse and a cow. There was also his barber's shop with enough razors and bowls to shave his guests.

INFLUENCE OF THE GUILDS

The production of food was strictly regulated by the victualling guilds, but this control was far from easy, as many different people had an interest in providing food and drink. The 1381 lay subsidy records 29 bakers in the city, eight cooks, 29 butchers and eight brewers. York residents were more likely to brew ale than bake their own bread. As a result tradesmen like glaziers, founders and barbers also appear in the records as bakers, brewers, fishmongers and innkeepers. It was not just the food providers in the city that were regulated, but also those from outside the city or not freemen, referred to as foreigners and aliens in the contemporary sources.

Each guild was headed by a master and a number of searchers elected at the annual meeting. Their ordinances, or rules, had to be approved by the Corporation and recorded in the city records. The guild searchers were the inspectors or internal police, enforcing all orders and assizes issued by the national government or the local Corporation, and checking the quality of goods sold at the markets or stored in the city. They had rights of access to the relevant properties.

The butchers had their own guildhall off Little Shambles, but other victuallers met at St Anthony's Hall from the late fifteenth century. The bakers, brewers, cooks, millers and fishermongers of Ouse Bridge met there on the feast day of St James the Apostle, 25 July, or within a few days of it. The fishmongers of Foss Bridge met in the hall at the feast of Corpus Christi, which fell between 21 May and 24 June. The innkeepers met on the feast of St Mary Magdalene, 22 July.

The butchers were the most prosperous of the victualling guilds and gained the freedom of the city in large numbers. Surviving butchers' wills contain bequests of livestock or show possession of grazing land. Butchers also had grazing rights in the Forest of Galtres in the early fourteenth century and probably earlier. The dominance of the butchers over the area around the city by the end of the fifteenth century led to the Corporation preventing them holding grazing land within six miles of the city. The butchers often had run-ins with the Corporation and five were imprisoned in 1480 for unspecified obstinacy and disobedience. Competition from foreign butchers was generally encouraged, curbing the dominance of the city butchers.

It is often difficult to distinguish between the roles of millers and bakers. A baker who acquired the lease of one of the common mills in 1487 was ordered to find a miller to work it. This segregation was unusual and in Winchester it was commonplace for mills to be let to bakers. All the citizens, innkeepers, bakers and brewers had to have their corn ground by a member of the millers' guild and this monopoly was maintained by the imposition of fines on anyone owning a mill but not part of the guild.

There were various types of mill located around the city and in the Ainsty; an order of 1405 fixed the price of flour and malt and applied to millers having a 'windmill, water mill or horse mill within the city, suburbs and precincts of the same as well as the Castle Mills and others'. The Castle Mills were near the dam across the Foss and were the most important in the city. They were probably built soon after the Fishpool was created, as mills near the castle are mentioned from the twelfth century. In the early thirteenth century the mills did not use water from the dam, but from a ditch constructed in 1215/16 around the Walmgate area from the Fishpond to the Foss to a point beneath the dam.

Other water mills included Hob Moor (or Folly) mill on Holbeck, mentioned in 1563 as corporation property. Windmills around the city are often shown on old maps and recorded in descriptions of the city boundaries such as Clifton or Lady Windmill in Burton Stone Lane mentioned from the late fourteenth century to the early nineteenth century and another known at different times as the White Cross on Bootham Stray and Pepper Mill; other windmills on the Mount outside Micklegate Bar can be traced back to the thirteenth century.

Religious houses also operated mills around the city. St Mary's Abbey had a water mill and a windmill near Monk Bridge mentioned in the records of the city boundaries from the late fourteenth to the early eighteenth century. The abbey also had windmills near Clifton and Siward Mill Hill in Heslington; the earthwork known as Siward's Howe may be the mound associated with the mill. The surviving Holgate Mill, built in 1770, may be the successor of the mill owned by the Archbishop in 1366. Clementhorpe Nunnery owned two windmills near Clementhorpe and St Nicholas's leper hospital owned a windmill from the late fourteenth century, mentioned in the city bounds until the eighteenth at the junction of Tang Hall Lane and the Hull Road.

The cooks made up an important guild and in their ordinances of 1425 they called themselves the public cooks. The cooks provided cooked foods for general sale, prepared meals for private customers and baked customers' own dishes. They were a hard group to define and often overlapped with other trades, especially innkeepers and bakers. Many people cooked at home and sold their products. An ordinance of 1425 prevented the wives of other craftsmen from preparing food for sale. As well as cooking meat and fish, they also made tarts, cheesecakes and other paste meats, pies and pasties. If a cook was required for a feast such as a wedding, burial, guild feast or meetings within the city or the suburbs, a freeman cook had to be employed, otherwise a £1 fine had to be paid. The cooks' guild searchers were allowed to check the quality of rabbits and fowl brought into the city and ensure they were not hawked around the streets but sold in the markets. They also had the right to check the red or white herring, salted and fresh fish landed at the King's Staithe and charged 4d a year for the service. The cooks also received 4d from anyone other than the free fishmongers wishing to sell salt fish, salt salmon, eels, stockfish or herrings in the city.

A more specialised trade was sauce making, based around the Shambles. According to their late fourteenth-century ordinances sauce makers only sold their produce from their shops. The mustard and condiment sellers who also lived in the same area sold cheaper dressings.

Sometimes the cooks and other victuallers were employed for large-scale events like the day-long celebrations for 6,000 guests at the installation ceremonies of Archbishop Neville in 1467; these required 300 caskets of ale, 100 caskets of wine, one large bottle of wine sweetened with sugar, nutmeg and ginger, 104 oxen, six wild bulls, 1,000 sheep, 304 calves, 400 swans, 2,000 geese, 1,000 capons, 2,000 pigs, 104 peacocks, over 13,500 other birds, 500 stags, bucks and roes, 1,500 venison pies, 608 pikes and breams, 12 porpoises and seals, 13,000 dishes of jelly, cold baked tarts, custards and spices, sugared delicacies and wafers.

Bakers made bread from corn purchased either directly from the countryside or from the corn market. To prevent them monopolising the corn market they were only allowed to buy there after 1pm in summer and 2pm in winter. Once corn had been ground by the miller the baker measured it and then bolted it, by placing it in a canvas or bolting cloth and shaking it, effectively sieving it to different levels of fineness depending on the bread to be produced. In the fourteenth century the breads were called wastell, cockett and payndemayne which were the most expensive white breads. Bastard wastell and simnel were cheaper with pains integer the cheapest, made of whole wheat. The flour was mixed into dough in wooden troughs and made up into loaves of different shapes. Each baker had to mark his bread so it was clear if anyone was breaching the regulations.

The fishmongers were one of the largest groups associated with providing food for the city. They supplied sea and river fish, mussels and cockles. Some were men of importance within the City Council such as Robert le Meek, subsequently mayor, and John King, later one of the chamberlains recorded in 1304. This reflects the fact that fishing was largely controlled by the merchants; a similar situation existed in late thirteenth- and early fourteenth-century Winchester. In York in 1393, 1398 and 1404 the mercers Thomas Gare, Henry Wyman, Robert Savage and Thomas and Robert Holme imported herring, but also exported cloth and wool. In 1300 there were only seven fishmongers in the Register of Freemen, but this increased during the fourteenth century, perhaps reflecting separation or definition of roles within the merchants' guild.

MARKETS AND FAIRS

Having seen the food that was prepared and consumed, we should now investigate where it was sold. An open space in a town need not have been used for a market, so archaeologically markets are hard to detect, being without diagnostic deposits like buildings. Documents can tell us more about the sale of the goods that archaeology can identify.

Markets were the end point for the delivery of goods brought to the city by road or river for redistribution and sale. They were a vital part of the city economy and as a result were heavily regulated. Although the markets were meant to be the official trading places, under the watchful eye of the Corporation and the guilds, a lot of trade probably took place in private in the inns, staithes or even before goods entered the city.

Pavement and St Sampson Square had market crosses. These crosses could be either simple or ornate structures. We cannot be sure why markets had crosses – it may be because the church had a strong hand in the development of trade or they may have signified some form of divine protection. As the crosses often had high bases they were used for reading proclamations, news or other vital information to the gathered people.

Goods or food were also sold by hawkers and hucksters, usually women, who walked the streets. This unregulated business caused the Corporation to issue orders. In 1389 foreigners were forbidden from hawking their wares around the city or selling them from the hostel where they were staying; this may have been why the Corporation finally decreed that all foreigners had to stay at *The Bull*.

Food was sold throughout the week, as it was perishable. A sore point was Sunday trading and in 1428 York ordered shops to close on Sundays, with the exception of food sellers who could open for restricted hours. The city's freemen purchased goods from the markets, but were meant to trade from the shops in the houses they rented from the landowners. This may be why in the fourteenth century rows developed, to maximise the retail space, providing a steady income for the landlords as opposed to the intermittent profit from the market stalls. London had clearly zoned streets like Bread Street around Cheapside where particular produce was sold. Although not so easily identifiable in York, we know meat was sold in the Shambles and luxury goods in Stonegate, which was home to the jewellers, goldsmiths, bookbinders and glaziers.

An important factor in the running of the markets was the management of hours of trading. Regulations stipulated when they opened and when certain groups were allowed to buy and sell goods. The market at Pavement was opened and closed by the ringing of the bell of All Saints' Church or Ouse Bridge Chapel. Regulation of market time was tightened with the development of clocks. York's civic clock in 1370 was in the tower of St William's Chapel on Ouse Bridge and determined the timing for rings of the city bell. The association of clocks with the Church, which set the pattern of the hours of the day, and their prominent position in towers, was more than just practical; it implied religious approval of the activities of the town.

The markets were the point of sale for all manner of goods, including foodstuffs, craft products, raw materials and livestock. As markets developed they also became specialised, with products either sold in specific areas within them or on specific days; many towns would have more than one marketplace although one always retained a greater importance. We have few records of where goods like leather and wool were sold. Rules governed the marketplaces, stipulating that traders keep them clean and clear of rubbish. Once a market was over, the space was usually cleared of stalls. Towns like York which managed to become staples, where specific goods had to be traded, manufactured and transported, or particular services provided, secured regional dominance and prosperity.

York's two principal marketplaces were Pavement and Thursday Market (now St Sampson's Square). Thursday Market was first mentioned in the thirteenth century and may have been a new civic enterprise to facilitate a reorganisation of the market space within the city. It may be much older and form part of the area called the Marketshire in

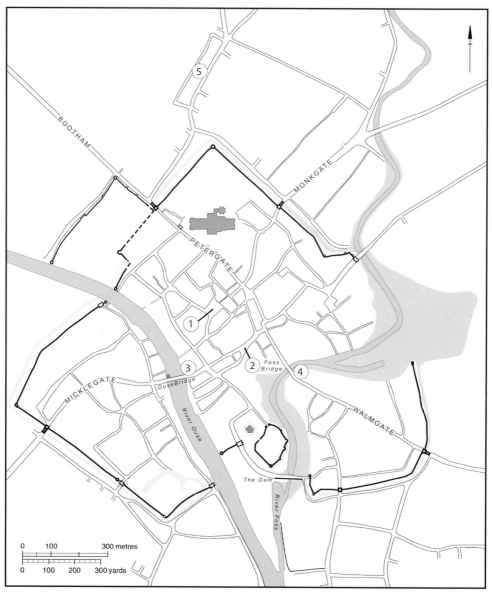

1. *Thursday Market*
2. *Pavement*
3. *Fresh/salted fish (Ouse Bridge)*
4. *Sea Fish (Foss Bridge)*
5. *The Horsefair*

57 The principal marketplaces

Domesday Book, a name used until the fourteenth century, denoting the area covering Pavement and the Shambles.

Today the marketplaces bear no relation to their appearance in the medieval period because of alterations to the city streetscape in the nineteenth and twentieth centuries. They were linked by Parliament Street, opened in 1836, that runs from the north-east side of Pavement to the south-west side of Thursday Market. Parliament Street cut across the line of medieval Jubbergate and a medieval lane that was the continuation of Little Shambles, originally acting as access for the properties fronting onto Pavement and Jubbergate. The south-eastern side of Pavement was altered further by the creation of Piccadilly in 1912; its north-eastern side was altered by the demolition of St Crux in the 1880s and the creation of the Stonebow in the 1950s. Thursday Market was also altered on its north-eastern side by the extension of Church Street across the churchyard of St Sampson's Church.

Using old maps to strip away the modern alterations to the streets we can see that originally there were two distinct open spaces with limited access, into which traffic was channelled, which no doubt greatly assisted regulation by the city and guild officials. Pavement was a triangular space with its south-western end dominated by All Saints and its north-eastern end by St Crux. Access into the market was from Coppergate, High Ousegate, the Shambles, Colliergate and Fossgate. There were probably numerous lanes running off the marketplace accessing the rear of the properties that fronted onto Pavement. Thursday Market was a square space accessed by Davygate, Feasegate, Little Hornpot Lane, Finkle Street, Three Cranes Lane and Silver Street, with access altered when Church Street was created.

By the sixteenth century markets were held in Thursday Market and Pavement three days a week on Tuesdays, Thursdays and Saturdays, coinciding with the days the courts of the sheriff were traditionally held. Pavement was perhaps the principal market, but its use before the fourteenth century, from which records date, is poorly understood. Its main function was the sale of the most important commodity, corn, which was carried out until 1946.

Most of the corn came from the area immediately around the city, but after the Black Death there were new opportunities for import and export of grain. Merchants exported it through Hull to Iceland and the Low Countries in the second half of the fifteenth century. At the same time city and alien merchants began importing corn and meal from Europe. In 1477 the oat market began at the ringing of the bell of All Saints and in 1505 the Ouse Bridge bell announced the start of the corn market. The idea of the segregation of goods within the markets can be seen in the eighteenth century when the corn market was arranged according to the grade of the grain: wheat (the most expensive) was sold on the north-east side, rye on the south-west, barley in High Ousegate, and the cheaper oats, peas and beans in Coppergate. There is no reason why a similar arrangement should not have existed in the medieval period.

Other goods sold in Pavement included dairy produce (until 1500 when it shifted to Thursday Market), herbs and vegetables. It was also used by small-scale producers for the sale of items like gloves and cloth and for the annual fair for hiring servants. Pavement was an important public space regularly used for formal proclamations. It was the site of the public pillory and occasionally for the execution of traitors. There was a bullring near the Shambles in the mid fifteenth century and Pavement was also the end point for the wagons of the Corpus Christi plays that culminated in the performance of the doomsday play by the mercers.

A wide variety of goods were sold at Thursday Market; an idea of the range can be seen in an order from 1519 for the thrice weekly sale of poultry, swine, dairy produce, oatmeal, salt, coarse cloth, herbs, vegetables, hemp and candles. Bread brought into the city by 'foreigners' was also sold there and from at least the fifteenth century foreign butchers were confined to Thursday Market.

A regulation of 1389 stated that all victuals in Thursday Market had to be sold openly and nothing could be sold before the market began. The city poulterers and victuallers were barred from making purchases before the market had been open for three hours and maximum prices were fixed for exotic goods such as woodcock, plover, teal, fieldfares and larks. No victuals were allowed to be taken away and sold.

Other markets existed within or around the city and for a period in the fourteenth century there was another corn market in Micklegate. The main cattle markets were held in the Horsefair on the north-east side of the city and on Toft Green within the walls at Micklegate Bar from 1416. The sale of fruit is not well recorded, but is indicated by the first reference to Gerard le Fruter, freeman, in 1322; Phillip le Fruter appears in 1335 and apples were sold on Ouse Bridge in 1418 near the fish market. Some fruit was grown locally, but fruit like dried dates, prunes and raisins from the Mediterranean were imported by the merchants through Hull.

Fish was brought into the city along the Ouse in ships called crayers (small sea-going vessels), keels or ketches, some of which were owned by the free fishmongers; it was unloaded at the *fyshelandyng* near Ouse Bridge. Non-freemen had to unload their boats downstream and pay 4*d* a year to sell their fish on Ouse Bridge. They also had to pay 4*d* per 12 barrels of white or red fish for searching by the fishmongers and the cooks, and a further 4*d* if they sold them in the common market.

Fresh and salted fish was sold on Ouse Bridge and sea fish on Foss Bridge. The city fishmongers who had taken out the freedom sold river fish such as salmon (both fresh and salted), oysters, mussels and cockles in the fish market in Ousegate. They also sold salt fish like herring. On Foss Bridge the fishmongers and panyermen supplied the city with fresh sea fish, most of which came from Bridlington, Filey, Scarborough, Whitby and Sandsend. This was predominantly an overland trade with the east coast, some 50 miles away. The fish was brought back in panniers on mules and the fishmongers were forbidden from meeting them outside the city in an attempt to bypass the markets.

The freemen fishmongers sold on the bridge, while the non-freemen sold their produce in the fish shambles on the Walmgate side of Foss Bridge and could only commence trading once the 'Skaite bell be Ronge at Fossebrigge' at 11am, after the freemen fishmongers had supplied the bulk of customers. The dominance of the sea fish trade by merchants is perhaps reflected in the fact it was sold on Foss Bridge in the heart of the commercial sector and near the merchants' hall.

Another important means of buying and selling goods from a wider region was the annual fair. The oldest annual fair was the archbishops', St Peter's or Lammas Fair which was one of the highlights of the year held from 3pm on 31 July to 3pm on 2 August. During the fair the city was under the jurisdiction of the archbishop whose bailiffs were responsible for maintaining order and collecting tolls at the gates and from the river. Some of these traditions survived into the early nineteenth century and petitions were made by the archbishop when the dismantling of gates and posterns in the city would limit his ability to levy tolls.

New fairs were obtained by the city in 1502. One was held on the Monday after Ascension and the five days following. The first two days were for animals, with cattle sold in Fishergate, horses outside Walmgate Bar and sheep on Heworth Moor. Another fair that was granted followed a similar pattern but focused on the south-west side of the Ouse; it was held on St Luke's Day and the five following days. The first two days were for the sale of animals in the area outside Micklegate Bar and the Knavesmire. On the remaining days goods were sold on designated streets on the south-west side of the Ouse. Goods on offer at these fairs included southern cloth in the Common Hall, and cloth from towns like Leeds, Halifax and Kendal in the streets nearby; in other parts of the city goldsmiths, jewellers, silk women, mercers and grocers, hatmakers, saddlers, glovers, turners and cartwrights sold their wares.

So the medieval residents of the city had access to a wide range of foods. What they ate was largely influenced by status and they could spend their money in the wide range of shops and markets within the city, with the highlights being the annual fairs. It is clear that the merchants and other city freemen were involved in the importation, manufacture and sale of almost every commodity, and regulations ensured that competition was kept to a minimum through the fines exacted on those not in the guilds. By the sixteenth century the freemen were dominated by a few York families. Much of the medieval system persisted into the eighteenth and early nineteenth century and it was not until 1835 that the Corporation was reformed and became the equivalent of the modern city council; after that date anyone could practise a lawful trade in the city.

6

A MATTER OF LIFE AND DEATH

We have looked at the people of York from the point of view of their daily actions and their consumption, but we can learn much about the residents of the city through analysing evidence from the many burials that have been excavated. Using this in conjunction with documentary sources, we can estimate the size of the population and gain some idea of people's appearance and health. But determining the size of a past population is not straightforward, and the best we can do is paint a broad picture of the residents of medieval York.

THE GREAT UNWASHED

The medieval population was recorded by heads of household so we have few hard figures relating to population for the most part. The civil registration of births, deaths and marriages only started in 1837. Parish registers do not begin until the late 1530s and don't record some elements of the population, such as infants dying before baptism. The problem is how to use the number of heads of household to determine the number of other people resident in a property. A household could comprise a single person, a couple or a family group. A household may also have had lodgers, apprentices and live-in servants.

It is not clear how medieval people defined 'a family', but it probably consisted of immediate kin such as a husband, wife and children. Marriage was one of the central cultural institutions of later medieval society and from 1215 was one of the sacraments of the Church. The family was a social and economic unit and, as such, marriage had far more implications than just the domestic, since husband, wife, sons and daughters could all be involved in the family business; the poll tax suggests that after the Black Death this household system was typical. As well as the family, an artisan might also employ workers for specific tasks.

It is difficult to calculate the number of servants and children. The 1377 poll tax for York, which is incomplete, shows very few children, but suggests that a third or more of households included an average of two servants. The number of servants in a household was related to income. Female servants were usually found in the wealthy households and, in 1381, 45 per cent of female servants were employed by mercantile traders and 23 per cent by victuallers.

We will never know precisely how many people lived in a household but estimating this number is vital to working out population figures not only for the city but also the country. It has been suggested that in Coventry an artisan household consisted of 4.6–4.8

persons, whilst poorer households consisted of no more than 3.2 persons. The poll tax data for late fourteenth-century York suggests household size within the walls ranged from 3.91 to 4.58 persons. An estimate of the population using these rough figures is only ever a broad guide. Figures for the poor are always elusive, because they often came to the towns seeking charity and perhaps employment.

From the estimated size of households it is possible to guess town and national populations, but these calculations are not an exact science. During the late eleventh to early fourteenth centuries the population of England grew from an estimated 2 million at the time of the Conquest to around 5 or 6 million by c.1300. The towns were growing at such a rate that by around 1300 c.15 per cent or even more of the population might have lived in them.

The earliest estimation of population for York uses Domesday Book, which suggests the city had a population of around 9,000. The urban population was rarely stable, subject to fluctuations caused by immigration from the hinterland as well as the impact of disease, in particular plague. It is thought that during the thirteenth century the population rose steadily overall and despite the plague may have been in excess of 12,000 by the fifteenth century.

The postulated economic decline of the early sixteenth century was thought to be mirrored in a fall in population to around 8,000 based on the 1524–25 subsidy and the chantry accounts of 1548, but these sources are far from reliable. Although beyond our period, the recurring problems with estimating population before the nineteenth century are shown in the 1670s when the parish registers, hearth tax and the Compton ecclesiastical census can be used to estimate the population; these suggest a population of 8,000–12,000 for the city.

Medieval towns are often viewed as 'urban graveyards' with populations declining at times through high mortality due to unsanitary conditions. However, as we have seen, the condition of the city actually improved during the medieval period. It could be that once exposed to the higher risk of disease in the town, those who survived had as good a chance of living to as old an age as their rural contemporaries. Plague was the biggest problem for towns after 1348, and it arrived in York in May of that year, peaking from June to August. However, there has been no direct evidence for the plague in the city (nothing to compare with the large plague pits recorded in London) and its impact on York is not well recorded.

Plague outbreaks continued through the late fourteenth and early fifteenth century, but by the sixteenth century plague was more or less an urban phenomenon, striking in a random manner. York seems to have faired better by the late sixteenth century than other towns, with only one occurrence between 1560 and 1670, whereas it struck Norwich seven times and Bristol five. The better-recorded plague in York in 1605 shows the speed at which the city could recover from an epidemic, with an increase in baptism rates and entry to the Register of Freemen in the next few years, similar to that seen in 1348. By 1610 contemporaries noted it was as though the plague had never happened. This ability of the city to replenish and sustain its numbers was due not only to children born in York, but also to migrants, drawn to the city from the surrounding countryside and sometimes much further afield. There is insufficient evidence to allow comparisons of urban birth and death rates to determine whether the increases in the population resulted from a baby boom or immigration.

The economy of the city and its population were linked. Most of the residents relied on York's role as a commercial, administrative and market centre for their livelihood into the mid seventeenth century, by which time it was a regional capital. It is suggested that the economy of the city slowed after the Civil War in the 1640s and this may be reflected in the lack of growth of the population until the 1750s. It was by the mid-eighteenth century that many other towns were experiencing the growth and development which can be associated with the Industrial Revolution.

It could be argued that York had a 'natural' population limit of 10,000–12,000, as a volume that its resources could easily support; this is based on the fact that this appears to be the average from the fourteenth to mid eighteenth centuries, despite economic, ecclesiastical and administrative changes. If the low population of the 1524–25 lay subsidy is seen as under-enumeration, then there was no major population decline just as there may have been no major slump in the city's economy. There was still much to draw people to the city and the problems of the urban poor saw the city obtain an act of parliament in 1572 to help deal with these issues, through measures such as the workhouses set up in St Anthony's Hall. Furthermore, it has been shown that if the city couldn't accommodate the immigrant poor they were sent back to their last known town.

WHENCE THEY CAME

Now we know how many people might have lived in the city we can also say something about the composition of the population. This information draws on the Domesday Book, poll taxes, the city records and the Freemen's Register. These documents allow us to trace changes in the names of people and also the areas from which they came.

Domesday Book shows clearly the difference between the invaders and the indigenous population of the town. The Normans were given 157 messuages or tenements within the city. The named households in Domesday Book suggest that 57 per cent of the people in York had Scandinavian names. One of the new lords, the count of Mortain, held 14 messuages, two stalls in the shambles and the church of St Crux. His tenants had clearly Anglo-Scandinavian names: Sonulf the priest, Morulf, Sterre, Esnarre, Gamel, Archil, Leung the priest, Turfin and Ligulf.

Other than the Norman lords, foreign settlers are reflected in the Bret element in Bretgate and Jubbergate, originally called Jubretgate, suggesting the presence of Bretons. It may be significant that St Sampson's, in modern Church Street, may be a new church or rededication to a 6th-century saint associated with Dol in Brittany.

The presence of Anglo-Scandinavian and Norman names does not necessarily imply a direct line of descent, but it may be an indicator of the prevailing political climate. This may be why there is a gradual change through the mid twelfth century to Latin and Norman names or names of biblical origin. For example, Lefwin, son of Thorulf, who married Juliana le Gras who may have been Norman, named his children Hugh, Gerard, Walter and Gilbert. The Register of Freemen recorded the first names and surnames of the inhabitants and these either relate to the trade they carried out or the place where they came from. However, by the mid to late fourteenth century surnames become fixed and often hereditary.

The Register of Freemen shows that the majority of York's immigrants were drawn from an area of 35 miles (56km) around the city. Fewer people came from the immediate area around the city and a similar pattern is seen at London, Norwich and Nottingham. York drew most of its immigrants from Yorkshire and the north-west, for example Cumbria, where it had established trade contacts. Even in the sixteenth century the few place names recorded show that the city was still drawing people from between 12 and 60 miles (20–100km) away. An even wider pattern of immigration is reflected in surnames such as James the Fleming, mayor in 1298, or John Colan, who may have come from Germany. More intriguingly, recent excavations in the cemetery of St Stephen's identified two individuals who may have come from Africa based on the shape and form of their skulls.

The reason why people migrated to the city are complex, but probably had much to do with exploitation of opportunities otherwise unavailable. This could be to work as servants, but also to take up apprenticeships with one of the city's master craftsmen, eventually setting themselves up as freemen in their own right or working as journeymen for other employers. This desire to move to the towns explains why urban populations could recover after periods of plague or other disease.

Migration wasn't necessarily a one-off event either. There appears to have been a steady turnover of young people, especially women, who worked as servants. Alice Dalton from Poppleton for example worked as a servant in the city before returning to her village after marriage. The rents from the College of Vicars Choral also suggest that tenants, especially female ones, were often short term, perhaps staying for a year.

Immigration must have made the larger towns somewhat cosmopolitan. Examination of the documentary records shows that there were a number of alien, or foreign, taxpayers in many fifteenth-century towns. In 1483–84 resident aliens constituted at least 6 per cent of the population of London and its suburbs, and in 1440 there were 82 alien taxpayers in Cambridge and York.

THE MEDIEVAL WAY OF DEATH

As in life, the Church exercised a considerable influence in death. There was a set of core beliefs surrounding the idea of death. With the development of the concept of purgatory came the idea of the soul, which was marked by rank, gender and occupation, and continued existence after death in limbo, awaiting full resurrection at the Last Judgement. The living could help the souls of the departed through prayer. Associated with these ideas was the concept of bodily resurrection at the Last Judgement.

These developments coincided with a growing sense of secular identity expressed through material culture but also through burial practice. People often chose to be buried with personal artefacts that were a display of piety, such as papal bullae. They could also show their rank by the materials used in the grave, ranging from stone coffins to simple shrouds. The majority chose to be buried in their local parish church, but some opted for burial in the monasteries or friaries. The latter were the most favoured, especially those within the walls, as shown in surviving York wills of 1370–1530. The least popular were St Andrew's Priory, Fishergate, and the nunnery at Clementhorpe. All of the urban churches had large burial grounds, which have been lost through later road improvements and building development. The graveyards were defined spaces with boundary ditches and walls, and the churchyard of St Helen, Stonegate, had an

58 The loss of urban graveyards means burials turn up in some unexpected places such as below modern St Helen's Square. © *York Archaeological Trust*

important footpath across it that led from Stonegate to Davygate, and they were also a place for the living and were used for markets and meetings. The churchyards could also contain detached priests' houses; one is mentioned in the building records for Our Lady Row in Goodramgate.

The Church taught that people had to prepare themselves for death. The soul was unaffected by bodily illness, but was subject to corruption through the desires of the body. This was shown through illnesses, some of which were considered punishments for sin; leprosy, for example, was seen as the result of sexual sin. To avoid sin leading to an extended stay in purgatory, the Church encouraged confession, repentance and penance. People were reminded of the need to look after their souls, the dangers of sin and about death and eternal afterlife, through sermons, stained glass and wall paintings.

Other ways to ease the burden of sin included good works, such as donations to the Church, pilgrimage and charitable work; these allowed people to have a 'good death', since they had made provision for their soul, and left their material and spiritual estates in good order. Another method for shortening time in purgatory was to purchase indulgences or 'pardons' from travelling sellers called pardoners.

It was also possible to have a 'bad death'. This occurred when an individual committed a mortal sin or was unable to prepare for death because of violence, accident or sudden illness. Anyone dying a bad death was treated separately as they might defile consecrated ground; they might be prohibited from burial in a cemetery, or be interred in a marginal place or an unorthodox position.

The burial of an individual would take place in the parish churchyard or the chosen religious house, and there were also designated burial grounds associated with hospitals and execution sites. Monks were laid out according to the traditions of their order. Dominicans were laid on ashes, and Cistercians on sackcloth, and the presence of ash was a sign of penance. The best place for a lay person to die was at home.

The processes of preparing for death can be found in the Book of Hours. This was a collection of psalms known as the Office of the Dead, to be recited for the soul of the dead in purgatory. Such books were hugely popular from the thirteenth to sixteenth century. Illustrations show the stages along the way, including the approach of death, with the gathering of family members and a priest, or fellow monks in the religious houses. When the person died the corpse was washed by the women and dressed, then wrapped in a shroud or placed in a coffin. The body would be taken from the house to the church on a bier or in a coffin carried by the men.

Sometimes people expressly stated that they did not want their families or representatives to prepare a coffin. John de Burton, for example, Rector of St Helen-on-the-Walls, insisted that the only covering for his body would be a sheet. The transportation of the body to the church was a visual display, involving a mourning procession from the house of the deceased made up of family members and in some cases led by monks or friars. Also present would have been candle bearers, a bell-man to announce the cortege and possibly members of the guild if the deceased belonged to a religious group. These displays could be very ostentatious for the wealthy who could afford to pay for a greater number of mourners to accompany the coffin. William Wylson, a goldsmith who died in 1517, requested in his will that a representative of the four orders of the friars accompany his funeral procession. In the same year John Wirral the fishmonger requested the presence of grey friars in his will. The carrying of a body into church was often a sign of prestige: the few pallbearers named in wills of the fifteenth and sixteenth centuries are almost all aldermen of the city.

The church bells would have been rung, with the length of the peal reflecting the status of the deceased. The coffin was placed before the altar the night before the burial and the wealthy might pay for a night vigil to be kept by the priest. In the morning, the mourners gathered for the requiem mass. The body was then taken to the graveyard and the sexton would place the body in the ground, with soil being sprinkled over the body by the priest or a family member. The grave would then be filled in after the mourners had left. After the burial there was a series of commemorative events in the church or at the graveside and a funeral feast.

The Jewish population were excluded from Christian burial grounds. Burial of the dead was a key religious obligation within Judaism, but we have no specific information for how the English Jews approached dying, death and burial. Information from the Continent shows they had a specialist burial society or fraternity. There are similarities with the Christian order of death, with the dying individual needing to confess sins and participate in prayers. Continental sources suggest that after death a funeral oration by a family member honouring the dead was delivered and the body was then carried on a bier or coach to the cemetery, accompanied by the family and mourners. In the cemetery was a wash house where the body was taken and thoroughly cleansed, reflecting the Jewish view that the body is unclean. Afterwards, the body was dressed in a shroud of white linen (men were dressed in prayer shawls) and then placed in a coffin. The coffin was placed in the grave and the mourners threw soil onto the coffin, psalms were recited and a male relative recited the Kaddish. Before leaving the cemetery for the funeral feast (the meal of recovery) all funeral guests washed their hands at a laver at the entrance to the cemetery. A period of mourning followed, lasting seven days after the funeral, when close relatives were forbidden to leave their homes.

York's Jewish burial ground, the Jewbury, was surrounded by a wall and accessed through gates. It was one of only 10 Jewish cemeteries in the country and had to serve a wide region. Other Jewish cemeteries were at Oxford, Winchester, Northampton and London, and were all outside the walls of the towns. The widely spaced nature of the Jewish cemeteries made it difficult for some Jews to conform to the Jewish law that required burial to take place as soon as possible after death, preferably the same day. It is possible that the Jews of Lincoln, Stamford and Northampton made use of the York cemetery before they acquired their own. The Jewbury is not mentioned until the 1230s, but was probably founded much earlier; it closed in 1290 when the Jews were expelled and was sold off by the crown and redeveloped.

A BODY OF EVIDENCE

The study of graveyards was not common until the 1970s, but since then it has produced a wealth of information on their organisation, and on the medieval residents. The use of different burial methods, changes in burial practice, marginal burials and displays of wealth and status have all been studied. The preservation of bodies, shrouds and coffins is a result of the soil in which they are buried. Waterlogged soil preserves material, but acidic soil causes decay. Depending on these circumstances, a body, with the exception of its skeleton, usually decays within 10–50 years.

Some burials stand out from the rest, especially those of the archbishops, examined at the Minster in 1968–69. They were buried in their robes which medieval written and artistic traditions suggest was to ensure they were properly attired to meet Christ. The tomb of Archbishop Walter de Gray (1216–55), opened during its restoration, contained a silver-gilt chalice and paten, a gold ring set with sapphire, emerald and ruby, a pastoral staff of walrus ivory, textile fragments including the remains of a cushion of silk and gold thread near his head, and the leather soles of his shoes. The almost complete destruction of his grave clothes suggests he was buried in linen rather than silk vestments.

59 Christian graveyards were busy places, as seen at St Helen-on-the-Walls. © *York Archaeological Trust*

The coffin of Archbishop Godfrey de Ludham (1258–65) was lead-lined and his body had been embalmed, which preserved the body tissue and surrounding textiles. His coffin contained a painted pastoral staff, a gold ring set with sapphire, a silver-gilt chalice and paten, the remains of a cushion, mitre, stole, woollen pallium with appliqué Maltese crosses and leather shoes. The majority of the population were buried far more plainly.

The city's graveyards are complex and contain a large number of burials. This results in many graves intercutting one another, despite the Church's views on bodily resurrection. The sexton and his gravediggers often disturbed earlier burials, some of which were not

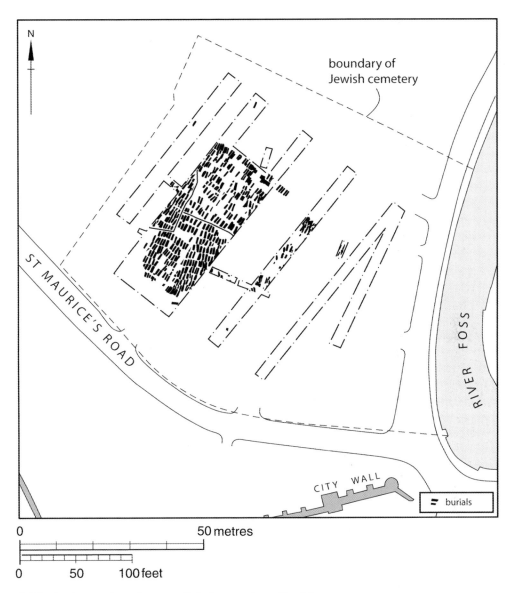

N

boundary of
Jewish cemetery

ST MAURICE'S ROAD

RIVER FOSS

CITY WALL

☞ burials

| 0 | | | | 50 metres |

| 0 | 50 | 100 feet |

60 The Jewbury, where there was little intercutting of burials

fully rotted, and articulated body fragments are found in graves as well as the loose bones from burials. Occasionally disturbed bones were reburied carefully in charnel pits and in the graveyard of St Wilfrid's charnel they may have been put into wooden boxes or containers.

The excavations at Jewbury showed that unlike the Christian cemeteries a great deal of care and attention was put into keeping the burials in rows, with little evidence for intercutting found. Analysis showed that only 12 per cent of the excavated burials were intercut and only 1.7 per cent had their bones disturbed. In contrast, at the Gilbertine Priory over 35 per cent of burials were intercut; at St Benet's over 60 per cent were intercut.

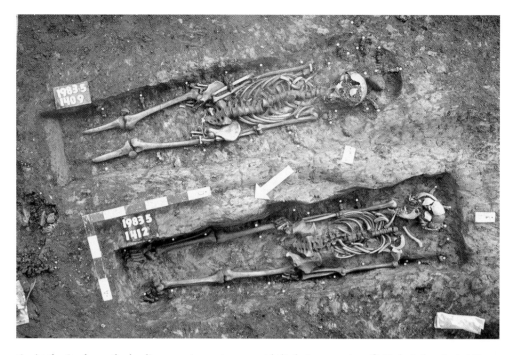

61 At the Jewbury the bodies were in neat rows with little intercutting. © *York Archaeological Trust*

The simplest graves were just holes dug in the earth, but there were many other forms of burial. Those that could afford it could be buried in the coffins used to transport them to the church. Many of the parish churches and religious houses had a communal coffin for the transportation of bodies, wrapped in their shrouds. Once at the graveyard, the bodies were taken from the coffin and buried.

Coffins don't always survive, but the shape of the grave and the position of the body can suggest their presence. Another indicator is the stain left in the soil by the decayed wood of the outline of the coffin. At the excavations of the graveyard of St Stephen's, which stood near modern George Street, 56 burials were assumed to be in coffins as they were in rectangular cuts, or the body had a parallel-sided appearance, or bones had rotated during decay implying that a coffin was present. Twenty-two burials had one or two iron nails in the backfill, interpreted as indicating the presence of a coffin. At St Helen-on-the-Walls, some graves had fewer than six nails per grave – medieval coffins only used a small number of nails in their production. At St Benet's wooden coffins made of oak or elm were held together by dovetailed joints, dowels and wooden pegs, with nails used only to secure the lid in place.

Coffins were also found at the Jewbury. Modern Jewish practice doesn't use iron, but medieval Jews were buried in coffins held together with iron nails. Sixteen burials used reinforcing and angle brackets, thought to suggest that the coffins had been moved some distance. Some of the coffins at Jewbury were charred, which may have been a deliberate attempt to ensure better preservation of wood.

Stone coffins, occasionally re-used from the Roman cemeteries, like St William's in the Minster, are usually found at religious houses and their use peaked during the twelfth

62 A wooden coffin from the churchyard of St Benet's. © *York Archaeological Trust*

and thirteenth centuries. These coffins took different forms: four from the Gilbertine Priory, dated *c*.1200–1325, had niches for the head, while later ones from the thirteenth and fourteenth centuries were long and tapering without head niches.

Graves lined with roof tiles have been found at Clementhorpe Nunnery and in the cloister of St Andrew's Priory dated to *c*.1200–75. Similar examples have been found at St James Priory in Northampton. We cannot be sure whether the care and attention required for the preparation of these graves indicates wealth or whether they were a cheap equivalent to a stone coffin or stone-lined grave.

Perhaps more common was the use of shrouds. Often little direct evidence of the shroud survives except for the occasional pin perhaps used as a fastening; the presence of antler toggles found above the heads of two burials at the Jewbury was thought to indicate the presence of shrouds. Historical sources suggest that the shrouds may have been tied rather than pinned, and this would explain the lack of evidence. A narrow grave cut and a skeleton with its arms tightly positioned against its sides, however, indicates the use of a shroud. The actual textiles of the shrouds or grave clothes rarely survive and rely on mineralization, waterlogging or desiccation.

Evidence for clothing has come from the archbishops who were buried in their vestments and green staining on the skulls of some of the female burials from Clementhorpe Nunnery was thought to indicate the wearing of a headdress, perhaps associated with the nuns. Excavations in 2006 in the waterlogged cemetery of St Sampson's Church found two burials dating to the late thirteenth or early fourteenth century containing a rare preservation of textiles. One, a female over 46 years old, was in a linen shroud of a type similar to that used in a well-preserved shroud burial from St Bees Priory, Cumbria, and another in St Mary's Abbey, Winchester. There was evidence for a strap of a finer-quality material for binding across the lower legs; it has been suggested that the bindings could be made from the person's chrysom (baptismal) band, saved specially for the purpose.

63 The use of large stone coffins was common on religious sites such as this one from the Gilbertine Priory. © *York Archaeological Trust*

The other skeleton, a young male aged between 19 and 25, had a coarse textile preserved on the hip comparable with cattle hair or the summer coat of goat. This is the coarsest textile in the medieval period, the medieval equivalent of sackcloth, usually found on quayside and warehouse sites around the North Sea, used as wrapping cloths for merchandise. Such material is usually associated with monastic burials of the eleventh to thirteenth century, such as at Cluniac Priory in Thetford, Wymondham Abbey, Norfolk, and Worcester Cathedral. The wearing of sackcloth may symbolise piety, in an emulation

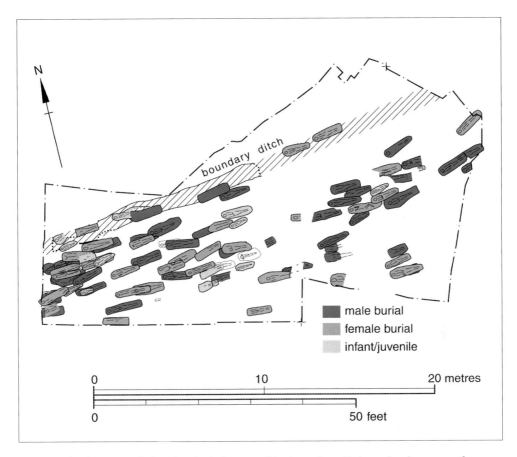

64 St Stephen's graveyard, showing the influence of the boundary ditch on the alignment of graves

of St Thomas Becket. Rare non-monastic use has been found at St John the Baptist Church at Newport, Lincoln, and this example at St Sampson's may also find a parallel in the will of John atte Battayle, a fourteenth-century London weaver, who requested that he be buried *in cilicio* (hair cloth), presumably as a sign of penitence.

The alignment of bodies within cemeteries was influenced by a number of different factors. At a basic level, the grave alignments could be influenced by topography or the alignment of the church. In many cases the Roman fortress had a prevailing influence as many of the churches were aligned north-east/south-west and burials respected these alignments, but were treated as if they were aligned on the standard Christian east–west alignment. At the Minster the Anglo-Scandinavian burials beneath the south transept respected the Roman north-east/south-west alignment which is also preserved in the proposed earlier alignment of the Minster Close to the north of the present church. Burials at St Sampson's, which follows the line of the fortress wall, also respected Roman orientation.

Other cemetery features such as crosses, walls and pathways were also influential, but evidence for these rarely survives. In St Stephen's churchyard, the boundary ditch exerted a strong influence on the alignment of the burials. The location of earlier burials may also have influenced alignments as seen at St Andrew's, Fishergate, where graves were consistently aligned within 10 degrees of one another.

The position of skeletons within the graves is affected by a number of factors which include the manner of burial, the process of decomposition, the effects of roots and animals, the rise and fall of ground water and disturbance by subsequent burials that redistributed or displaced bones. The majority are aligned with the head to the west and the feet to the east, which appears to be an ancient custom recorded in writings of the early twelfth century. The body itself could be in a number of different positions: arms straight and hands either by the side or one hand on the pelvis; both hands on the pelvis or over the groin which was the most popular across the city; one or both arms at 90 degrees at the elbow joint; or both arms fully flexed at the elbow.

Some burials that don't follow this pattern may reflect punishment; a decapitated burial from St Andrew, Fishergate, had his feet to the west. However, some burials with clear evidence for a violent death were buried in the normal manner. Another anomaly was seen in the later priory cemetery where an infant lay on its side and another had its arms flexed above its head.

The excavation of Jewbury revealed a different pattern of burial alignment. A comparison with other Jewish cemeteries shows that there was no standard alignment for burials; it was influenced by the boundaries of the cemetery. The bodies of the Jews in York were laid out north–south, with heads at the south, and fully extended arms and legs. A few outside the main cemetery area were in unusual positions. In one case the arms were folded at 90 degrees across the body while another had the left arm on the right pelvis and the right arm across the chest. These may have been burials of the socially excluded such as apostates, suicides or baptized Jews.

Within the cemeteries there may have been zoning, perhaps reflecting status or family groups. Something of this segregation can be seen in contemporary writing. The Augustinian John Mirk in the late fourteenth century identified groups such as those out of favour with the Church, thieves who died during the theft, those who had committed adultery, thieves who had not confessed their sins, suicides, and women who had died in childbirth and were buried in the churchyard while their children were buried outside the churchyard. There are also some instances of women buried with foetuses. Criminals could sometimes be given church burials – religious houses tried to ensure the proper burial of felons. In York those executed on the gallows were buried in St James's Chapel on The Mount.

Burials within churches were rare until the thirteenth century and were reserved for the clergy or very wealthy individuals who might be buried within the main body of the church, in side chapels or in the chancel. In the later medieval period favoured positions included in front of the high altar, in the nave or in the aisles.

Evidence for zoning burials within the cemetery and the church was seen at the Gilbertine Priory. Within the priory church, four of the burials in stone coffins were within the north chapel and dated to the thirteenth or early fourteenth century. Other burials in stone or wooden coffins were in the cloister alley; this may have been the favoured area for the laity. One thirteenth-century burial within the nave of the church re-used a Roman sarcophagus and was presumably for someone of high social status.

Some of the burials within the church appeared to be without coffins, but their position in the crossing implies they were individuals of some status.

Family groups may have been buried within the church, as suggested by the presence of males, females and children. There was also uniformity in the numbers of male and female burials within the chancel and the cloister alley suggesting the burial of wealthy patrons and their wives. Four double graves were identified, one of which contained a male and female lying side by side, another male and a 10–12 year old child.

Outside the church, on the east and north-east side, there was an area that was probably used exclusively for the canons. The southern part of the cemetery was still dominated by men, but the presence of females and young adults was thought to suggest that it formed the burial ground for the priory servants and their children.

Within the parish churches there were also divisions. At St Helen-on the-Walls three zones were identified: north-west of the church which had equal numbers of men and women, the south corner of the churchyard that had more juveniles; and south-east of the church which contained higher numbers of females and juveniles. The significance of this arrangement is far from clear. The division of space was also seen at the Jewbury where there was a clustering of infant burials in the north-eastern part of the cemetery. In the Jewish cemetery in Winchester infants were mainly buried to the east of the boundary ditch.

ALL DISEASES GREAT AND SMALL

The skeletons from cemeteries can tell us much about the health and well-being of York's medieval residents and shows that there were broad similarities between the Christians and the Jews. Towns were inevitably subject to high rates of disease, due to the effects of a dense concentration of people, and everyone was affected, rich and poor alike. Perhaps common to all people were the problems of intestinal parasites, which would not have unduly affected the individual; the eggs of whipworm and maw worm have been found in cess pits. Lice were a problem and the skeletons show that many people also suffered from sinusitis, perhaps due to air pollution.

Some form of healthcare was clearly carried out, as some skeletons show evidence of injuries healing without infection. Broken bones were probably the most common injury for medieval residents of the city and of these rib fractures and broken spinal vertebrae were most frequent; broken arms, legs, ankles, feet, fingers, shoulder blades and collar bones are also recorded.

The York Jews seem to have been less prone to injury, with bodies displaying a lower number of fractures of the long bones. One skull showed evidence of surgery: an incision had been made for cleaning a wound or removing bone splinters. Fractures were probably due to the general wear and tear of a life of physical work. Although breaks and fractures are common they are not always well set and, although they healed, resulted in misaligned bone, which in extreme cases produced crippling effects.

At the Gilbertine Priory there was clear evidence for some form of medical treatment for a mature adult male who had been buried in the late thirteenth or mid fourteenth century. He had a rotary fracture of the right knee and the excavators

65 Copper plates support the injured knee of a man buried at the Gilbertine Priory. © *York Archaeological Trust*

found two copper-alloy plates either side of his injured knee. These plates were horseshoe-shaped rather than round; there was evidence for binding or stitching, and the corrosion preserved parts of the leather covering. Similar plates have been found at Reading from the leper hospital of Mary Magdalene and at the hospital of St Mary Spital, London, and it is thought they were bound to the injured leg as a form of support.

Many diseases or medical problems leave little direct evidence on the skeleton. Indirect evidence for problems with people's feet comes from the shoes recovered from excavations. The foot leaves its mark on the shoe through the pressure points at the ball of the foot and the heel. Friction of the toes on the shoes leads to problems like corns and, to relieve the pressure, the leather was sometimes cut.

A disease that does leave its mark is tuberculosis, which can be identified by marks on the rib cage. Syphilis also leaves its mark on the bones and both diseases were displayed on skeletons from St Helen-on-the-Walls; other cases have been seen at St Stephen's and outside the walls at St Helen's, Fishergate. Paget's disease, which results in the thickening of the bones, has also been found on some skeletons. At St Stephen's lesions on the ribs not characteristic of tuberculosis may represent some other form of lung infection or infection of the organs of the lower abdomen.

Perhaps the most feared disease in the medieval period was leprosy. Around 200 hospitals for lepers were founded in the thirteenth century. A clear case of leprosy was found in the cemetery of St Stephen's. The individual had a deformed nose, a porous and extremely thin palate, some wasting of the finger and toe bones and infections of the lower legs which are features consistent with a diagnosis of leprosy. Other cases from the city may include one from St Helen-on-the-Walls and another from St Helen, Fishergate, where a skeleton had severe infection of the lower legs, as well as wasting of the toes.

Degenerative joint disease and osteoarthritis were quite common although as with so much of the skeletal data it is problematic to compare different cemetery sites from York, because recording techniques and standards have varied enormously. The majority of joint disease comes through wear and tear, and usually affects the spine joints (such as the hips), knees, hands, shoulders and elbows. As it is today, joint disease was experienced mostly by the older members of the population, with very few young adults affected.

As we have seen, diet was probably largely influenced by the seasonality of foods as well as rank and social status. A disease thought to be associated with being overweight is diffuse idiopathic skeletal hyperostosis (DISH), characterised by additional bone growth. This is often found on the spines of individuals associated with a monastic or high-status lifestyle and may reflect a richer diet. The occurrence of DISH was most prevalent at the Gilbertine Priory, amongst burials thought to be associated with the religious community.

Rickets is caused by a deficiency of vitamin D and leads to a distortion or curving of the long bones; deficiency of vitamin C can cause scurvy. Anaemia brought on by lack of iron was another problem and is thought to have been a bigger problem for women due to menstruation. A lack of iron is usually thought to be indicated by *cribra orbitalia*, small pits in the roof of the eye socket, but no clinical causal link has been identified. These diseases are seen on skeletons from several cemeteries in York including St Helen-on-the-Walls. The health of medieval residents may also have been affected by the inadvertent consumption of toxic substances. Lead was used extensively in glaze for pottery and in pewter. In some studies the deposition of lead on the long bones has been recorded in X-rays, displayed as dense white lines on the ends of the bones.

Diet also influenced the level of caries, tooth decay, which although prevalent in the medieval period was not as common as in modern populations. The medieval diet did not contain high levels of sugar and was coarser than modern diets, with more grain that probably also contained bits of the millstones. The comparatively low levels of sugar explain why many ancient skeletons exhibit evidence of having had healthier teeth than we do today; the coarse diet explains the wearing down of medieval teeth.

Additional to tooth decay as a dental problem was the build-up of tartar (calculus) which reflected a lack of tooth cleaning and is seen in cemeteries across the city. The varying levels of calculus may reflect diet or patterns of dental hygiene. Some people did go to the effort of trying to clean their teeth and some from the Gilbertine Priory displayed wear patterns suggesting the use of a toothpick. Gum disease was also a problem for many of the medieval residents, as were abscesses. One individual from St Helen's Fishergate had dental surgery for the extraction of a tooth which had clearly healed.

Blade wounds are not uncommon in medieval cemeteries although they were probably rarely the result of violent death. The exception seems to be a group of young men found at St Andrew's Fishergate and in the later Gilbertine Priory where a total of 19 individuals were found with clear evidence for sword wounds; these dated from the late eleventh or early twelfth century and from the late twelfth or early thirteenth century. Most were young males aged 20–30, with a few aged 30–40. Some at least must have been injured or died in single events as they were buried in double graves.

VITAL STATISTICS

The skeletal evidence can also tell us about the height, sex and age at death of an individual. The majority of these statistics rely on quality of the osteological data, but there are known problems with assigning age and sex to individuals. The majority of analysis relies on the fusion of figures from epiphyses (the ends of the long bones), tooth wear and bone degeneration; it is only possible to positively assign sex in adults where the pelvis and the skull survive. Work at the eighteenth-century crypt of St Mary Spital in London highlighted the problems of skeletal ageing leading to over- or under-representation of individuals of a particular age or sex whose details were known from coffin plates.

Although diet was an important factor, height probably owes a lot to genetics, and the increase in average height is a modern phenomenon as many burial assemblages show little variation in height over 900 years (for example at Barton on Humber); there was actually a decline in height in the nineteenth century, arguably associated with the increase of industrialisation. The evidence from York shows that there was very little difference in the height of residents from across the city. At St Andrew's and the Gilbertine Priory in Fishergate, women between the eleventh and sixteenth centuries were 1.58m (5ft 2¼in) and men were 1.72m (5ft 7¾in). The burials from the Jewbury were slightly shorter than their Christian contemporaries, with females averaging 1.56m (5ft 1½in) and males 1.67m (5ft 5¾in).

The statistics obtained on age of death of residents are affected by factors such as the preservation of the skeletons and the different methods used to calculate age. It seems fair to assume a high mortality rate for babies and infants but these are often under-represented because their skeletons are disturbed by subsequent burials, or because they were excluded from the cemetery as non-baptized children, or because infant bones are less dense and can dissolve away.

Comparisons between parishioners of St Helen-on-the-Walls and the lay and ecclesiastical cemeteries at St Andrew, Fishergate, suggested that overall about 35 per cent died before reaching adulthood (about 20 years old). At St Helen-on-the-Walls 56 per cent of women died before they reached 35 compared with 36 per cent of men, whereas at Fishergate 35 per cent of women died aged 20–30, nearly 20 per cent at 30–40 and just over 40 per cent at 40–50. If the group with blade injuries is excluded, 40 per cent of males died aged 20–30, 28 per cent at 30–40 and 13.5 per cent at 40–50.

66 A guarantee of a short stay in purgatory? A papal bulla from All Saints, Peasholme Green. © York Archaeological Trust

The seemingly low level of life expectancy was also seen in Jewbury, based on 476 individuals from around 1,000 burials. This showed that 60 per cent of women died aged 20–40; the figure for men was 53 per cent. This suggests that there were peaks of mortality in the period from childhood to adolescence and again in adults in their thirties but if one survived these periods one had a chance of surviving past 40. The information from St Helen-on-the-Walls suggests the majority of people died before they were 60. The Register of Freemen also implies that many individuals survived at least into their 40s.

EARTHLY POSSESSIONS

Although grave goods are uncommon in later Christian burials a few artefacts do survive that shed some light on the lives of the medieval residents. Religious belief is shown through papal bullae found in some graves. These were lead seals attached to papal documents. They can be dated from the issuing pope and the majority found in

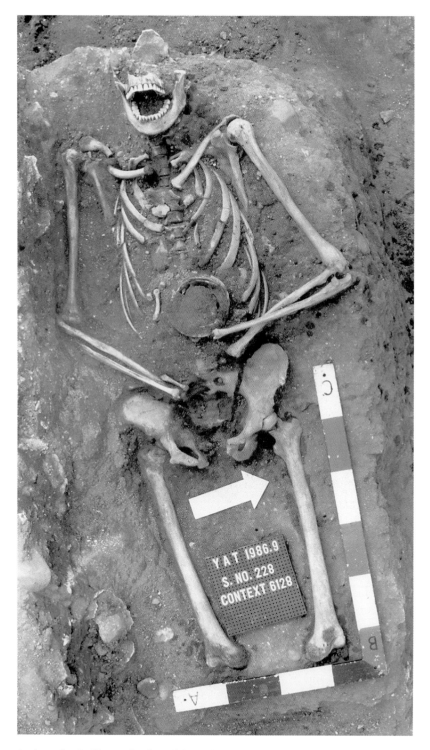

67 A mark of office with a burial from the Gilbertine Priory holding a chalice and paten. © *York Archaeological Trust*

68 The chalice and paten after conservation. © *York Archaeological Trust*

excavations are from the twelfth to fifteenth centuries; they appear to be limited to England and Wales.

The documents sealed by the bullae were probably indulgences or pardons for sins, aimed at minimising the time the soul spent in purgatory. The number issued may have declined with the development of chantries or when it was realised that forged pardons were being sold. Some of the pardoners who sold forgeries were put on charge in Nottingham in 1379 and in 1384 two officials were authorised to search for smuggled bullae at Scarborough. There was also a changing mentality towards purgatory and Chaucer condemned the pardoners in the *Canterbury Tales*; these sentiments were also expressed by the Lollards.

Individuals may have hoped that the bullae seals with which they were buried would prove their worthiness to spend less time in purgatory. Two burials at All Saints, Peasholme Green, were buried with papal bullae; one clasped the seal in the left hand and the other was found near the head. One bore the mark of Pope Urban III (1185–87) and the other one of the many Pope Clements.

Other displays of religious belief may include a possible pilgrim's badge from St Helen-on-the-Walls and scallop shells which were a symbol of St James interred with an individual from St Helen, Fishergate – this may suggest he had made a pilgrimage to Santiago de Compestella in Spain or to another site associated with the saint. Another unusual find from graves are keys. There were two possible examples of this from St Helen, Fishergate, but the concept they symbolise is unclear. They may represent the keys of St Peter but they might equally symbolise a means of escape from purgatory, which was sometimes known as God's prison.

Many of the clergy were buried with marks of office such as a chalice and paten of pewter or other base metals. The chalice and patens found are hard to date as styles change little over time, but they are found in burials predominantly from the thirteenth and fourteenth centuries, with one example found at the Gilbertine Priory. Some are later such as the late fifteenth- or early sixteenth-century burial at St Mary in the Horsefair. The largest number was recovered from burials in the nave, transepts and crossing in York Minster, with a few also found in the presbytery, during the excavations of 1967–73.

Advances in the study of evidence from medieval cemeteries show that much has been learned, but that there is still much scope for further analysis. While the historical sources can tell us something of the size of the population and the origins of individuals, it is archaeology that gives us clues to their physical appearance, state of health and the complex system of social and Christian beliefs depicted in treatment of the dead. This includes burial methods and the inclusion of artefacts associated with aspects of those beliefs. We also gain an insight into the other faiths, particularly Judaism, which had its own rituals and preparations for dealing with the dead. Despite their religious differences the Jews were otherwise very similar to their Christian neighbours, suffering from the same diseases and health problems overall, although less prone to breaking bones.

The marks left upon skeletons show that life was, by modern standards, strenuous. Both sexes carried out hard physical work throughout their lives and may have suffered from joint disease. Children were also included, carrying out physical work from a young age. Although disease was rife there was a good chance that if you survived childhood you could live a reasonably long and active life.

7

LIFE IN MEDIEVAL YORK

The 500 or so years spanning the medieval period, from the Norman Conquest to the Dissolution of the 1530s, saw the city of York undergo many changes. Using archaeology to supplement the historical sources, we can piece together a much fuller picture of life in medieval York. The swings in religious and political views in the mid sixteenth century marked the end of the medieval period and the start of a new era in the city's history.

Combining historical and archaeological information we can see how the economy of the city developed, while learning about the goods people traded and the skills of the master craftsmen. We can also build up an impression of the daily lives of the residents: the food they ate, where they worshipped, where they could buy food and goods, and the impact of religious belief on both daily life and the treatment of the dead.

Life in the city wasn't all hard work, and free time was used for entertainment and playing games. Artefacts associated with the pastimes of the medieval residents included an ash bowling ball found in fifteenth-century levels at Coppergate, gaming pieces, and a board game scratched onto a wooden coffin from Swinegate. There were some chess pieces made of jet, with simpler gaming tokens made of bone or antler. Dice have also been found, even at the Vicars Choral site where gambling was banned.

Music featured in the lives of the medieval residents. There were complex instruments indicated by tuning pegs found at the College of Vicars Choral and simple whistles from Coppergate. Archaeology also gives us a glimpse of the personal lives of the medieval residents through the set of wax tablets found at Swinegate. They are the size of a small matchbox and were kept in a decorated leather cover. Conservation work showed that they had been written upon and their subject matter included a range of topics. One tablet was in Latin and was the draft of a legal document, another a set of accounts and another was far more personal: a poem with perhaps a love theme, written in Middle English with the repeated line, 'She said nothing to me not no'. The tablets suggest that some of the medieval residents of York were literate. Excavations at the College of Vicars Choral and Gilbertine Priory have also uncovered a number of styli with iron tips and parchment prickers to mark out the lines for writing. Copying out texts was an important part of the ecclesiastical life. Lead alloy points have been found and these may have been used in the same way as modern pencils. Other artefacts associated with literacy include book mounts, which were protective, and decorative clasps for keeping the books closed.

The study of medieval York is still relatively new. Until recently much reliance has been placed upon the historical sources. There is a growing body of archaeological evidence

69 Evidence for leisure pursuits: a die and game counter. © *York Archaeological Trust*

70 A simple game board scratched onto a coffin. © *York Archaeological Trust*

that sometimes supports and sometimes challenges this; integration of the two forms of evidence can provide new openings for study and understanding of the city.

For example, the archaeological evidence suggests the streets were, by the later medieval period at least, in a better state of repair than has generally previously been believed. Environmental evidence also shows that the city gradually became cleaner, and probably healthier. Buildings also underwent significant changes from earth-fast and plank-built structures to fully timber-framed buildings. During the fifteenth century these were slowly fitted out with accessories such as chimneys, and became drier and cleaner. Even though it is the well-built rows that survive, the one surviving example of a small house on the corner of the Shambles suggests that even the lower-class buildings were fairly well built.

The disputed issue of urban decline in York also requires review, because the evidence suggests that 'decline' and 'decay' may be far more complex than often believed and are tied up with changes to the social structure of the city. It is clear that a flat reading of the

71 A glimpse of the personal life of one fourteenth-century York resident from these wax tablets.
© *York Archaeological Trust*

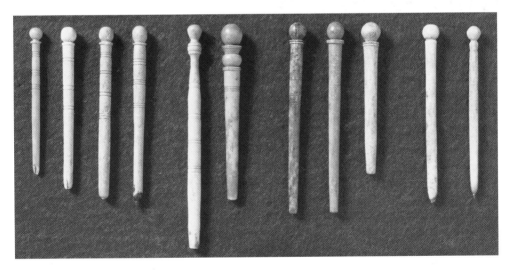

72 Evidence for literacy: styli made from bone. © *York Archaeological Trust*

sources can give a distorted view of the issues concerned. There is perhaps evidence to suggest that little changed in the city's economy until the late seventeenth and eighteenth centuries, when developments are reflected in the trades listed in the Register of Freemen. Archaeology also indicates that a different role was then had by the city, with areas of the waterfront given over to gardens. Perhaps it is necessary to look at the medieval city from both a historical and an archaeological perspective to gain a fuller understanding of why changes occurred.

73 Barley Hall: from hostel for monks, to home of William Snawsell, to archaeological interpretation. © *York Archaeological Trust*

The evidence also suggests that the city had a population level in the region of 10,000–12,000 which was the optimum volume for it to support. This suggests a stability of population levels until the nineteenth century when the first census of 1801 records a population of just over 16,000. It is not until the nineteenth century that there is a clear, rapid growth of population, resulting in areas of open land formerly occupied by the monasteries or the marginal areas of the city like Hungate and Walmgate being filled in with housing.

Combining sources of information has been attempted in projects like that carried out upon Barley Hall in which archaeology, the standing building and historical references have all been brought together to give an impression of a large house in the city in the late medieval period. The historical sources record the development of the building from its construction in the 1130s as a hostel for St Nostell Priory to the home of one of York's wealthy late medieval residents, William Snawsell, a goldsmith, registered as a freeman in 1436 and sheriff in 1464–65. Examination of the building confirms the date of its construction and periods of alteration. Excavation showed the great hall had an elaborate glazed floor and a central hearth in the fourteenth century. Excavation also exposed the foundations for the stairwell that gave access to the great chamber. The will of another York goldsmith was used to recreate the interior to include authentic fixtures, fittings and furniture.

The analysis of medieval Coppergate used historical and archaeological sources to trace the development of the neighbourhood from an Anglo-Saxon production centre

74 Copying
the rich?
Copper alloy
brooch, similar
to the one
made in gold
wire. © *York
Archaeological
Trust*

to a residence for some of York's wealthiest citizens According to the incomplete poll tax assessment of 1381 these residents included drapers, bakers, shoemakers, weavers, tailors, taverners and labourers; some such as the merchants, cooks and bakers were able to make wills. Some of the residents were among the elite of the city, like William Alne and Andrew de Bolynbroke who was mayor in 1309. This shift to an affluent residential area is seen in the archaeology, with an absence of industrial or craft activity and the presence of high-status objects such as glass wine goblets.

The significance of buildings and use of space are topics that need further exploration, which can further our understanding of how the medieval city functioned. A study of the York guildhalls has shown that they were much more than just meeting places for guilds or a display of wealth. The topography of the city also merits further investigation to reveal more about the Roman influence on the medieval city. The re-use of space, such as the *principia* area for the Minster, may have been part of exploiting an established focus of power or influence. Divisions of space within the city also played an important part in ordering the city, but also expressed social standing; at the same time it is clear that the city streets could contain individuals of all walks of life, from nobility to the poor.

Another aspect that is largely neglected is the influence of the Christian world view on the plan of the city. It may be significant, for example, that a church dedicated to St Michael, the guardian angel, stands on the north-west side of Ouse Bridge at the entrance to the commercial heart of the city.

A major shift has taken place in the study of artefacts; they are no longer used solely to date sites and assign status, but are increasingly valued for the information they can give about the function of particular buildings. Based on work in post-medieval archaeology of the eighteenth and nineteenth centuries, often in America, artefacts are being seen as indicators of people's economic and social power. The pottery, metal artefacts like clothes fastenings, scallop shells or tin ampullae are all expressions of wealth, status and belief. Aspirations to higher social status may find expression through the food people ate, or the wearing of decorative items that imitated gold jewellery such as brooches. This expression was continued into death through the founding of chantry chapels or altars and in funerary practices.

The story of medieval York is being constantly rewritten as new discoveries are unearthed during modern development of the city. This new information will no doubt challenge some of the views put forth in this book. There is, therefore, great potential to take study of the city further, through the combination of the many strands of evidence becoming available to us. Hopefully then we may be able to shed further light upon our knowledge of medieval York.

SELECT BIBLIOGRAPHY

The following abbreviations have been used:

Archaeol. J.   *Archaeological Journal*

AY   *Archaeology of York fascicule series*

AYS   *Archaeology of York Supplementary Series*

AYW   *Archaeology of York web series (http://www.iadb.co.uk/resources/ayw.htm)*

YAJ   *Yorkshire Archaeological Journal*

GENERAL SOURCES

1972–2000 *Interim: Archaeology in York* (Bulletin of the York Archaeological Trust)
2000– *Yorkshire Archaeology Today* (Magazine of the York Archaeological Trust)
The York Archaeological Trust Sites Gazetteer (www.iadb.co.uk/gazetteer.htm)
Giles, K. & Dyer, C. (eds), 2007. *Town and Country in the Middle Ages. Contrasts, Contacts and Interconnections 1100–1500*, Society of Medieval Archaeology Monograph 22 (Maney)
Palliser, D. (ed.), 2000. *The Cambridge Urban History of Britain, 600–1540*. Cambridge University Press (Cambridge)
Royal Commission on Historical Monuments of England, *An Inventory of the Historical Monuments in the City of York*. 1. *Eburacum* (1962); 2. *The Defences* (1972); 3. *South-West of the Ouse* (1972); 4. *Outside the City Walls east of the Ouse* (1975); 5. *The Central Area* (1981) (HMSO London)

PREFACE

Auden, G.A., 1906. *A Handbook to York and District* (York)

INTRODUCTION

Bartlett, R., 2000. *England under the Norman and Angevin Kings 1075–1225* (Oxford)
Daniell, C., 2003. *From Norman Conquest to Magna Carta. England 1066–1215* (Routledge)

Hall, R.A., 1994. *Viking Age York* (London)

Hall, R.A., 1996. *York* (London)

Hall, R.A., Rollason, D.W., Blackburn, M., Parsons, D.N., Fellowes-Jensen, G., Hall, A.R., Kenward, H.K., O'Connor, T.P., Tweddle, D., Mainman A.J. & Rogers, N.S.H., 2004. *Aspects of Anglo-Scandinavian York*, AY 8/4

Hill, D. & Cowie, R. (eds.), 2001. *Wics – The Early Medieval Trading Centres of Northern Europe*, 92–94 (Sheffield)

Nuttgens, P.J., 2001. *The History of York: From Earliest Times to the Year 2000* (York)

Ottaway, P., 2004. *Roman York* (Stroud)

Raine, A., 1955. *Medieval York: A Topographical Survey Based on Original Sources* (London)

Schofield, J. & Vince, A., 2005. *Medieval Towns. The Archaeology of British Towns in their European Setting* (London)

Sheeran, G., 1998. *Medieval Yorkshire Towns. People, Buildings and Space* (Edinburgh)

Tillott, P.M. (ed.), 1961. *The Victoria County History of the Counties of England: A History of Yorkshire, The City of York* (London)

1: LIE OF THE LAND

Addyman, P.V., 1975. 'Excavations in York, 1972–1973 First Interim Report', *The Antiquaries Journal* LIV, 200–31

Addyman, P.V., 1979. 'Vernacular Buildings below the Ground', *Archaeol. J.* 136, 69–75

Addyman, P.V., 1988. *The Waterfronts of York* (York)

Addyman, P.V., 1989. 'The archaeology of public health at York, England', *World Archaeology* 21/2

Bran, M., 1988. 'Queen's Hotel: Excavations', *Interim* 13/4, 5–12

Clarke, A., 1989. 'Albion Wharf – All Muck and Magic', *Interim* 14/1, 7–12

Cooper, T.P., 1904. 'The medieval highways, streets, open ditches and sanitary conditions of the City of York', *YAJ* 22, 271–86

Dobson, R.B., 1996. *Church and Society in the Medieval North of England* (London)

Finlayson, R., 1987. 'Oh! What a Lovely Waterfront', *Interim* 12/3, 3–9

Grenville, J. 1997. *Medieval Housing* (London)

Hall, R.A., MacGregor, H. & Stockwell, M., 1988. *Medieval Tenements in Aldwark and other Sites*, AY 10/2

Hall, R.A. & Hunter-Mann, K., 2001. *Buildings and Land Use around Medieval Coppergate*, AY 10/6

Lilley, K.D., 2002. *Urban Life in the Middle Ages 1000–1450* (Basingstoke)

Macnab, N., 2003. *Anglo-Scandinavian, Medieval and Post-Medieval Urban Occupation at 41–49 Walmgate, York, UK*, AYW 1

Norton, C., 1998. 'The Anglo-Saxon Cathedral at York and the topography of the Anglian city', *Journal of the British Archaeological Association* 151, 1–42

Ottaway, P., 1996. 'New Streets for Old? Recent work in the Sewers of York', *Interim* 20/4 12–21

Palliser, D.M., 1978. 'Medieval street names of York', *York Historian* 2, 2–16

Palliser, D.M., 1990. *Domesday York*, Borthwick Paper 78 (York)

Palliser, D.M., 1997. 'Thirteenth Century York: England's Second City', *York Historian* 14, 2–9

Rawcliffe, C. & Wilson, R. (eds), 2004. *Medieval Norwich* (London)

Short, P., 1980. 'The fourteenth century rows of York', *Archaeol. J.* 137, 86–136

Wilson, B. & Mee, F., 2002. '*The fairest arch in England*': Old Ouse Bridge, AYS

2: PORTCULLIS AND PALISADE

Addyman, P.V. & Priestly, J., 1977. 'Baile Hill, York: a report on the Institute's excavations', *Archaeol. J.* 134, 115–56

Barber, B., 1986. 'Walmgate defences Foss Islands Road', *Interim* 11/1 22–9

Butler, L., 1997. *Clifford's Tower and the Castles of York* (London)

Cooper, T.P., 1911. *The History of York Castle* (London)

Creighton, O.H., 2005. *Castles and Landscapes. Power, Community and Fortification in Medieval England* (London)

Creighton, O. & Higham, R., 2005. *Medieval Town Walls: an Archaeology and Social History of Urban Defence* (Stroud)

Davidson, A., 1987. 'Tower 28', *Interim* 12/1 46–8

Dean, G., 2007. *Excavations at Robin Hood's Tower, York* (York Archaeological Trust unpublished report)

Evans, D.T., 1999. 'The former female prison. Skeletons in the Cupboard', *Interim* 23/1 17–22

Lilley, J., 1992. 'Beneath the Castle Car Park', *Interim* 17/1, 3–6

Morris, M., 2003. *Castle: A History of the Buildings that Shaped Medieval Britain* (London)

Ottaway, P., 1981. 'Castle Garage', *Interim* 7/4, 7–8

Pearson, N., 1982. 'Tower 11', *Interim* 8/3, 16–20

Rees-Jones, S., 1987. *Property, Tenure and Rents: Some Aspects of the Topography and Economy of Medieval York*, unpublished PhD thesis, University of York

Wilson, B. & Mee, F., 2005. *The City Walls and Castles of York: The Pictorial Evidence*, AYS

3: FOR THE LOVE OF GOD

Barnett, C.M., 2000. 'Commemoration in the Parish Church: Identity and Social Class in Late Medieval York', *YAJ* 72, 73–92

Brewster, D., 1993. 'The Solved Mystery of the Sac Friars', *Interim* 18/1, 8–9

Brown, S., 2003. *An Architectural History of York Minster* (English Heritage)

Butler, R.M., 1997. 'Notes on the Minster Close York', *York Historian* 14

Clarke, A., 1993. 'The Search for the Lawrence Street Lepers', *Interim* 19/1

Cullum, P.H., 1991. *Cremetts and Corridies: Care of the Poor and the Sick at St Leonard's hospital, York in the Middle Ages*, Borthwick Paper 79 (York)

Dobson, R.B., 1996. *Church and Society in the Medieval North of England* (London)

Dobson, R.B. & Donaghey, S., 1984. *The History of Clementhorpe Nunnery*, AY 2/1

Hall, R.A., 2004. *Bedern Hall and the Vicars Choral of York Minster.* Exploring York: 1, York Archaeological Trust (York)

Hall, R.A. & Stocker D. (eds.), 2005. *Vicars Choral at English Cathedrals* (Oxford)

Hunter-Mann, K., 1990. 'St George's Chapel', *Interim* 15/3, 14–20

Hunter-Mann, K., 2001. 'The Quest for the Minster Precinct', *Interim* 23/2, 17–23

Hunter-Mann, K., 2003. 'From Roman Fortress to Medieval Hospital: Excavations at St Leonard's', *Yorkshire Archaeology Today* 8

Johnson, M., 2000. 'St Leonard's at the Theatre', *Interim* 23/2, 9–16

Kemp, R.L. with Graves, C.P., 1996. *The Church and Gilbertine Priory of St Andrew, Fishergate*, AY 11/2

Newman, P.R., 1994. *The History of St William's College* (York)

Norton, C., 2001. *Archbishop Thomas of Bayeux and the Norman Cathedral at York*, Borthwick Paper 100 (York)

Ramm, H.G., 1976. 'The Church of St Mary Bishophill Senior, York: Excavations, 1964', *YAJ* 48, 35–68

Rawcliffe, C., 2006. *Leprosy in Medieval England* (Boydell Press)

Richards, J.D., 2001. *The College of the Vicars Choral of York Minster at Bedern: The College at the Bedern*, AY 10/5

Richards, J.D., Heighway, C. & Donaghey, S., 1989. *Union Terrace: Excavations in the Horsefair*, AY 11/1

Rodwell, W., 2005. *The Archaeology of Churches* (Stroud)

Spall, C.A. & Toop, N.J. (eds), 2005. *Blue Bridge Lane & Fishergate House, York. Report on Excavations: July 2000 to July 2002*, http://www.archaeologicalplanningconsultancy.co.uk/mono/001/index.html

Stocker, D.A., 1995. 'The Priory of the Holy Trinity, York: Antiquarians and Architectural History' in L.R. Hoey (ed.), *Yorkshire Monasticism. Archaeology, Art and Architecture*, BAA Conference Transactions XVI, 79–97

Ware, P., 2001. *Excavations at All Saints Church, Pavement, York 1995*, MAP Archaeological Consultancy (English Heritage)

Wilson, B. & Mee, F., 1998. *The Medieval Parish Churches of York: The Pictorial Evidence*, AYS

4: MERCHANT, BUTCHER AND CANDLESTICK-MAKER

Badham, S., 1989. 'Monumental Brasses: the Development of the York Workshops in the Fourteenth and Fifteenth Centuries' *Journal of the British Archaeological Association* IX 165–189

Bartlett, J.N., 1960. 'The expansion and decline of York in the later middle ages' in *Economic History Review*, 2nd ser. 12, 17–33

Blair, J. & Ramsey, N. (eds), 2001. *English Medieval Industries* (London)

Bridbury, A.R., 1981. 'English provincial towns in the Later Middle Ages' in *Economic History Review*, 2nd ser. 34 (1), 1–24

Dobson, R.B., 1977. 'Urban decline in late medieval England', *Transactions of the Royal Historical Society*, 5th ser., 27, 1–22

Dyer, A., 1995. *Decline and growth in English Towns 1400–1640* (Cambridge University Press)

Dyer, C., 2005. *An Age of Transition? Economy and Society in the Later Middle Ages* (Oxford)

Finlayson, R., 2004. *Medieval Metalworking and Urban Life at St Andrewgate, York*, AY 10/7

Giles, K., 2000. *An Archaeology of Social Identity: Guildhalls in York, c.1350–1630*, BAR British Series 315 (Oxford)

Giles, K., 2003. 'Reforming corporate charity: guilds and fraternities in pre and post reformation York' in R. Gilchrist & D. Gaimster (eds), *The Archaeology of Reformation 1480–1540* (Oxford), 325–340

Hogarth, S., 1986. 'Ecclesiastical Vestments and Vestment makers in York, 1300–1600', *York Historian* 7, 2–12

Kaner, J., 1988. 'Clifton and the Medieval Woolhouses', *York Historian* 8, 2–11

MacGregor, A., Mainman, A.J. & Rogers, N.S.H., 1999. *Craft, Industry and Everyday Life: Bone, Antler, Ivory, and Horn from Anglo-Scandinavian and Medieval York*, AY 17/12

Mould, Q., Carlisle, I. & Cameron, E., 2003. *Craft, Industry and Everyday Life: Leather and Leatherworking in Anglo-Scandinavian and Medieval York*, AY 17/16

Ottaway, P. & Rogers, N.S.H., 2002. *Craft, Industry and Everyday Life: Finds from Medieval York*, AY 17/15

Reeves, B., 2006. *Excavations at 62–68 Low Petergate, York*, AYW 7

Richards, J.D., 1993. *The Bedern Foundry*, AY 10/3

Slater, T. (ed.), 2000. *Towns in Decline AD 1000–1600* (Ashgate)

Swanson, H., 1989. *Medieval Artisans* (Oxford)

5: EATING, DRINKING AND SHOPPING

Arnold, H., 1999. 'The Kitchens of Medieval York – the Evidence of the Inventories', *York Historian* 16, 2–10

Bond, J.M. & O'Connor, T.P., 1999. *Bones from Medieval Deposits at 16–22 Coppergate and other sites*, AY 15/5

Dyer, C., 2000. *Everyday Life in Medieval England* (London)

Laing, L., 2003. *Pottery in Britain 4000 BC to AD 1900* (Greenlight Publishing)

Murray, H., 2003. *A Directory of York Pubs 1455–2003* (York)

Richardson, H., 1961. *The Medieval Fairs and Markets of York*, Borthwick Paper 20 (York)

White, E. (ed.), 2000. *Feeding a City: York* (Devon)

Woolgar, C.M., Waldron, T. & Sarjeantson, D., 2006. *Food in Medieval England: Diet and Nutrition* (Oxford)

6: A MATTER OF LIFE AND DEATH

Daniell, C., 1996. *Death and Burial in Medieval England, 1066–1550* (Routledge)

Dawes, J. & Magilton, J.R., 1980. *The Cemetery of St Helen-on-the-Walls, Aldwark*, AY 12/1

Dean, G., 2007. *New Electricity Sub-Station, Silver Street, York* (unpublished report)

Galley, C., 1998. *The Demography of early modern Towns: York in the Sixteenth and Seventeenth Centuries* (Liverpool University Press)

Gilchrist, R. & Sloane, B., 2005. *Requiem. The Medieval Monastic Cemetery in Britain* (Museum of London Archaeology Service)

Goldberg, P.J.P., 1996. *Women, Work and Life Cycle in a Medieval Economy; Women in York and Yorkshire, c.1300–1520* (Oxford)

Goldberg, P.J.P., 2004. *Medieval England. A Social History 1250–1550* (Arnold)

Grauer, A.L., 1989, *Health, disease and status in Medieval York* (UMI Dissertation Information Service)

Hadley, D.M., 2001. *Death in Medieval England* (Stroud)

Jewell, H., 1996. *Women in Medieval England* (Manchester University Press)

McComish, J., 2008. *Roman, Anglian and Anglo-Scandinavian activity and a medieval cemetery on land at the junction of Dixon Lane and George Street, York*, AYW 9

Ottaway, P., 1992. *Archaeology in British Towns from the Emperor Claudius to the Black Death* (Routledge)

Stroud, G. & Kemp, R.L., 1993. *Cemeteries the Church and Priory of St Andrew, Fishergate*, AY 12/2

7: LIFE IN MEDIEVAL YORK

Gerrard, C., 2003. *Medieval Archaeology* (London)

Hall, R.A. & Ottaway, P., 1999. *2000 Years of York. The Archaeological Story* (Bradford)

Hinton, D., 2005. *Gold and Gilt, Pots and Pins* (Oxford)

Kyriacou, C., Mee, F. & Rogers, N., 2004. *Treasures of York* (Landmark)

INDEX

Numbers in *italics* refer to plates and **bold** to plans

Alabaster, craft 129
Anglian 10–12
Anglo-Scandinavian 12–15
Archbishopric, development of 11
    Archbishop, role of 11, 14, 16
    Palace 73, 141
Archbishops (see also burials)
    de Gray 71, 161
    de Ludham 162
    de Pont l'Evêque 71
    Ealdred 15
    Greenfield 27, 66
    Melton 66, 93
    Neville 148
    Plantagenet 66
    Scrope 16, 96
    Thomas 71, 73, 86
    Thurstan 93
    William (see saints)

Baile Hill 15, 47, 50, 54, 56, 61, 66–7
Bedern, College of the Vicars 74–8, **75**, *77*, 117, 118,
    129, 145
Bedern Foundry 32, 117, 118, 119, 120, *121*, 125, 126,
    133, 138
Black Death 16, 106, 109, 131, 132, 136, 151, 155
Bone working 115, 126
Bridges (see also Ouse Bridge and Foss Bridge) 10, 12,
    19, 21 2, **22**, 24, 31, 33, 35, 36, 37, 38, 59, 106, 135
    Monk Bridge 32, 46, 103, 147
Buildings (see also Craft and Industry; Trade; Colleges;
    Castles; Minster) 9, 10, 11, 12, 19, 32–9, *36, 39*, 40,
    42, 44, 45, 46, 49, 51, 61, 63, 66, 69, 73, 80, 86, 90,
    93, 94, 99, 100, 103, 120, 132, 133, 178, 181
    Barley Hall *180*
    chimneys and fireplaces 38, 178
    floors 37, 93, 103, 112
    floor tiles 84, 93, 101
    foundations 33, *34*, 35, 54, 71, 72, 73, 82, 83, 84, 85,
    94, 112, 114, 180

hearths 103, 112, 115, 119, 120, 121, *123*, 140, 156, 180
living space 34
materials 10, 36, 38, 109, 115, 135
Norman House 35
plots 12, 23, 31, 32, 33, 34, 36, 44
regulations 33
roofs 21, 33, 35, 37, 65, 72, 78, 94, 114, 116
Rows 35, 36, 38, 149, 178
shops 21, 30, 33, 34, 35, 38, 130, 136, 139, 140, 146,
    147, 149, 153
sill walls 35, 76, 116
stone houses 35
storeys 34, 133
timber framing 21, 33, 35, 36, *37*, 59, 65, 76, 87,
    114, 178
uses 35–6
Building crafts 33, 115–6
Burials 10, 45, 61, 70, 82, 83, 91, 93, 103, 109, 118,
    147, 155, *159*, 161, *162*, 171, *174*, 176
    Archbishops 161
    chalice and paten *174, 175*, 176
    family groups 169
    Grave goods 173
    Jewish 161, 163, **163**, *164*, 165, 168, 172, 173
    keys 176
    papal bullae *173, 175*
    position 167, **167**, 168
    practice 158, 160, 161, 164
    sackcloth 160, 166
    scallop shells 176
    shrouds 158, 161, 164, 165
    stone coffins 158, 164, 165, *166*, 168
    tile lined 165
    wood coffins 81, 164, *165*, 168, 177
    zones 169

Castles (see York Castle and Old Baile)
Cemeteries 10, 161, 163, 164, 169, 172, 176
    St Helen-on-the-Walls *162*, 164, 169, 170, 171, 172
    St Sampson 151, 165, 167
    St Stephen 103, 158, 164, **167**, 170, 171
    St Wilfrid 82, 163

Chantry Chapels 82, 104, 182
Chapels 44, **79**, 96–7, 168
   St Anne 31, 96
   St Catherine 96
   St George 62, 64, 96, 109
   St James 96, 168
   St William 27, 96, 97, 109, 149
Clockmaker, seal of 124, 125
Cooking 139–40, 141, 142
Corporation, The 28, 31, 49, 69, 96, 97, 104, 106, 109,
   133, 149
   areas outside control 105
   civic seal 49
   county status 61
   end of 153
   guilds 146
   independence from the crown 106
   regulations 23, 40, 41, 46, 105, 106, 130, 136, 145,
   149
Council of the North 16, 17, 88, 134
Craft and Industry *116*
   main groups 115
   workshops 21, 34, 108, 118, 120, *121*, 128
   zoning 130–1

Defences (see also Roman, Anglo-Scandinavian
   Castles and St Mary's Abbey) 21, 31, 40, 43, 44,
   47, **48**, 50, 51, *52*, 54, *57*, 58, 107
   barbicans 19, 49, 54, 59, 60
   Biche Daughter Tower 56
   Bootham Bar 31, 40, 45, 51, 54, 58, 59, 86
   Castle Postern 53, 62
   chain towers 53
   Elrondyng 52
   Fishergate Bar 35, 44, 51, 58, *58*, 60, 94, 137
   Fishergate Postern 57, 60
   Micklegate Bar 31, 45, 50, 51, 59, 60, 97, 147, 152, 153
   Monk Bar 40, 45, 51, 54, 59
   North Street Postern 60
   ramparts 51, 52, 53, 54, 58, 100
   Robin Hood Tower *56*, 56
   Saddler Tower 56
   Skeldergate Postern 60
   Tower of the Tofts 54, 56
   Walmgate area 53, 54, *55*, 57, 59, 60, 121
   Walmgate Bar 44, 53, 59, 60, 80, 82, 150
   Wards 21, 50, 66
Death, medieval beliefs 158–61
Defoe, Daniel 17
Diet (see also food, cooking and health) 135, *138*,
   171, 172
   birds 139
   church restrictions 136
   dairy 139
   environmental evidence 137, *138*
   fish 138–9
   food sources 135–9

   meat 138
   social differences 136
   spices 139
Diseases 169–72
   caries 171
   cribra orbitalia 171
   DISH 171
   intestinal parasites 169
   knee plates 169–70, *170*
   leprosy 171
   medical treatment 169, 170
   osteoarthritis 171
   pagets disease 170
   rickets 171
   syphilis 170
   tuberculosis 170
Domesday Book 14–6, 21, 28, 47, 61, 67, 86, 135, 151,
   156, 157

Economy (see also Markets and Fairs) 17, 50, 53, 70,
   104, 105, 115, 135, 144, 148, 156, 157, 177, 179
   development 105
   fee farm fifteenth and sixteenth century 'crisis'
   131–4, 156
   foreign traders 24, 105, 108, 145, 146, 149, 152
   imports and exports 106–7
   regional and international 107
   regulation 105
   staple town 107
   tolls 21, 24, 32, 42, 49, 50, 53, 106, 107, 115, 117,
   153

Ferries 22, 51, 53
Fishpool **22**, 28–30, **29**
Food and drink brewing 144
   alehouses 145
   bread 145, 148
   influence of the guilds 146–8
   inns/hostelries 145–6
   seasonality 141–3
   serving 141, *141*
   status 143–4
Forests, Galtres 15, 46, 64, 91, 136, 146
Foss Bridge 12, 27, 30–1, 96, 107, 146, 152
   properties along 30
   St Anne Chapel 31
Freemen 24, 105, 106, 119, 122, 134, 135, 136, 149,
   152, 153, 158
   non-freemen 152
   Register of 32, 107, 108, 116, 119, 130, 134, 144,
   145, 148, 156, 157, 173, 179
Friars 24, 90 2, 104, 108, 158
   Augustinian 70, 92, 109, 168
   Carmelite 28, 30, 38, 91, 92, 101, **102**
   Dominican 91, 92, 160
   Franciscan 24, 30, 62, 65, 91
   Sac 92

Games 177, *178*
Gardens 30, 33, 36, 42, 44, 77, 94, 96, 97, 102, 111, 112, 114, 115, 134, 136, 137, *137*, 179
Guilds (see also Guildhalls) 14, 41, 69, 85, 97, 108, 109, 128, 138, 146–8, 153, 181
   leather 124
   religious 108, 109
   textile 116
Guildhalls 12, 19, 105, 106, 108–115, **110**, 131, 146, 181
   Common Hall 106, 109–11, *111*, 153
   Merchant Adventurers 28, 32, 35, 104, 108, 109, 111–2, *113*
   Merchant Taylors 113–4
   St Anthony's Hall 114

Harrying of the North 15
Health (see also diseases, diet) 97, 135, 144, 155, 169, 171, 176, 178
   age of death 172–3
   blade wounds 172
   broken bones 169
   height 172
Hinterland 10, 15, 156
   Ainsty 15, 136, 147
   Bean Hills 15, 44
   Bishopfields 15
Horn working 129, *130*
Hospitals (see also Leper hospitals) 44, 45, 46, 69, 97, **98**, 104, 144, 160, 170
   Guild 112, 114
   Maison Dieu 27, 97
   St Leonards 41, 49, 51, 52, 53, 69, 70, 78, 97–101, *99*, **100**
   St Mary in the Horsefair 101–2, *101*, **102**
   St Mary Magdalene 45, 97
   St Thomas 45, 97
Household 108, 115, 136, 140, 141, 143, 144, 155–6, 157
   children 122, 132, 144, 155, 156, 157, 168, 172, 176
   emulation *181*, 182
   family group 169
   servants 108, 115, 145, 146, 151, 155, 158
   women 119, 121, 132, 142, 144, 145, 149, 158, 160

Jews 62, 64, 70–1, 161, 176
   Jewbury 46, 161, **163**, 164, *164*, 165, 168, 169, 172, 173

Leather working 124–8, *126, 127*
Leper Hospitals 44, 102–3, 170, 171
   St Catherine 45, 103
   St Helen 103
   St Loy 46, 103
   St Nicholas 44
   skeletal evidence for 103, 147
Liberties 21, 49, 105, 128, 145
   St Peter 73

Malmesbury, William of 16, 106
Markets and Fairs 27, 31, 32, 42, 45, 69, 85, 106, 107, 119, 128, 135, 136, 143, 146, 147, 148–153, **150**, 156, 159
   cattle 152
   Corn Market 151, 152
   fish market 152
   Horsefair 45, **150**, 152
   Lammas Fair 152
   Pavement 31, 82, 111, 149, **150**, 151
   segregation of goods 151
   servant fair 151
   Thursday Market 149, **150**, 151, 152
Merchants 22, 38, 69, 105, 106, 107, 108, 111, 112, 115, 128, 131, 132, 133, 134, 135, 136, 145, 148, 151, 152, 153, 181
Metalworking (see also Bedern Foundry) 14, 118–24, *120, 121, 122, 123*, 131, 133, 140
   copper alloy 119
   precious metals/jewellers 122–4
Mills 44, 45, 62, 64, 147
Minster 9, 11, 21, 31, 32, 56, 59, 69, 70, 71–4, 76, 86, 90, 96, 99, 104, 105, 107, 120, 124, 130, 161, 176, 181
   Anglian 11
   Anglo-Scandinavian 14, 167
   Chapter House 72
   Close 73–4, 167
   excavations 19–20
   Norman 71
Monasteries, Dissolution (see also Reformation) 7, 94, 177
Monmouth, Geoffrey of 50
Mystery Plays 69, 109,

Our Lady Row, Goodramgate 38, 159
Ouse Bridge 12, 19, 23, 24, 27, 30, 31, 32, 71, 82, 96, 97, 109, 146, 151, 152, 181

Parishes 12, 16, 23, 44, 50, 78, 80–2, 111, 117, 155, 160
Parish churches 14, 21, 74, 78–86, **79**, 96, 104, 105, 108, 131, 158, 160, 164, 169
   All Saints, North Street 92
   All Saints, Pavement 14, 31, 85, 149, 151,
   All Saints, Peasholme Green 70, 78, 82, *83*, *173*, 175
   St Andrew 80, *80*, 92
   St Benet's 14, 80, 82, 163, 164, *165*
   St Crux 81, *81*, 83
   St Gregory 11
   St Helen-on-the-Walls 14, 81, 84, **84**, 160, *162*, 164, 170, 171, 172, 173, 176
   St John del Pyke 59, 74
   St John in the Marsh 39
   St Margaret, Walmgate 28, 31, 103
   St Mary-ad-Valvas 74, 80
   St Mary Bishophill Junior 10, 14, 80

St Mary Bishophill Senior 10, 82–5
St Mary Castlegate 14, 61, 70, 91
St Mary Layerthorpe 83
St Mary, Walmgate 31
St Michael le Belfrey 74, 81, 140
St Michael Spurriergate 14, 31, 40, 82, 131
St Nicholas 88
St Peter-in-the-Willows 82
St Peter the Little 131
    wall paintings 104, 159
Pilgrimage 70, 160, 176
    of Grace 104
Population 19, 43, 47, 104, 131, 132, 140, 143, 155,
    176, 180
    immigration 157–8
    Jewish 70
    names 157–8
    size 156–7
Pottery 128–9, *129*
Property 32, 36, 40, 136
    definitions 34
    ownership 33, 70, 76, 94, 100, 104
Purgatory 38, 69, 70, 158, 159, 160, *173*, 175, 176
    chantries 38, 69, 74, 75, 76, 80, 85, 104, 175

Reformation (see also Dissolution of the Monasteries)
    16, 72, 87, 96, 102, 103, 104, 109, 138
Religion, beliefs 30, 38, 104, 158, 173, 176, 177,
    182
    Holy Wells 70
    Influence on life 69–70
Religious houses 16, 21, 44, 70, **89**, 96, 107, 144, 147,
    160, 164, 168
    Clementhorpe Nunnery 92–3, 104, 147, 158,
    165
    Gilbertine Priory 44, 93–6, **95**, 118, 129, 138,
    144, 163, 165, *166*, 168, 169, *170*, 171, 172, *174*,
    176, 177
    Holy Trinity Priory 11, 69, 88–90, 104
    St Mary's Abbey 14, 19, 21, 24, 41, 45, 49, 52, 54,
    55, 86–8, *87*, *88*, 104, 137, 147
River Foss (see also Fishpool and Foss Bridge) 9, 12,
    13, 21, 28–30, **29**, 30, 40, 44, 47, 49, 51, 53, 61, 65,
    92, 94, 112, 147
River Ouse (see also Ouse Bridge) 5, 9, 11, 13, 14,
    15, 21, 22–6 *25, 26*, 31, 40, 47, 49, 50, 51, 53, 65, 66,
    83, 93, 96, 106, 107, 135, 136, 152
    Common Crane 24
    King's Staith 24, 25
Roman 9, 11, 21, 31, 34, 51, 52, 54, 56, 59
    civilian settlement/*colonia* 9–10

St William (see also chapels) 27, 70, 71, 72, 93, 164
St William's College 74, *74*, 76
Saints 69, 80, 103, 104, 136, 175
    relics 70, 72
Sanitation (see also pits) 39, 41, *41*
    cess pits 40, 137, 169
    King's ditches 40, 44
    rubbish disposal 40
    rubbish pits 13, 30, 34, 129, 138, 139, 143
    stone drains 41, *42*, 88
    water supply 30, 41, 144
Schools 11, 70, 73, 87
Seals 124
Shambles 39, 40, 111, 148, 149, 150, 151, 152, 157,
    178
Simeon of Durham 15
Streets and Lanes 16, 19, 21, 27, 28, 30, 31–2, 33, 34,
    35, 39, 111, 151, 36, 38, 39, 40, 42, 44, 45, 69, 111,
    133, 149, 151, 153, 178, 181
    maintenance and surfaces 32
    Pavers 32, 115
    principal routes 31
    street names 131
Suburbs 13, **43**, 42–6

Textiles 11, 14, 115, 116–8, 119, 126, 131, 134, 161,
    162, 165, 166
    dyed 117, 131, 137
    tailors 113–4, 133, 134, 181
    weavers 108, 116, 118, 181
Tile 45, 94, 101
    industry 115–6, 165
Topography 21, 31, 40, 49, 51, 66, 69, 104, 181

Union of Parishes, Act 104

Vitalis, Orderic 15, 47

Wars of the Roses 16
Wics 11
Writing 129, 177, *179*

York, study of 18–9
    antiquarians 9, 27, 53
    archaeology in 19–20
    artists 19
    map evidence *17, 18*, 18
York Castle 15, 21, 28, 30, 31, 44, 47, 49, 60, 62–5,
    70, 91, 96
    Clifford's Tower 15, 31, 47, 49, 53, *63*, 64, 65
    pre castle activity 61